YAKS
and
CATARACTS

YAKS

and

CATARACTS

MEDICAL MISSION
AT THE TOP OF THE WORLD

Monica Bass and Ada Burroughs

Design and tyesetting: Aga Karmol

Cover photo: A road in Spiti.
Photo on the title page: Henry and Ada Burroughs at Hammerwood.

First published in the UK in 2018 by The Cloister House Press

ISBN 978-1-909465-83-1

CONTENTS

PREFACE

This book is my mother's and my grandmother's. This is the story in their words. My mother never managed to publish the book she worked on so I decided to do it for her.

When I was eight I gave up sugar on my cornflakes, in tribute to my grandmother's self-discipline. As a much-travelled adult with my own family, I am in awe of her achievements, and I am intensely proud of my grandparents' devotion to the service of others.

Gillian, Lady Crofton
2018

INTRODUCTION

The idea for a book about Western Tibet had been in my parents' minds for many years. It first occurred to them in Khalatse, where my mother started taking extensive notes. Tourists would visit Ladakh for a few weeks then write a book, often being kind enough to send a copy to my parents. These books were very readable, but my parents thought they often lacked accuracy. As far as they knew, there had been no authoritative publication in English since A. H. Francke's 'A History of Western Tibet' in 1907. They did not aspire to a work of scholarship but felt a book on the everyday life in this comparatively unknown part of the world might be of interest.

Their unexpected return to England in 1926 put an end to my mother's on-the-spot research and the project was shelved while they built a new life for themselves, but they kept in touch with Dewazung, who wrote about twice a year with the news from Khalatse and Leh. They also corresponded with their successors and read the Moravian Missions' monthly magazine, The Moravian Messenger. Their own memories were kept alive by giving talks and lectures, for which they were both in great demand.

My father died in 1957, leaving my mother desolate and without a purpose for living. However, with characteristic courage, she started giving lectures and talks once more, partly to augment her tiny income, but chiefly to get out and about. She was asked so often if she had written a book that she revived the idea. By now she was no longer so inhibited about narrating the personal experiences that seemed to interest people. These writings form the core of the book.

However, my mother's health began to deteriorate and she had two spells in hospital so, when my husband was posted as British Deputy High Commissioner to Southern Rhodesia[1] in 1959, we invited her to join us in Salisbury for an extended visit. She let her flat, boarded an aeroplane and at the age of seventy-two set out for a new continent. She enjoyed every minute, especially when we were able to take her on a tour of Nyasaland[2] and Northern Rhodesia[3]. A serious heart attack at this time left her frail and forgetful and I believe she destroyed a number of papers, which may have contained details that have subsequently been difficult to verify.

She moved with us to South Africa in 1961. There she was able to meet up with an old friend from Douglas House days, Miss Evelyn Richardson, who lived in a retirement home in Rondebosch, not far from our home in Cape Town. Miss Richardson had been a missionary in Swaziland, where she had introduced education for girls and subsequently took on the early education of the Queen Regent's son, who became King Sobhuza the Second. These two old ladies thoroughly enjoyed comparing notes.

One of the wives at the British Embassy became interested in my mother's story and also knew some of the Moravians in Cape Town so, one day, she arranged a visit to one of them. The door of the house was opened by a woman with a happy, smiling face, beaming with hospitality. It was Lisl Hettasch, the little girl from Dresden who had been so shy and hostile all those years ago. Her cousins, Werner and Siegfried, also lived in Cape Town and so, after nearly fifty years, my mother was able to renew their acquaintance.

Early in 1962, my brother Ronnie wrote to say that he had been appointed Counsellor at the British Embassy in Brazil and that he would like to see his mother before he went. We persuaded her she should go home. By now she was very frail and we thought she might not live to see Ronnie and his family again unless she took this opportunity.

---

[1]   Now Zimbabwe

[2]   Now Malawi

[3]   Now Zambia

She returned to England and was cared for in turn by each of her sons until her death in March 1963.

Although I now had her papers, there was little opportunity to research and expand the story before my husband retired, as I, the papers, and access to books of reference never seemed to be in the same place at the same time. I had very clear memories of Khalatse, and my mother had spoken often about her life there, but there were still some points that needed to be clarified. Eventually, in 1981, my husband and I visited Ladakh. In Leh I met and talked with the Reverend Puntzog Razu, then Superintendent of the Moravian church in Ladakh and, in Khalatse, I met Madtha the son of Chospel, and we sat and drank tea outside my old home which is now a police post. Both these men remembered my parents but, most particularly, they remembered my father for his dedication as a pastor and a man of God. Each of them expressed a wish that they could have the support and inspiration of missionaries of such calibre.

Monica Bass
1982

PEOPLE IN THE STORY

LEH

Ada Moore – single sister (later Burroughs)
Dr. Reeve and **Dr. Kathleen Heber** – doctors
Revd. Henry Burroughs (Harry) – minister
Pagspa – the first Tibetan Ada met
Yoseb Gergan – headmaster of the Mission School
    and guide from Srinagar
Puntsog – a government official who helped escort the party
    from Srinagar
Drogpa – cook on the journey from Srinagar
Miss Birtill – single sister
Revd. F. E. Peter – Mission superintendent
Zodpel – Christian and translator at the hospital
Dewazung – Tibetan tutor
Yeshas (Ishe) – sisters' gardener
Denyed – sister's maidservant, who later moved to Srinagar
Deskyd – the Hebers' cook
Chondzin – mission servant, who also looked after
    the Hebers' children
Madtha (Tsodnam Puntzog) – Harry's manservant
Gordon – the first Burroughs child

PU

Mr. and Mrs. Marx, Ellie, Werner and **Erika** – fellow
   missionary family
Tarchungma – maid and cook
Dewa – Pu headman
Ronnie – second Burroughs child
Gyalstan – mail runner
Choskyid – Gyalstan's wife
Samdan – nursery boy
Chotob – steward
Rigdzin – cook
Monica – third Burroughs child
Chungste-ma – nursemaid
Mr. and Mrs. Mortimer – Salvation Army missionaries
   at Chini

KHALATSE

Tsering Yangzdom – cook
Elisabet – housemaid
Tsodnam – gardener, groom and handyman
Chospel – evangelist and Elisabet's father
Drambuchan – old grandfather
Geoffrey – fourth Burroughs child
Miss Warne – the children's guardian
Miss Rudd – escorted Monica to England
Mrs. Rudduck – became a family friend and benefactor

After a mile or so we came to Khalsi, the home of the Moravian missionary. His little house lay in a well-wooded compound. He made us very welcome, gave us tea, lettuces grown by himself … and the best brown bread, made from rough country flour, that I have ever eaten. He was a small man with strange, light-filled eyes which seemed always to be gazing at something far away. He told us much of his life. It must have been desperately lonely, for he and his wife saw no Europeans during the seven snow-bound winter months. … Often he was away for as long as a month or six weeks, visiting remote villages in the mountains, trekking over rubble and rock, and at the end of a long journey having to find the inspiration to preach. During these times his wife was left alone.

He had four children. … At the birth of these children he had acted as both nurse and doctor. He admitted that the life had told on his wife and himself, that sometimes their longing for the society of Europeans was almost unbearable, and that he and she had become nervy and were increasingly afraid of abnormality. Then he showed us his dispensary, for Moravian missionaries, although unqualified, have studied medicine and have many patients from among the native populations of the countries where they teach. His church was a long room with a few chairs, a desk and a piano. In the dispensary he showed us a tube of serum which he used for leprosy cases, saying he was attending at the moment to fifteen lepers.

"Religion and medicine," he said, "The two are indissoluble." …

Around this priest hung an atmosphere of simplicity, devoid of self-satisfaction. He and his wife had lived for twelve years in this wild, mostly snow-bound world, brought up children under hard conditions, seen little result of their labours, and sacrificed the companionship of their fellow Europeans. (Even that of the missionary in Leh was denied to them in winter.) They had suffered heat, cold, and perhaps even the physical hunger born of the utmost frugality, yet it was obvious that hope was still alive in their hearts.

Extract from *Mountain Magic* – Eve Orme

PLACES IN THE STORY

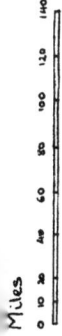

KASHMIR AND WESTERN TIBET

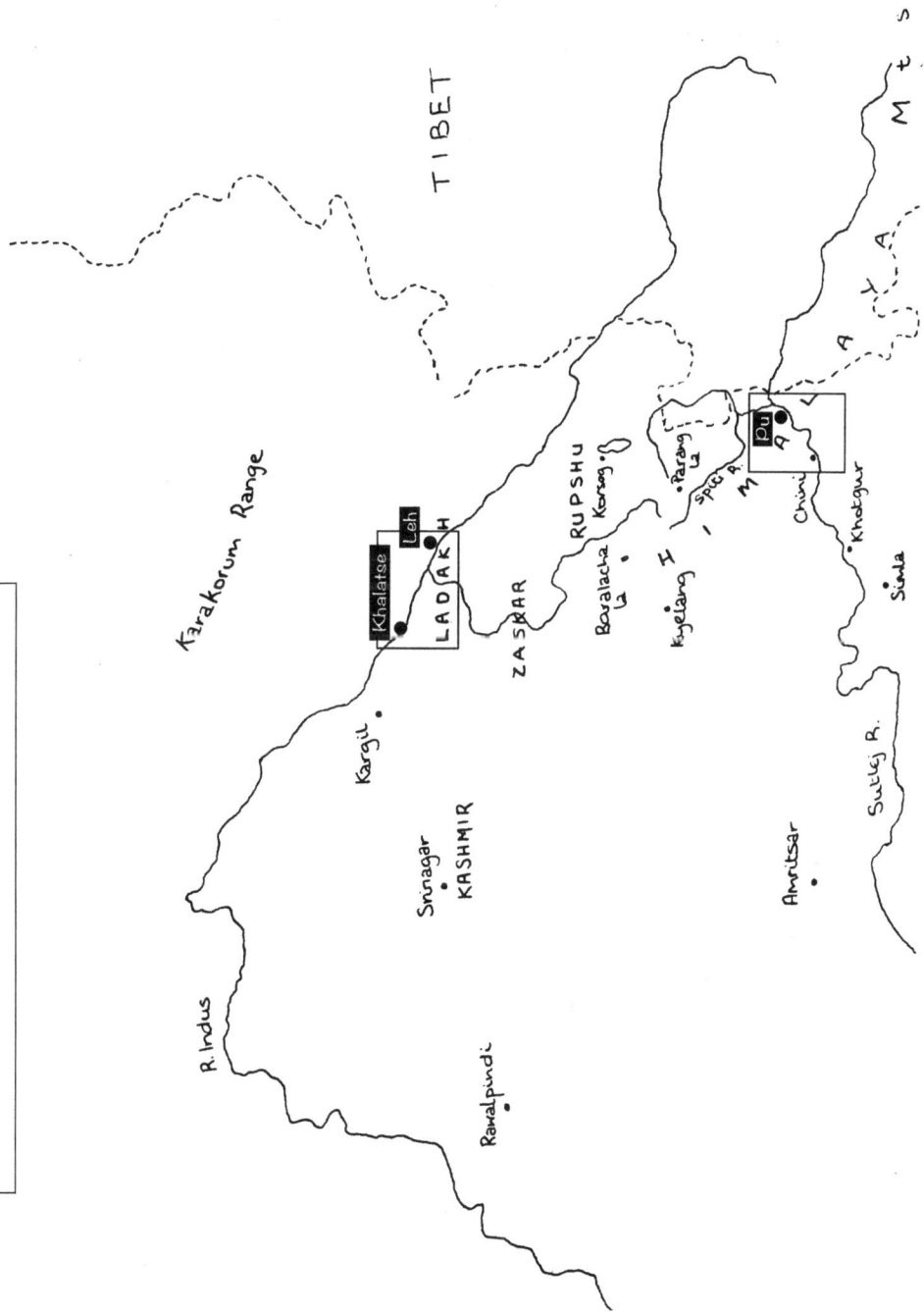

Miles

0 10 20 40 60 80 100 120 140

TIBET

Karakorum Range

Khalatse

Leh

LADAKH

ZASKAR

RUPSHU

Baralacha La

Koksar

Spiti R.

HIMALAYA Mts

Pu

Chini

Khotgur

Simla

Kyelang

Kargil

Srinagar

KASHMIR

Amritsar

Sutlej R.

R. Indus

Rawalpindi

LEH AND KHALATSE

PU DISTRICT

CHAPTER 1

Revelation

Ada Moore was seventeen in 1903. Her life plan, arrived at after many hours studying the Bradshaw guide in the outdoor privy at her home, was to cross China in a wheelbarrow, shoot the rapids on the Yangtse River, then ride on into the unknown beyond. One wild, wet morning she forsook this dream and vowed to go to Tibet instead.

She had left the Hostel for Women and Girls in Scarborough, known as Douglas House, just after seven o'clock, on her way to her job at the Springfield Laundry. Despite the weather she made her usual detour to read the headlines on the posters in the newsagent's shop. If the main news item was from abroad the newsagent would open the large atlas displayed in one of his windows at the appropriate page and Ada loved to study the maps. Her imagination had been fired by talks and lantern lectures given by missionaries at the chapel her family attended and she loved stories from far-away places.

She scurried along, trying to avoid the worst of the puddles for her boots needed re-soling. She held tight to her shabby skirt and the wind snatched at her cape, but she watched everything going on around her with sharp-eyed interest. When she came near enough to read the placards in the window, she stopped dead as if thunderstruck. She read and re-read the words, 'Younghusband Enters Lhasa'[1]. "It was a moment of blinding clarity", she wrote in later years, "In that moment I knew I **had** to go to Tibet".

She had no time to study the atlas then, but she felt transported with excitement at this wonderful revelation. She wanted to shout to the

---

[1]   Sir Francis Younghusband led a British expedition to Tibet in 1903

passers-by, "Look! Isn't it wonderful? Younghusband is in Tibet and I'm going there too!"

She managed to contain her excitement until dinner-time at the hostel then, after grace had been said and people had settled in their places, she suddenly burst out, "I'm going to Tibet!" There was a momentary silence. Some of the girls giggled at this latest of Ada's jokes; others snorted and turned away muttering, "Oh Ada! You and your daft ideas!" Ada looked at these scoffers with her green, deep-set eyes, which usually sparkled with mischief but now held a steely glint, and said, "You wait. I'll show you."

The Principal of the hostel, Miss Yelland, had listened to these exchanges. She said nothing but, noticing the stubborn set to Ada's jaw, realised that, for once, this mischievous, humorous girl was in deadly earnest. She decided she must take her in hand.

Later that day she called Ada into her private sanctum. "Tell me Ada, what gave you the idea of going to Tibet?" she asked. Ada explained what had happened that morning, and Miss Yelland drew her out to talk about her childhood and her aspirations. It was the first time that anyone had considered that she might have aspirations and Ada was encouraged to expand her ideas. Miss Yelland was impressed by the girl's sincerity. She warned her, however, that her faith and patience would be tried and tested and she would have to continue with her normal life until it was clear what she should do next. She must use that time, Miss Yelland said, to deepen her spiritual life, learn self-discipline and widen her education as much as possible by reading and observation, but, "Whatever you do," she added, "You must never lose your sense of humour. It is the most wonderful balancer."

The other inhabitants of the hostel were eager to know what had transpired in the 'holy of holies', but Ada fobbed them off with a flippant remark. In bed later, she lay marvelling at this great sense of purpose. She felt that she, Ada Moore, had been chosen by God to serve Him in Tibet. From then on she prayed every night that the Tibetans would stay just as they were and the country remain wild and unknown until she could get there and see it all for herself.

Ada's childhood had not been an easy one. Her parents, John Moore and Emily Milnes, had married against their parents' wishes. The Moores

Ada's mother, Emily

Ada's father, John

disapproved of the marriage because they thought Emily would not be able to manage a working man's household as she had been educated by a governess and had 'never done a hand's turn'. The Milnes's dissociated themselves entirely from such a socially disastrous alliance. Nevertheless, the marriage was a happy one. It lasted all too short a time, however, as John caught a chill which turned to pneumonia and he died within a week, at the age of thirty-two. Ada was eighteen months old.

Emily was heartbroken but had no time to indulge her grief. She had three children to support and was expecting another. There was no social security in the 1880s and she had to find somewhere to live and some means of earning money. A family friend came to the rescue and recommended Mrs. Moore for the job of caretaker at the County Court Offices in Queen Street. Thankfully, Emily moved into the spacious basement flat. She was allowed free fuel and light, so she could keep good fires going, even in the bedrooms, to counteract the damp.

She soon found, however, that she could not manage on the small wage and she had to resort to taking in washing to bring her income up to ten shillings a week. Even so, Ada and her sister Mary grew up in clothes provided by a local charity and suffered the humiliation of having the children of the town tagging after them calling "Charity Bulldog! Charity Bulldog!" All the children from a very early age had to help with the work but, when they had finished, Emily would gather them round the fire and tell them stories. Bible stories often featured in these sessions. She was a lively raconteuse, so they remembered the tales she told for the rest of their lives.

Emily found her lively family a handful but discipline was strict. Ada and her older brother John always seemed to cause the most trouble, as they both wanted to rule the roost and were continually fighting. However, they had fun too. Sometimes, after they had all been sent to bed, the boys would creep out of their room into the one Ada shared with Mary. One of their favourite games was to re-enact the death of Sir Richard Grenville aboard his ship, the *Revenge*. A picture of the scene hung above Ada's bed, so that became the deck and gave her the right to declaim his final words: "Sink me the ship, Master Gunner, sink her! Split her in twain! Fall into the hands of God, not into the hands of Spain". On the occasions her eloquence exceeded her wisdom, Emily would hear what was going on and the sound of her footsteps on the stairs sent the children scrambling in all directions, the boys diving for their room with their hands behind to protect themselves from attack.

Nonetheless, Emily taught them good table-manners and made the girls curtsey to their elders and betters, and the boys to raise their caps. Above all, she dinned into them that they had to be absolutely truthful and scrupulously honest. As soon as they were old enough they went to Sunday school at St. Sepulchre's Primitive Methodist Chapel, where they were grounded in the teaching of both the Old and New Testaments. Older still, they attended the Chapel services too. None of this early teaching, however, was nearly as effective as the standards Emily set.

Emily had what she thought was a good idea to teach Ada lady-like ways. She arranged with a friend for her daughter, who was nice and quiet, to be Ada's companion. Ada hated her. The girl always wore gloves, seldom spoke, was very dull and had no imagination and Ada felt she was like a hump on her back, to be carried about wherever she went. The only interesting thing about her was that she lived on a terrace high above the sea. Often, when Ada walked home with her, the sun was setting and Ada longed to run across the broad golden path over the water to visit other lands.

The deprivation that Ada felt most keenly throughout her childhood was a lack of education. At school she was so far ahead of her contemporaries that she was put into the top standard when she was ten. To her chagrin, the following year all the pupils in the lower standard were transferred to the new Girls' High School. Her mother tried to help and spared one penny a week for her daughter to get a library book, but that was quickly devoured.

When she left school, just before she was twelve, her mother found her a place as an apprentice in the millinery department of Rowntree's shop. Not unnaturally, Ada hated it. She disliked being cooped up all day in a small dark room where she seemed to spend most of her day on the floor picking up pins. She was found unsuitable and soon dismissed. She hated all the domestic jobs she was sent to do as well. There was one nice house whose owners were kind and gave Ada the only birthday present she had ever received – a piece of hair ribbon – but they had too many books and Ada would be distracted from her duties and too often found with her nose in a book rather than working.

Ada was sixteen when her mother announced her intention of marrying again, this time to a man who was the exact opposite of John Moore. All the children begged their mother not to marry him but Emily's mind was set, although she wavered slightly when Ada refused to go and live in the Watson house. It was a significant point in the girl's life, because from then on she made her own decisions.

She applied for a job at the laundry. Miss Mackenzie, the manageress, looked scornfully at her shabby appearance and said, "The situation advertised is for a clerk, not a cleaner".

"Yes, I know", replied Ada "I am applying for the job as Manageress's clerk." Something about her manner must have made a good impression, as she was appointed and given a wage of sixteen shillings a week.

It was fortunate that she came under the influence of someone as wise and good as Miss Yelland at the hostel, who recognised that she had in her charge a highly intelligent young woman, bursting with character and humour, who was struggling, not so much against material poverty, as for a richer intellectual and spiritual life. The girl also craved for love and affection. She found in Miss Yelland a substitute for her mother, whom she felt she had lost. She always, in later years, addressed her letters to 'My dear Second Mother'.

Many of the residents at Douglas House attended Holy Trinity Church and Ada, out of interest to begin with, occasionally went with them. She found that the dignified liturgy of the Church of England appealed to her aesthetic sense and she became a regular member of the congregation. After a while she decided to affirm her Christian faith by taking instruction and being confirmed.

Her family were quite as sceptical of Ada's declaration that she was going to Tibet as the girls in the hostel had been. They were also displeased by her behaviour. They did not like the fact that she had left the Chapel. Her mother was horrified, too, that her daughter should be working at the laundry where a number of the town's prostitutes were employed and when, one day, the news got round the town that Ada had been seen driving one of the delivery vans, her sister cut her dead.

Ada was doing such a shameful thing because she had gone to look for Joe, one of the van drivers, who had not reported back from his round. He had taken to the bottle since his little daughter had died and Ada had often comforted him when he was maudlin and kept him safe in her office when he was in no fit state to be out. She suspected he was drunk again and knew roughly where he might be so, anxious to keep him out of trouble with the police or Miss Mackenzie, she set out by herself to find him. He was huddled on a doorstep, dead to the world, with the horse waiting patiently nearby. She managed to haul him into the van then took the reins and let the horse find its own way back to the laundry-yard.

Ada had become very fond of the workers at the laundry. One way or another, most of them were social outcasts; prostitutes, drunkards, simpletons, or people whom life had treated badly. She always maintained that she never again met a body of people who were so kind and com-passionate to each other. It occurred to her that none of them attended any place of worship, so she asked one or two of the women whether they would like her to conduct a short lunchtime meeting. They gave grudging approval to the idea. Rather nervously at first, Ada started a well-known hymn and followed this with a Bible reading, then a few short prayers and another hymn. The women asked her to continue with a weekly meeting. Some of the men started to lurk in the shadows, caps in hand. It was obviously appreciated and Ada knew she had succeeded when she heard the women discussing the little service and referring to her affectionately as "that religious bugger".

Six years passed then, one Monday morning, when Ada arrived at the office, she was surprised to find Miss Mackenzie already there and an elderly man installed at the clerk's desk. Miss Mackenzie announced tersely that the man (who later turned out to be an elderly relative of hers) was to take over the accounts and the records, which Ada was so proud of keeping well. At the end of the week it was obvious he was quite incompetent and Ada had to sort out the mess, the books she had kept so beautifully being full of mistakes and blotches. Matters did not improve. In the end she confided her troubles to Miss Yelland, who agreed that the situation was intolerable. After a pause, she said, "I think the time has come for you to take the next step."

Events now moved quickly and, in what seemed no time at all, Ada took up her place at the Missionary Training College at Chelsea. She was sponsored by the generosity of the congregation of Holy Trinity. After she had paid her fees and compulsory extras she had one shilling and sixpence a week left, out of which she had to find money for shoe repairs, bus fares, collection money, and postage – indeed everything. She once remarked wryly, "I never seemed to have anything to spare, not even a farthing for the odd bun, which the other girls occasionally indulged in." Realising that life as a missionary would involve greater hardship she began a rigorous course of self-discipline, cutting out unnecessary luxuries like sugar in her tea, just to prove to herself that she could.

Poverty, however, did not spoil her pleasure in her new life. To Ada everything was thrilling. London exhilarated her – the crowds, the bright lights, the movement, the shops and buses – this was all the entertainment she needed. She loved the pageantry, the art galleries, the great churches and memorials.

An experience she treasured all her life happened at this time, when she was chosen to sing as one of a quartet representing the college at a choral festival at the Albert Hall. She had a good ear and a pleasing contralto voice ("All t'Moores can sing", remarked a great-aunt) but Ada

Ada at Chelsea

couldn't believe it was happening to her, and she never lost this heightened capacity for enjoyment of new experiences that came her way.

Above all she relished the opportunity to improve her education. She realised she had a very great deal to learn, not only from her books, but from everything and everyone around her. She was still a very rough, uncouth girl, with a broad Yorkshire accent and an uncompromising Yorkshire attitude, but mercifully she was perceptive and adaptable and her good humour and zest for life endeared her to people.

The students at Chelsea were all young women who hoped someday to become missionaries or, failing that, Church workers. They came from every walk of life, some, like Ada, with very little education, so the curriculum included arithmetic, English grammar and hygiene. Also, because it was thought important that a missionary should have some interest other than her daily occupation, they had classes in botany and geology. The students had to do most of the housework at the college and help in the kitchen, to learn practical skills. Ada was used to hard work and would always try to swap light duties, such as dusting the parlour, for cleaning the stairs and hallway, from where she could keep an eye on what was going on. Later in the course they helped in the local

Future missionaries: Ada's year at Chelsea

Miss Brook

Miss Grapes

Sunday Schools and with women's meetings and they undertook house to house visiting. Above all, the course set out to make the students completely conversant with their Bibles and to understand the history of the Christian teaching, so that they themselves in time could teach.

Ada had the gift of making the stories in the Bible come alive. She attributed this to the brilliant teaching of Miss Frances Brook, the lecturer on Old Testament history, who inspired her to know the Old Testament thoroughly and to understand its deepest significance in laying the foundations of the Christian faith. Miss Brook was scholarly and inspiring as a teacher and a quiet, kind woman with a magnetic personality. Ada adored her. At first Ada would reproduce the facts she learnt verbatim, thanks to her excellent memory, but Miss Brook encouraged her to write essays in her own style and eventually Ada was achieving the highest marks of anyone in the class.

Her high spirits were still inclined to get her into trouble. The students were all terrified of the Principal, Miss Grapes, and, when they had some request to make of her, there was a long discussion about who would be brave enough to go and see her. Eventually, Ada was nominated and, putting a brave face on it, she went clowning down the stairs, watched by all her friends. At the bottom the mat slipped under her feet and she went skidding across the polished floor, bang into the Principal's bedroom door, which crashed open. Ada sailed through on her mat and landed at the feet of Miss Grapes, who was clad only in her stays. Stunned for a moment, Ada then collapsed with laughter at the ridiculous situation, until an icy voice suggested she remove herself and report to the study when she was in a proper frame of mind.

Ada's slender means prevented her returning to Scarborough for holidays. Sometimes a friend called Grace Bond would invite her to stay in Norwich, where she had been brought up by two maiden aunts. The 'Aunties Bond' were dear, good people and Ada made life-long friends of them.

Another holiday, when she thought she was to act as companion to an old lady, nearly ended in her expulsion from the college. The old lady was called away a few days after Ada's arrival, leaving Ada in the house with the maid, who took the opportunity to go out and about on her own business, while warning Ada to stay out of the main house and the kitchen. Unfortunately, there was only one key, so Ada was virtually a prisoner in her hot attic bedroom. The window had been nailed shut but, in desperation, Ada managed to force it open to get some air and in doing so made the acquaintance of a black cat that seemed at home on the roof. The cat was her only company until the old lady returned.

Hoping that at last she would have someone to talk to and a decent meal, Ada was surprised and upset to be summoned for evening prayers before being dismissed once more to her room without anything to eat. The following day she was told to pack her bags and return to the college, where Miss Grapes wished to speak to her. Ada presented herself in Miss Grapes' study, where her erstwhile hostess was already seated. She received a lecture on her ingratitude and was so appalled and mystified that she only heard odd words, such as 'stealing', 'damage' and 'filling the house with cats'.

She was ordered to apologize but Ada could only stammer, "But what have I done?" She was ordered to kneel with the other women, who prayed that her hard heart would be softened and that she should see the folly of her ways. This really put Ada's dander up and, when it was suggested that she might join in a prayer asking for forgiveness, she remained absolutely silent. With a grim face, Miss Grapes escorted the old lady out. On her return she told Ada to sit on the sofa and consider her wickedness and, when she was in a proper state of mind, she was to admit to her sins.

Ada flared up, "If I sit here for the rest of my life I shall never confess to something I have not done!"

Whereupon Miss Grapes replied, "I can see I shall have to write to Miss Yelland and see about sending you back to Yorkshire." She sat there for the rest of the day and late into the evening. Eventually, Miss Brook quietly opened the door and came in.

Sitting beside Ada on the sofa she said, "Tell me what happened, Ada." Ada was reluctant to speak at first, but Miss Brook coaxed the story out of her. The threat of expulsion had been a severe shock, but she never did discover what she was supposed to have done and the subject was never referred to again.

The following term Ada was once again summoned to Miss Grape's study. She anxiously thought of all her possible misdoings. No one was more surprised than she when she was told she had been elected by the votes of the students and staff to be Senior Student. Her predecessor had always appeared perfect in every way and Ada's reaction was, "What? ME? Me – follow 'Holy Maude'? You can't mean it!"

Towards the end of the second year, the students had to submit applications to the missionary societies of their choice. Ada's options were narrow as there were only two missions working in Tibet: one was the China Inland Mission, which had a small station on the Sino-Tibet border, and the other was the Moravian Missionary Society, which operated at several stations in Western or Little Tibet. Ada's application to the China Inland Mission was unsuccessful as they had no vacancies for single women. She then wrote to the Moravian Missions and was downcast to be told that there were only two posts for single sisters, as the unmarried women were called, and these were both filled. She prayed earnestly for a miracle to happen. A week or two later she received a letter from the Moravians calling her to an interview with the Board, as one of the single sisters in Leh had fallen ill and had to be recalled. Ada was duly accepted by the Board to go to Leh, in Ladakh, the following autumn. She could hardly believe her good fortune and was more than ever convinced of Divine Guidance.

There were still three months of training to undergo at the Mildmay Mission Hospital in Bethnal Green. Here prospective missionaries were taught the rudiments of nursing, setting broken bones, stitching wounds, pulling teeth, doing dressings, assisting at operations and dispensing. Ada should also have been taught some midwifery but somehow Sister Edith, who was her supervisor, always directed her into other departments when she should have been in the midwifery section, despite her pleas and protests. She left without even seeing a baby delivered, an omission she felt keenly in later years.

The Mission Board confirmed her appointment at a salary of £100 a year. It was also decided that she should spend three months in Germany, at the Moravian centre at Herrnhut in Saxony. She was to stay with a family called Hettasch, while she familiarised herself with the Moravian way of life and learnt German, as many of her future colleagues would be German-speaking.

For the first time in two years Ada returned to Scarborough, to prepare for her departure. The Mission Board had given her a grant of £20 to equip herself for her first ten-year tour, with which she had to buy everything she might need. Even Ada, who was used to living on a shoestring, found the sum quite inadequate. Her good friends at Douglas House and the congregation at Holy Trinity came to her rescue. Someone presented her with a French carriage clock, which accompanied her on all her travels and never needed repair. A group clubbed together to give her a camera, fitted with a special lens. Everyone suddenly became generous. Her Uncle Abraham, who was prospering now, gave her a handsome sum of money with which to buy clothes. Her brother John gave her a fountain pen, which she used for the rest of her life. Her mother gave her four silver spoons and forks she had had from her own home and Ada joyfully equipped her tiffin basket[2] with them and was deeply upset when they were later stolen in India. She also gave her an enamelled fob-watch. Ada felt wonderfully rich.

For the first time it seemed that everyone had accepted her and her 'daft ideas'.

---

[2] Tiffin is a word used in India for a light meal, so picnic basket

CHAPTER 2

Journeys' beginning

It was spring 1913, almost exactly ten years since she first believed that God wanted her to go to Tibet, when Ada said goodbye to her family and friends in Scarborough. She was met in London by an official from the Mission Board who put her on the boat train on the first leg of her journey to Dresden, where she was to wait a day or two for the local connection to Berthelsdorf. Despite being dreadfully hungry, as her packet of sandwiches was soon eaten, the journey was uneventful as far as Leipzig. She had expected the train to go straight through to Dresden so when she was turned out at Leipzig Ada was very worried, especially when she discovered there were several hours to wait and she would not arrive in Dresden at the time she was expected. Anxiously trying to identify her luggage in the luggage van and wondering how she was going to manage to find out what to do next, she was unnerved when a little man, dressed in a black suit and bowler hat, came up to her. He added to her unease by clicking his heels, seizing her hand and kissing it, saying, "Miss Moore?" Then, before she had time to recover, he started talking in voluble German, of which she understood nothing except for two words, Hettasch and Dresden. At this she sighed with relief. A meal made her feel much better but as the long day wore on she found her companion's formal manners made her uncomfortable. He seemed to be for ever bowing and clicking his heels, which seemed to her absurd and ludicrous. She had to keep reminding herself that it was bad manners to be critical and she must accept a different way of behaving but the day passed slowly and the relief was probably mutual when she and her guide eventually parted company.

Herr Hettasch's brother was waiting for her at Dresden and she was thankful to find that he spoke a little English. He and his wife were most kind and hospitable. However they had a small daughter, Lisl, who in her childish way resented this strange foreigner in her house. Ada, who must have been feeling rather unsure of herself, found that this caused her considerable hurt and upset. She was glad to go on to Herrnhut, where she was most warmly welcomed by the whole Hettasch family.

There was Grossvater, with a round rosy face and a long white beard, who sat in the corner by the stove smoking his curly pipe, watching everything that was going on with a twinkle in his eye. Ada came to love him dearly. There were Pappa and Mutti, and there were four children, two boys, Siegfried and Werner, and two girls, Elisabeth and the youngest who was always affectionately known as Putti.

Putti quickly took Ada in hand and pounced on any mistake she made. "Nein, nein, nein, Schwester Moore, du musst nicht *so* sagen, du musst *so* sagen."

On the other hand, Grossvater liked to practise his pedantically correct English on Ada, or recite his favourite poem, "Brrreakk, brrreakk, brrreak on thy cold grey stones, oh Sea!" which always made her giggle. One day he caught her giggling and was most hurt, "Did I not say it correctly?" he demanded.

"Oh yes," said Ada, "It was perfect."

"So why do you laugh?"

"It was too perfect."

He stiffly rejoined in his most German manner, "It is not possible to be too perfect", and was a little huffy with her for several days.

Life in Herrnhut was quite different from anything she had ever known. It was quiet and peaceful and everyone tried to live a simple, communal life with as little contact with the outside world as possible. Ada found the Moravian liturgy to be similar to that used by the Church of England. The hymns they sang were mostly the beautiful old German chorales and the sermons were immensely long. Ada was very happy there.

However Germany was obviously preparing for war and even the Moravians, whose creed was to live demonstrably in a state of love and charity with their neighbours, believed that Germany must go to war with England. All the fine black cattle belonging to Count Zinzendorf, on whose land Herrnhut was built, were replaced by cavalry horses during Ada's stay and soldiers were billeted on the estate. Siegfried and Werner pointed out Zeppelins to her and announced that they were going to bomb England. It seems unbelievable that in England itself there was little realisation amongst ordinary people of the coming crisis.

By the time her three months were up Ada had a working knowledge of the German language and had absorbed the traditions of the Moravian Church. But, even more important, she had come to love and respect the people of the Herrnhut community, who had so hospitably received her and made her one of themselves.

Two young doctors, Reeve Heber (who was of German descent) and his wife, Kathleen, were also posted to Leh. As they were still on their honeymoon they welcomed the trip to Herrnhut to collect Ada. From there they all travelled to Trieste where they were to embark on a Lloyd Triestino liner for Bombay. Everything was so novel and so different from her former life that Ada enjoyed every minute. The ship was a few days late and so, nothing loath, this young missionary trio had to spend three or four days in Trieste.

Ada's room was on the second *piano*, next door to the landlady's son. He would sit on a mat outside his door each evening with his guitar and serenade her, much to her enjoyment. The Hebers teased her unmercifully, especially when he turned up to see her off on the ship.

The ship docked at Bombay, from where they set off up-country by train. The party for Leh was to foregather at the house of a lady missionary, also a doctor, at Ambala but the Hebers had been invited to spend a day or two visiting a mission hospital, which meant leaving the train before it reached Ambala, so Ada carried on alone. The fourth member of the mission going to Leh was a young minister by the name of Henry Burroughs, usually called Harry.

Ada was on her own at the house when Harry Burroughs arrived, as the doctor had been called out to attend to a case some distance away. The bearer brought the new sahib to her on the verandah. She couldn't resist acting as hostess and seeing how long she could pretend to be the lady missionary, so Harry spent the whole day misunderstanding who she was. Fortunately, he took it well when Ada introduced their real hostess on her return and explained she was to be one of his colleagues in Leh. As soon as the Hebers joined them the party set off once more, first by train to Rawalpindi. After that the going became wilder and

Ada at Ambala

more hazardous and they had to hire a light cart called a *tonga*, the
only sort of transport that could negotiate the mountain roads. Srinagar,
their next objective, lay three days ahead, which meant spending three
nights at rest houses on the way. Their driver was a white-bearded
Mohammedan, who drove at a cracking pace and refused to give way
when another *tonga* approached from the opposite direction. The other
driver was equally obdurate, so the two carts collided and they were all
thrown out into the road. Without so much as a glance in his passengers'
direction, the old rascal of a driver jumped off his seat and threw his
arms round the other driver's neck and they clutched each other in a
warm embrace. Shaken though they were, the young missionaries had
to laugh at the sight of the two bearded men bear-hugging each other
in the middle of the road.

When the *tonga* had been put to rights, they set off again at the
gallop. It was bumpy going for the passengers, but must have been even
worse for the boy who lay on the roof, whose job it was at each bend
in the road to blow a few notes on a horn to warn other traffic of their
approach. Every five miles the horses were changed, though Ada could

see little difference between the sorry beasts that were unharnessed and those that were harnessed up again.

On the second day they crossed a bridge that was the boundary between India and the princely state of Kashmir. Here they were held up by a clerk whose job it was to see that everybody entering Kashmiri territory signed a promise and declaration that they would not cross into the Forbidden Territory of Tibet, the boundaries of which had been defined in the treaty drawn-up by Younghusband in 1904.

The third day of the journey was the most exciting, as they were all looking forward to reaching Srinagar, the doorstep to their future life. They were bowling along a lovely road, lined all the way with trees, admiring their beauty, when something startled the horses and they bolted. Ada was sitting next to the driver and set up a wail of, *"Thairo, thairo"*, which she thought meant "stop", while the poor man struggled to get the frightened animals under control. He said nothing but he looked as if he would like nothing better than to see her thrown out. At length they arrived in Srinagar, that beautiful yet squalid city.

Srinagar

The very next day Ada met Pagspa, who was the first Tibetan she had set eyes on. It was the moment she had dreamed of for ten years and she was nearly intoxicated with delight, but she was also mildly disappointed at seeing a Tibetan so neat and clean. The vision she had stored up was of shaggy, unkempt hair and a dirty, shabby robe leaving the right arm bare, but here was Pagspa, with his kind, fatherly smile and gentle mien, dressed in his tidy homespun gown held at the waist by a bright woollen sash. His legs were bound by black homespun puttees and he wore the Kashmiri leather shoes shaped like canoes. His hair curled out from underneath his cap and was tied in a neat pigtail behind. He wore large earrings fashioned in filigree silver, in the centre of which was a large coral, with a turquoise on either side, a design that was repeated in his necklace. As he turned to leave, however, she saw that there was a large greasy patch on his back, where the oil or butter from his hairdressing had stained his gown and she felt a little mollified. Pagspa had accompanied one of the missionary ladies, who had come down to Srinagar to send her child home to school. He was not joining their party on this occasion but he later became Ada's dear friend and guided her on many a difficult journey.

The men who were to escort them to their new home arrived the following day, having walked two hundred and forty miles from Leh. Immediately, they set about buying stores for the return journey and for the missionaries' use in the coming months. They also had to arrange the hire of ponies, for riding and to carry the luggage. The young missionaries did not realise at the time how fortunate they were to have all the arrangements made for them. There was nothing for them to do but to be happy and enjoy the experience.

The leader of the party was Yoseb Gergan, who had been educated in Srinagar at the school founded by Canon Tyndale Biscoe, and he took the opportunity to visit his old school. Puntsog, his helper, was a tall loose-limbed fellow with a ready sense of humour and a wide smile that revealed perfect white teeth. He was of aristocratic descent and had a place in the Tehsil, or government office in Leh. The third man was called Drogpa, who was an orphan brought up and taught by the Mission and he accompanied the party as cook. They were all members of the Christian Church at Leh and so did not wear the Buddhist pigtail.

The members of the Church Missionary Society made their colleagues very welcome and Ada found comfort in the knowledge that these neighbours, although sixteen days' march away, would always provide lodging and assistance if there was any reason to go down-country. The missionaries visited schools and hospitals and watched a regatta organized by the rowing club of the Church Missionary Society School on the River Jhelum. They were also given injections against typhoid and other diseases. Ada looked about in complete wonder at the shimmering leaves of the autumnal chenar leaves and the sparkling of the sun on the ice on the mountain range, dominated by Nanga Parbat, and felt that such scenes could only induce a silence of adoration of the Creator of all beauty.

On 1st October, 1913, after about ten days, the party left Srinagar on the last leg of their journey. Their Ladakhi guides, led by Yoseb Gergan, took the ponies round by land while the four young missionaries made an idyllic journey across the lake in a *shikara*, a kind of punt, attractively equipped with colourful hand-embroidered cushions and an awning to shade them from the sun. The *shikara's* crew paddled rhythmically with their heart-shaped paddles, skilfully negotiating the boat under stone bridges and through a network of narrow waterways overhung by willows, past wooden houses built on stilts, until they came to the huge Anchar lake, where the ponies were waiting for them on the lake-shore at Ganderbal.

The Hebers were experienced riders and mounted their animals cheerfully. Harry had not only grown up with horses but had ridden quite a lot during his years in the army in India. He had brought his own English saddle with him, but even the biggest pony looked rather like a small boy wearing his father's jacket. Harry was so careful of his saddle, which was his pride, that during the journey it became nicknamed 'Mrs. Burroughs'. Ada, however, felt a little queer about the idea as she had never been astride a pony before, though she had often jogged along the sands at Scarborough on a donkey. She eyed her pony with interest, not altogether reassured except as to its size, but thought that if she could not ride him then she ought not to have left the cradle. He was very small and had only one eye. The saddle was high and made of wood, with ragged stuffing in places, and for reins and bit there was a rope.

There was some hilarity at Ada's attempt to mount and everyone made different suggestions. It was Harry who gave her a leg up and got her settled. At last they set off – luggage ponies with their loads, riders and walkers. A fair-sized caravan, they were all excited and happy. The way soon led through fields, where the paths were the narrow banks of watercourses, a few inches high. They were picking their way along one *bund* between two water-courses when Ada felt her pony slip and her confidence evaporated. She yelled, "I'm off!" and flung her arms round the pony's neck rather than fall into the water, which frightened the pony into a run. From this position there was no recovery. Puntsog was delighted. He rode up behind and smacked the pony each time it showed signs of slowing up and Ada was so convulsed with laughter at her ridiculous position that she couldn't sit up. This was never forgotten by the Tibetans, who love fun, and they decided that Ada was worth teasing. They played all sorts of jokes on her during the trip, including one day loosening the girth so that Ada felt herself gently sliding to the ground as the saddle slipped. It all helped to enliven a dull march.

Ada decided that even the ponies had entered into a conspiracy against her when one day, when she was feeling quite experienced, they were ambling along in the warm sunshine on the outskirts of a village and horse and rider must both have been dreaming. When the road took an unexpected turn round the wall of a field he went straight into the wall and Ada was pitched over it into the field beyond.

They wound up the beautiful Sind valley for four days. At Baltal they crossed the river, a tumbling mountain torrent. This was a favourite camping spot, both for travellers and fishermen. The road wound on up through the hills, following the valley the whole way. At first they rode through forests of deodar and pencil cedar, which gradually thinned out and gave way to scrub and silver birch. They were climbing up to the Zoji La, which crosses what is known as the back-bone of the Himalayas at an altitude of 11,500ft. The road eventually became less steep and they rode across an alpine meadow covered in flowers. On top of the pass Yoseb Gergan suggested that they should dismount and look back on the beauty of the Vale of Kashmir, for, he said, they would not see such fertility again. He explained that the monsoons break against this vast mountain barrier and few clouds ever rise above the peaks, so that the

The Zoji La

land to the south is fertile and green whereas that beyond is dry and rocky. Yoseb went on in his quiet voice to say that, though they were leaving so much beauty behind, he hoped that in the new land they were about to enter they would find sufficient kindness and interest to compensate for the barrenness of the landscape. Yoseb also pointed out the winter route across the pass, on which many men had lost their lives. At an almost unbelievable height, to keep them above the winter snow, they could see telegraph wires running from crag to crag.

The party turned to go over a snow bridge on the summit of the pass, with crystalline water flowing below, and Yoseb showed them the glacier from which the watershed is formed. They had seen the rushing mass of water that was the Sind River and here was its source, tiny trickles running down the mountain, slipping into runnels, where a small stone in its path would decide which way, north or south, the water would flow: to Kashmir from the Sind to the Jhelum, or by the Ladak Chu[3] to join the Zangskar River which later joined the Indus in the mountains of Pakistan. The Tibetan name of the glacier was *Acho nos chu Lgos,* – the separation of the water brothers.

---

[3]   Chu: water

The road from Srinagar to Leh was one of the longest and oldest roads in the world. Herodotus wrote an account of collecting gold from the desert along its way. The ancient Greeks also knew of this country for Megasthenes, Greek ambassador to an Indian court, tells how the Indian ants dug gold out of the earth, not for the sake of the metal, but in making burrows for themselves. The old gold diggings were still there and, as the missionaries rode along, they were shown traces of them. Ptolemy too wrote about the rivers and people in the district of Western Tibet. Ada loved the sense of history and was fascinated by the stories of the people who had travelled that way before her.[4]

It was only a mountain track, so narrow in most parts that travellers had to journey in single file. The missionary party found their ponies had a disconcerting habit of walking on the extreme edge of the precipice, so that every now and then a hind foot would slip over the edge, which was nerve-wracking for the rider until he became accustomed to it. The ponies, which often

Descent from the Zoji La

carried bulky loads, knew it was safer, for if they bumped the load on an overhanging rock they might lose their balance and go plunging down the *kud*.[5]

---

[4]   This route, which had remained substantially unchanged for centuries, is now built up and made into a military road suitable for vehicles, since Leh is a strategic point in India's defence against the Chinese and Pakistanis.

[5]   Kud: ravine

There were large caravans of pilgrims travelling to Mecca, Mohammedans from Turkestan, with their wives and children. For forty-two days these people had travelled under hazardous conditions to Leh, where they sold or bartered such merchandise as coarse white cotton cloth, woven and raw silk, dried currants, pistachio nuts, dried mares' milk and garlic. In exchange they got flour, mutton, salt and leather, which they needed for the next sixteen days' journey to Kashmir. In Kashmir they would sell their *numdahs*[6], which the Kashmiris would then embroider with traditional designs in gaily coloured wool and export again. Ada wrote, 'The men were of huge stature, tall and haughty. Many of the women were beautiful, but wore black *yashmaks* over their faces, a custom which, I learnt later, caused much amusement to the Tibetan women'. After selling their goods and with money in their pockets, they would travel to Bombay or Karachi and take a boat on the next stage of their journey to Mecca.

They also met Ladakhi men with ponies and donkeys laden with *charas*, which was a narcotic resin produced by the hemp plant. The resin was secreted by the bracts surrounding the flowers and the finest came from Yarkand and Kashgar. Ada found the method of collecting the resin interesting. Men clothed in leather walked in amongst the plants and, as they did so, the resin stuck to the leather, from which it was later carefully scraped off. The Indian *bhang*, or hemp, which was smoked, was prepared from the leaves and fruit of the hemp and the narcotics *gunjah* and *hashish* were prepared from the leaves and flower tops of the same plant. The sticky resin from Turkestan was packed in leather bags and then in sacking, but under the hot sun much of it exuded. It looked like black treacle and was equally sticky to the touch. There was a heavy customs duty to pay as it was brought into Indian territory through the Leh gate, which provided a useful form of revenue for such a poor province as Ladakh.

There were few places where the road was wide enough to allow two caravans to pass, so one or other of them had to give way and urge the ponies up the mountainside. The men shouted greetings and badinage to each other and exchanged bits of news they had picked up. Meeting

---

6   Numdah: felt saddle pad or rug

people relieved the monotony of ambling along hour after hour. Not all the travellers were on horseback; some were on foot and these automatically gave way to the ponies, except for the mail runners. Everyone gave way to the Royal Mail.

The runners carried a stout staff, at the top of which some little bells were tied and these jingled a warning as the man loped along. The precious bag of mail was tied on to his back with a shawl, which left his hands free to negotiate difficult places. Every five miles or so, at a convenient spot by a stream or a spring, there was a rough shelter built out of stones, or in the lee of a projecting rock, where the mail-runners made their rendezvous. The first arrival lit a fire, striking a flint on the metal edge of his tinder wallet, or *chakmak*, and set a pot on the fire to boil up some tea. He then rested until the runner from the opposite direction arrived. They drank tea together while they talked, giving each other the news and gossip from up and down the road, until it was time for them to exchange bags and set off again in the direction from which they had come. Before they left, they made sure that there was a little pile of fuel, dried dung or scrub, for the next comers. Throughout the winter, in the most appalling conditions of bitter winds and blinding snowstorms, with the constant danger of falling rocks or avalanches, the mail-runners faithfully carried the mail. Many lost their lives.

Dak[7] bungalows were staged about ten or fifteen miles apart, the normal distance for a day's march. People travelling light often did double stages but with heavily laden pack-ponies progress was naturally slower. Although these were convenient places to stay, some of the bungalows were not well-kept and it was wiser to pitch tents. It was nearly always wiser to use one's own bed, to avoid the vermin which thrived in the public rooms.

On the fourth day after crossing the Zoji the party arrived at Kargil, an historic crossroads for caravans from China, Tibet, Yarkand and Kashmir. Here the road branched, one way to Leh and the other to Baltistan. Up to this point the predominant religion (left behind after the Dogra invasion) was Mohammedan. Beyond Kargil they entered Buddhist country, with its monasteries and lamas, *chortens*[8] and prayer flags. At

---

[7] Dak bungalow: accommodation for travellers

[8] Chorten: a memorial structure

Kargil village

Mulbek the monastery dominated a solitary peak, which rose
straight up from the ground and
stood apart. Below it ran a
stream, which provided an
unfailing source of pure water for
the lamas. Here too, they saw for
the first time a massive effigy of
Chamba, otherwise known as
Maitreya, the Future Buddha,
carved out of solid rock in the
7th or 8th century.

They climbed up the Photu
La, a pass of 13,000ft, and
then dropped down again to
the river valley to a place called
Lamayuru, where they stopped
to see the monastery built into
the pinnacles of the mountain.

Kargil

The Monastery at Mulbek

They spent the night in the guest house there and were interested to be told the story of how Lamayuru received its name. A lama, centuries ago, was on a pilgrimage. One night, as he slept by the stream, he dreamed that he saw a *Yungdrung*, or swastika, in that place. So he rose quickly and looked around until, after patient searching, he found the spot where he saw the sacred sign in the sand. This, he said, must be a holy place. He therefore sought help and, after many years, founded a monastery there, which was named Lama Yungdrung. In the course of time, however, the name became shortened to Lamayuru.

When they were out walking in the evening in a field below the monastery wall, they were greatly entertained to see two billy-goats having a fight, which appeared almost like a pre-arranged match. Looking like two high priests with solemn faces and long beards, they each stood on their chosen sites about sixteen feet apart, then the two of them lunged forward simultaneously and met with a resounding whack on the forehead. Withdrawing, they backed with deliberate steps, paused, and then went in again for another crack. It was the solemnity with which they carried on their sparring match that made the whole thing so ludicrously funny to the onlookers.

Lamayuru

Lamayuru

The party had not travelled very far the following day when they saw an old, grey-haired woman by the roadside, supported by two men. The men said that they had heard that a doctor was travelling along the road and that they had brought her to be healed. Doctor Heber examined her poor old eyes and could see that there were cataracts in both. It seemed heartless to leave her but his instruments were packed away and he could only promise to come back to her village one day to perform the operation. How they longed to have the power to heal by touch! Later, Doctor Heber made numerous medical journeys and brought healing and sight to many people in need of help.

Lamayuru

Beyond Lamayuru, the Indus River takes a sharp turn to the north, after having flowed west from Tibet for 130 miles. The name 'Indus' is never used by the Tibetan-speaking peoples as they have their own descriptive names for the great rivers. The River Indus is *Senge ka Babs* or 'the water that flows from the mouth of the lion'; the Sutlej is *Langpo ka Babs*, meaning 'the water which flows from the mouth of the elephant'; and the great Brahmaputra River is known as *Mabya ka Babs*, or 'the water which flows from the mouth of the peacock'. The Tibetans were imaginative story-tellers, as they had no books to read, and Ada reflected

Wire rope bridge and fort at Khalatse

The bridge at Nyemo, one stage before Leh

that these names must have arisen from a fund of traditional folk-tales, handed on from generation to generation.

By this time they were used to crossing streams by typical Tibetan bridges, usually consisting of the trunks of two poplar trees lashed together and supported on piles of stones. If the trees were not particularly straight there were yawning gaps, sometimes plugged with a large stone. Here, however, there was a good suspension bridge to Khalatse.

As they rode along the river they passed two ancient fortresses. The one called Balukar had been a fortified customs house, which guarded the bridge. It was believed that the traders from Yarkand were taxed here, for although no coin has ever been found, many cowrie shells, which were used as currency, have been discovered at this site. There was an inscription carved on a rock below the castle and, from the orthography used, it has been estimated that it was carved in 800-1000 AD. Further along were large ruins at Basgo.

Typical bridge

Beyond this they came to a steep valley up which they rode or walked. It was so steep that the ponies climbed about four steps, rested, and then went on again, until at the top they arrived on the Ladakh plateau.

CHAPTER 3

First experiences of home

They spent the last night of the journey at Spitug, from where the next morning they rode across the flat, sandy plain which lay outside Leh. At such an altitude it was possible, in the clear and rarefied atmosphere, to see caravans moving a great way off and Ada reflected on the story of King David waiting anxiously for the news of his son Absalom. It must have been a gate very like the one she was riding towards from where he could see runners 'a great way off' bringing the news of Absalom's death. From the northern gate the road leads to the Karakoram Mountains and onwards to Yarkand, Kashgar, Tashkent, lands sealed off by Russia after Tibet was taken by the Chinese. The southern gate gives access to the route to India and the west, to the Changtang plateau and Tibet in the east. From China came brick tea, from Tibet wool, salt and borax, while from India came rice, cotton cloth, iron and brass pots and pans, as well as things from the West, including mirrors, horse-shoes, needles and tobacco. The gate had a large door and a little stairway leading to a room above, so that the customs officer could see anyone approaching the town.

It was an unforgettable experience passing through the town gate into the walled city. They were greeted at the gate by a kind little man, who led them through. Emerging from the shadow of the gatehouse was like awakening from a dream, for instead of austere desert and the mountains they had moved among for eighteen days they were in the heart of a busy town. Indians in white turbans and loose robes sat amongst their goods in their open-fronted shops; pigtailed Tibetans were unloading animals; Ladakhi women, wearing head-dresses with large, black lambskin ear-flaps making them look rather like teddy bears, were

The town gate, Leh

selling turnips and other vegetables, or moving about their business, carrying their children on their backs.

Pack horses in the serai, Leh. They had come about one month's journey from Yarkand, Central Asia

Leh bazaar

Everyone paused in their work to watch the new missionaries ride by, greeting them with welcoming smiles, as they were glad that the hospital was to have a doctor again. The hospital had been there as long as the oldest could remember and they missed its help when it was closed. Ahead of them was a Mohammedan mosque and, as it was noon, the Mullah came out on to the balcony and they heard the ancient cry meaning "There is no God but Allah".

Soon they saw a plump Englishwoman coming to meet them. This was Miss Birtill, the other single sister, whose jovial face and forget-me-not blue eyes welcomed them to their new home. She conducted them to the Mission Compound where they dismounted, travel-stained and stiff, but intensely excited. The newcomers were taken directly to meet the Superintendent of the Mission, the Rev. F. E. Peter, of German-Swiss birth, later Bishop Peter, who had been in the country for many years.

As Ada awaited her turn to be introduced, something sprang at her and gave her a fearful blow on the back, nearly knocking her down. It was Mr. Peter's fierce Tibetan dog, which had broken loose and obviously did not approve

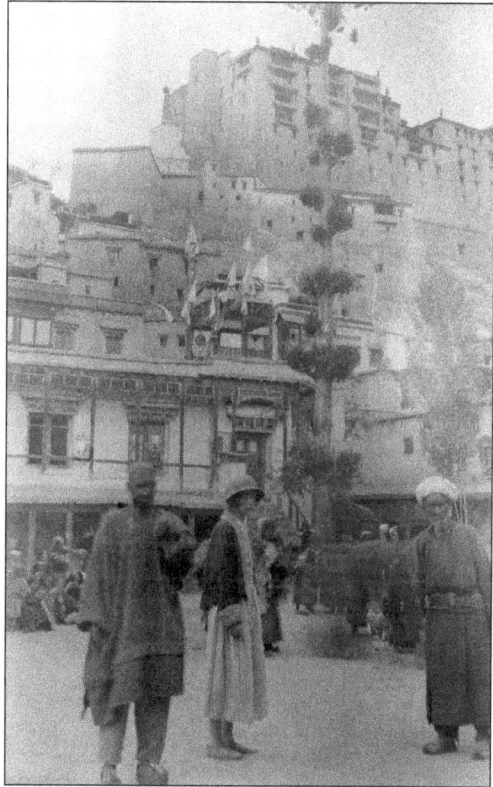

The Mosque at Leh

of strangers. A strip was torn out of her riding coat, from the shoulder downwards. Beyond giving Ada quite a fright, no further harm was done, but she reflected ruefully that her journey had begun with her falling off a very small pony and ended with being knocked about by a very large dog!

After this episode, the party dispersed to their own quarters. The four bungalows were neat, white-washed buildings, with verandahs and flat roofs, built in Tibetan style, with thick walls of mud. Unlike the Tibetan houses, however, the windows were glazed, indeed double-glazed, and the entrance was at ground level. The houses faced south, looking towards the range of mountains across the Indus. As well as the houses in the compound there was a library, a printing-press, a storeroom and stables, a school, the hospital and, of course, the church.

It was a wonderful feeling when Ada woke up the following morning to realise that at last she was in the place she had longed to reach for so many years. As she looked around her tiny, whitewashed bedroom, she thought she must be the most fortunate person alive. She wanted to get up and look at the snowy peaks through the little window set in the thick wall but caution held her back for a moment. After eighteen days' riding her saddle sores were painful. Then, throwing caution to the winds and telling her aches and pains they could look after themselves, she jumped out of bed and was soon chatting at the breakfast table with Miss Birtill about the day's programme.

Miss Birtill

The day was Sunday so, after their simple breakfast, Miss Birtill, whose chief responsibility was the mission school and Sunday school, took Ada across to the small, white-washed church, where children were excitedly awaiting their beloved teacher and the new Miss Sahib. Children of all sorts and conditions were jumping about like puppies, their brown eyes shining like lollipops with excitement and pleasure. Ada had never seen a Sunday School like it and she realised it was ideal for the circumstances. An amazing mixture, not only of nationalities and languages but of religious backgrounds all came together. Ada recalled that on one occasion she counted people who spoke nine different languages or dialects. The teacher was an English Christian, two children of missionaries were Swiss and spoke German, the Yarkandi Consul's son spoke Turki, a small girl, who had come with her father's caravan from Nepal, spoke Nepali and was a Hindu; others came from India, Kashmir, Afghanistan and Baltistan and, of course, there were the local Ladakhi children. So they all met, Hindu, Buddhist and Moslem at the Christian church to be taught by an English Moravian in Tibetan, which to some degree they all understood.

The regular members of the Sunday school loved to come, but some of the newcomers felt strange and shy, so Miss Birtill organized a game

School children

The mission team at Leh (with two unknown men)

Ada and Miss Birtill with the Sunday School

for them all. Ada wrote, 'I can see in my mind's eye a little Balti boy, kneeling inside a ring of children with his tiny hands up like the ears of a rabbit, while the rest circled round and round him singing:

"*Riong tsangs i nangna*
Nyid lokste duk, nyid lokste duk
Riong zurmo pok bina
Riong drong mi tub in
Da chongs!"

Which, roughly translated, meant:

"Rabbit in your nest,
Fast asleep, fast asleep,
Are you ill? Are you not able to jump?
Now JUMP!"

On the word "*chongs*" up sprang the little boy to choose another child as the rabbit. After one or two more games silence was called and the children clustered round the church door, where they kicked off their shoes, if they had any, and quietly went inside.

Ada came to love the children. They were in the main children of illiterate parents and neither they nor their parents had had any teaching previously, but they were lively and intelligent and would soon point out any inconsistencies in, or bits left out of, stories which they had been told before. They enjoyed singing too, although the tunes the missionaries taught them were quite different in character from their own music. Ada also liked them because they were full of fun and mischief and was inwardly delighted one day when she caught one small boy making the others giggle during the lesson by producing a rock partridge's foot and pulling the sinews to make the claws open and shut.

Sunday school had to finish in time to leave the church empty and open, to air before the main service. At that altitude oxygen was scarce and quickly became used up in an enclosed building. It was impossible to have the church full of people at Christmas and have lighted candles too for any length of time, as the lights slowly dimmed as the oxygen ran out.

Soon the adult congregation began to assemble and what a kaleidoscope of colour it was! The floor of the church was covered with yellow straw matting and, instead of the chairs or pews of a European church, there were strips of dark-grey homespun matting for the people to sit on. The men were on one side of the church and the women on the other, with the children in front. The missionaries had chairs at one side. The Minister stood before a draped table and Miss Birtill sat at the harmonium. Quickly and unobtrusively the men filed into their places, took off their caps, which they placed on the floor in front of them, and sitting cross-legged bowed in prayer. Their gowns of either undyed or mulberry-red wool were bound round the waist by a coloured *skyarak*[9]. Their caps, with points above the ears, were lined with sheepskin and turned up at the back and sides to show the wool. In bitter weather, or in times of mourning, the earflaps were turned down at the back. They could also be turned round to shade the eyes in bright sunlight.

The church at Leh

The women came in in a more stately manner, because of their heavy headdresses. Their thick, woollen dresses were of the same mulberry-coloured homespun material as the men's and edged with gay, woollen embroidery from Kashmir. They, too, wore coarse white cotton shirts, wrapped over at the neck and cuffs, and the woollen *skyarak*,

---

[9]   Skyarak: a long piece of fabric used as a belt

slipped through a circular brass ornament which they wore over the left hip and from which dangled a brass needle case, an implement for cleaning the ears, keys and leather thongs threaded with cowrie shells. The married women wore dark trousers, wrinkled tightly from knee to ankle but voluminous in the seat and tied with a cord. The unmarried girls wore white trousers. These trousers, when not being worn, were so long in the leg and broad at the top that they looked, for the entire world, like the arch of a viaduct. In the winter-time each woman and girl wore a goatskin on their backs with the hair inside for warmth. The smartest had a fringe of long hair showing round the edges. In summer-time, they wore thin, gaily-coloured shawls, worn under one arm and fastened on the other shoulder, where the ties were emphasized by a triangle of velvet. Their shoes were made of embroidered wool, well turned up in front to prevent the stubbing of toes against the stones, and soled with yak skin.

Their chief adornment was their headdress. Some of the Christians had adopted the white *burka* of the Mohammedan woman, which was made as an attractive cap from which flowed snowy white cotton down to the waist. On the front of the cap the Mohammedan women wore the Star and Crescent upon a red ground but the Christian women placed a cross of seed pearls on a red ground instead. The majority, however, wore the traditional *bcragh*, a stiffened red cloth shaped like a cobra. The head hung over the forehead and was adorned with a large turquoise or coral. A row of gold or silver amulets decorated the crown and on the body of the cobra, which fell to the waist, were row after row of neatly sewn turquoises. The wealthier the family, the larger and more numerous were the stones. Many women wore side extensions covered with corals. At each side of the head were black lambskin earflaps, which could be folded over the ears in bitter or windy weather. A former Ladakhi queen was said to have suffered from ear-ache and as the Leh palace was perched high up over the town all the bitter winds whistled through, so she had the earflaps made to protect her ears. The fashion caught on and became part of the national dress.

Beneath their headdresses, the women plaited lengths of wool into their hair, black for the married women and white for the unmarried. The plaits passed under their woollen girdles, till the many tiny plaits ended in a large tassel which hung at the bottom of the long gown. Small silver and brass bells were attached so that they tinkled as she walked. If the woman was rich she wore a lot of jewellery: filigree silver earrings, threaded with turquoise and coral; necklaces of silver and coral; rings; cowry shell bracelets and dangling silver ornaments, wherever they could squeeze them in on their heads. There were no banks in the country in which to accumulate wealth so that jewellery was bought or bartered and the wife carried it about on her person. Ada commented that she never heard of a case of robbery, so the system was obviously respected.

She was most struck by the dignity and beauty of the women as they filed into church that morning and, like the menfolk, sat down and bowed their foreheads to the ground in prayer. Everyone remained seated for the singing of the hymns. She could not help feeling how strange it was to hear the old chorales and hymns she had so recently learnt in German sung in slow, nasal Tibetan.

The strangeness did not last for long however, for, after the service, outside in the warm sunshine, the new missionaries were greeted in turn and the kind, open faces of the members of the congregation beamed with friendliness. Their manners were dignified and charming. Many of them were of high rank but all were naturally courteous and their happy smiles made the newcomers feel that they were at home and surrounded by friends.

Children's games

Playtime at the primary school

On Monday morning the missionaries each went to their appointed tasks. Children came to the compound for lessons and games, which took place in the sunshine. The parents thought it foolish that the missionaries taught the children Tibetan grammar and language, "Why teach them something they know and speak every day?" they asked, adding, "What they need is to be taught Hindustani or Turki, so that they can conduct their trade more intelligibly." They ridiculed the idea that children should be taught to read as only lamas should read. The girls were also taught to knit, and this was approved of, but as only men sewed it was not right that the girls, too, were taught to sew. The children loved to play together, too, which they did not have the opportunity to do at their homes.

Harry began to study the language, as it was essential that he should learn quickly. As he had had some medical training, he was also made responsible, under the doctor, for visiting the few lepers who lived outside the town. At that time there was very little that could be done for these unfortunate people who lived as outcasts. All Harry could do was to dress their sores and try and bring them some spiritual comfort and help.

The doctor went to the hospital, where crowds of people were waiting to see him, and Ada went too to help with the dressings and dispensing.

Knitting class

Sewing class

Not knowing the language was a serious handicap and the doctor had to depend on Zodpel, a Christian man, to translate for him. Zodpel had previously worked with a German missionary as a dresser but he knew no English. He listened to the patient's troubles in Tibetan, Turki, Urdu or Kashmiri and then translated them into the little German he knew. Dr. Heber spoke German but his mind worked in English, so that progress was necessarily slow and he had to rely largely on physical examination and intuition in discovering what ailed his patients.

Learning the language was the missionaries' primary duty and, each afternoon, they worked at it. Yoseb Gergan, their guide from Srinagar, was the schoolmaster of the mission School. He was the son of a lama of the Red Cap order, who had also been on the staff of the thirteenth Dalai Lama. The family had had to flee from Lhasa. They came into contact with Christian missionaries and when the father fell ill he gave Yoseb into their care, asking that he should receive a good education. Yoseb attended the CMS[10] School in Srinagar, where he turned out to be a brilliant scholar, but he decided to return to his homeland where, after some years, he was ordained the first Tibetan Christian minister. He started to teach the two doctors. Harry and Ada were taught by Dewazung, also later ordained, who knew a good deal of English, which was a great advantage.

At the end of twelve months they all had to be examined by the Superintendent, who had been in the country for nearly thirty years and knew Tibetan very well. Dewazung warned Ada that she might be asked to translate the story of the Prodigal Son into Tibetan up to the verse where the lost son returned home. As she had a good memory, she learned it almost off by heart. Unfortunately for her this plan of hers leaked out and when she entered the examination room she was asked to translate the second half of the story, where the elder brother came home and asked angrily why there were such rejoicings. As she had not studied, let alone learned, this part of the story she had to go stumbling through it, much to Mr. Peter's amusement and her discomfiture.

The Tibetan language is a difficult one, not least because it has three forms. All religious ceremonies were conducted in *Choksad*. The honorific *Tralskat* is used when addressing people of high rank, or those held in great respect, while *Palskad* is the common language used by the ordinary people in the daily course of their lives. The language is based on Sanskrit and the present alphabet was introduced into the country during the eighth and ninth centuries. In Ladakh the language of the original inhabitants, the Dards and Mons, has also been absorbed. The

[10]   Church Mission Society

art of printing came from China, where for many centuries whole pages of books were engraved on long wooden tablets. The Tibetans in Lhasa adopted this method, printing on paper imported from Nepal. However, at that time there was no Tibetan literature available for the common use of the people, as the only books in the country were religious books, written in *Choksad*, the language of religion, which were kept and read exclusively by the lamas.

The first record of the introduction of Lamaist literature into Western Tibet was in the 13th century. A king named Lhargyal, circa 1250 AD, whose name has been preserved on an ancient sculpture near the village of Daru, ordered a treatise about his favourite god to be copied in gold. Besides this, he ordered two other Lamaist works to be similarly copied on indigo-tinted paper. During the reign of his son the old Bon religion of Ladakh received its death blow after he introduced a system whereby novices were sent to central Tibet and Lhasa thus became the literary centre, instead of Ladakh. This meant that the province of Western Tibet, which had a great aptitude for poetry and a wealth of folklore, was prevented from developing its own literature. In accordance with his plan

Lama 'making religion' by reading

to bring central Tibetan literature into prominence in his country, this same king ordered that the colossal Tibetan Encyclopaedia of Lamaism, called *Kangyur*, a collection of one hundred and eight volumes, should be copied twice, and a book of secret spells to be copied many times.

Unfortunately, instead of the written language becoming a source of knowledge and true learning, the aim of the study of the country's literature became only to accrue merit and reading degenerated into the rattling off of syllables without considering the meaning. Many times in Tibetan homes Ada saw lamas reading aloud from different pages of the same unbound book, believing that it was the act of reading alone that would bring about the desired result.

To a certain extent the history of the country had been kept alive by travelling beggars, who wandered round the villages. They sang some of the ancient ballads and epics, which had been passed on for centuries and for which the country was once famous. To accompany the singing a man tapped with his finger tips on a tiny drum, or, more often, he had a little drum with swinging knobs which could be made to produce rhythm. Occasionally the instrument was a one-stringed fiddle, to which a woman sang. Old and new tales were also told by men around the camp fires and on the flat roofs of the houses in winter as the women spun their wool in the sunshine.

As part of their language study, Yoseb Gergan would teach the missionaries about Buddhism and local beliefs. The Tibetan Buddhists believe that there were a thousand Buddhas before the one they knew as Sang-gyas, whom they reckon was the perfected one. He was reincarnated five hundred times in a sinful state and five hundred times in a sinless state, Buddha, or Sang-gyas, being the last of the thousand. Before his retirement and emergence as Buddha his personal name was Gautama, in Sanskrit, and Dondrub in Tibetan. He lived at his own house and his family name was Shakgya Dukpa, which means the Conqueror. He was liberal and gave alms freely. In fact he gave away all that he had, even his wife, and the most precious jewel which he wore on his head. His father became angry with him and expelled him from his house so that he had to go and live in the forest. As the sisters showed sympathy with their brother they were also turned out of their home. Seeing them the Lha, or God, sent word to Buddha that he might marry his sisters.

Another story Ada found most interesting was a Tibetan theory of the Creation of the World, which in some ways resembles that of the Book of Genesis. Nestorian Christians had certainly arrived in China by the sixth century, so Ada wondered if they had had some influence on this story. Evidence of an early Christian presence is also to be found at Drangtse in one of the many ancient stone carvings to be found in Ladakh[11].

Ada and Miss Birtill shared the single sisters' bungalow. This had two small bedrooms, a living room, a kitchen and a store room. They also had a garden in which to grow vegetables and flowers. Yeshas was the gardener and odd-job man. The more common form of this name was Ishe, meaning wisdom, which in this particular case was not entirely apt.

Women selling barley beer

He was a Buddhist and wore a very long pigtail and he had a fondness for the local barley-beer, or *chang*. Whenever either of the sisters spoke to him, he always replied, "O-le!" in a deep voice, which was a polite way of saying, "Yes". The more *chang*

---

11   Ladakh is rich in ancient stone carvings. The most important of these to the Christian world is at a place called Drangtse. In 1906, when one of the missionaries was on a medical tour he found some crosses carved on a rock accompanied by a strange inscription. He consulted Dr. Francke, the missionary at Khalatse and a famous archaeologist, who suggested that the crosses might be evidence of Christianity. When Dr. Francke was later in Berlin he discussed the matter with a Professor F. M. Muller who, on seeing a photograph, declared that it was in Syriac script over a thousand years old. It read: 'One year on 215 halting places: I, the man from Samarkand, Charansar, have arrived here to Tubot." Above the cross was inscribed the word 'Ysax', declared to mean 'Jesus'.

At the sisters' bungalow

Kathleen Heber and Ada in the sisters' garden

he had imbibed, the longer the "O" became, so that it was easy to assess his condition by how deep and long drawn out were the affirmatives to their requests. However, he was a mild and kind man, who enjoyed gardening and was skilled in growing vegetables.

In the summer, when the garden was invaded by hordes of caterpillars he would break off a cabbage leaf and go round carefully picking them off the plants. Then he dropped them over the wall. Being a good Buddhist he could not take life and even after all his patient labour to get rid of them he did not seem to mind how fast the caterpillars formed queues on the wall to get back into the garden again.

Their other servant was Denyed. Despite being younger than Ada and Miss Birtill, she was as kind and thoughtful as any mother could have been. She belonged to a Tibetan family who had come from Kyeling, on the Tibetan side of the Rotang La in Kulu. Ada thought her family were splendid people and she regarded Denyed as a saint on this earth for her sweetness of mind.

The Hebers had a delightful cook, called Deskyd, meaning Happiness. She came of a good family and her lively face certainly radiated happiness and merriment. She enjoyed a little chaff and, with her ready wit, could give a very spicy repartee. She was always beautifully dressed and wore magnificent jewellery. Her headdress was heavy with turquoises and gold amulets, and she wore many necklaces and bracelets. She lived in a large house in the town with her brother. He was a tall, slim, elegant young man, who was also always well dressed and who wore his shirt-sleeves long enough to cover his hands as an indication of his rank. He was responsible for the customs post at the northern gate of the city, through which passed all the goods from Yarkand, Tashkent, and Russia. He was a good Christian and a man much honoured for his integrity.

The various household servants were constantly going to and fro, for none of them lived on the compound but in their own homes in the town and they went home for meals. The missionaries had to adapt their mealtimes to suit the cook for, if it were a woman, she would have to go home in time to cook again for her own family.

The mission stables were situated by the gate to the compound, near the stream. One day, a new arrival appeared there, a beautiful *rkiang*, or Tibetan wild ass, which Mr. Peter had acquired. He was a lovely animal, nut brown in colour shading to white underneath, and his graceful motion as he ran was a delight to behold. He was wild and hated being shut up and he was always seeking a way to escape. One day Ada saw him careering round the compound with a gate round his neck. On another occasion he ate their tea-cloths, which were hanging out to dry, leaving only a few ribbons of cloth for domestic use. He spent a short but eventful time with the missionaries and they were sad to see him taken to a collector, to be sent to Europe or America.

The autumn days in Leh were sparkling clear. The sun was usually very warm in a cloudless blue sky and the view from the verandah was over a wonderful range of snow-capped peaks, which never looked the same two days running. Sometimes spirals of snow caught by the wind could be seen on the peaks. Shadows moved, melted and re-emerged as the sun crossed the sky, while below the light on the River Indus sparkled and shifted. Often at midday a spiral of dust could be seen approaching, bringing a great wind in its wake.

A stream fed by a glacier ran by the path outside the compound gate. There was a pool, too, where the women assembled to fill their tubs and to enjoy meeting and chatting with their friends. Beside it was an ancient, gnarled tree in whose shade, it was said, the mother of Christ sat when she came to Ladakh. The pool was called Ama Miriam, which means Mother Mary.

The compound was a busy place and there was always something to see. Merchants came to borrow money with which to trade and in return they would give a promissory note sealed with their thumb-print. The debt was usually repaid with grain, which the missionaries could use to pay their servants. Money was useful only to the traders who traded with India but

Ladakhi traders

to the local people grain was of far more value, either for their own use or for further bartering. Sometimes traders came to sell their wares: wool or jewellery or curios to interest the Europeans. The missionaries sometimes bought wool for the Mission school, or cloth for themselves.

People who had no actual business there but who had never seen Europeans and were curious about them and their ways often came to the compound. They made themselves quite at home, sitting on the ground and staring all around them. No one took any notice of them once friendly greetings had been exchanged and they stayed as long as they wished, until their curiosity was satisfied. Sometimes, they became interested in the church services or listened to the Gospel preached at the hospital. As soon as Harry had mastered a smattering of the language he would try and converse with these visitors. He also took to visiting the caravanserai in the evenings, where, with the help of a Ladakhi evangelist and poster-sized pictures, he would try to explain the gospel message.

A familiar and sad figure was the old Gyalpo of Ladakh, a king without a kingdom. He had only a small pittance to live on but it was not fitting that he should work. Nor was he a common man to sit in the bazaar and chat. So he used to come to the mission compound to sit on a doorstep in the sunshine and dream. His appearance was elegant, with a fine-featured face and

The king of Ladakh with his son

beautiful hands, which he placed on his knees, displaying long, delicate fingers. He wore a yellow brocade cap edged with fur and, under his mulberry-coloured gown, a white cotton shirt with the long sleeves befitting his rank. His yellow scarf, or shawl, was of fine homespun, as was his white girdle. From his seat on the compound step he could see, stretched before him, the lovely mountains of the Ladakh range, the beautiful peaks rising magnificently above the Indus plain. The sun glistened on the snowy crests and glaciers, while lower down the snow lay thinly around the dark rocks, edging them with lace.

The best time to see this sight was a frosty winter's night. Then the dusky sky was full of stars and as the moon rode slowly across the sky moonbeams picked out diamonds of ice, which glistened and flashed, almost putting the stars to shame. Ada watched this wonderful scene on many a winter's evening and had to turn away, unable to comprehend or contain such grandeur and purity. She believed that this is how the king saw it, as he sat, day after day, dreaming the time away. As the sun set, the king would rise and climb stiffly up the hill to his empty palace, no longer the glory of Ladakh, but an empty shell.

Dominating the town of Leh, high above the bazaar but so close that every rock and indentation was familiar to the people below, was a great hill. On the very top of the hill was the Buddhist Monastery, known as the Red College. This monastery was built in prosperous times, about the year 1400 AD, by a king who was known to be good and gentle. His aim was to make this place as beautiful as possible, in honour of the Buddhist deities. All around, brightly-coloured frescoes were painted and many statues of Buddhist deities made of gold and silver, or brass and clay, once sat beautifying the monastery. The most important of them was an enormous statue of Maitreya in a sitting position, made of wood and clay, which was so large that the head reached through the ceiling of the first floor to the upper storey. Most of the frescoes and the small statues had disappeared but Maitreya remained. During the century when the image was made the land was so rich and prosperous that, according to the records, a popular song was sung which said that all the people wore hats of gold and their mouths were never empty of tea and beer.

The king's palace stood on the shoulder of the same hill. It actually formed part of the town, but was raised high above it. In the clear, rarefied

Leh monastery

Lamas and novices at the monastery

atmosphere it was possible to call from a window in the palace and be heard far below in the bazaar. Built in the usual Tibetan style, with beautiful straight lines, the palace leant backward slightly, to break the force of the wind. It was a very large building, nine storeys high, windows without glass and a few small window verandahs, gaily painted in blue, green, red and yellow. A colder or draughtier place to live in would be difficult to find.

The newcomers had not been long in Leh when the ladies were told that they should go and pay a courtesy call on the queen and, according to custom, take her a present. Worriedly, Ada looked through her few belongings and confirmed what she already knew, that she had nothing fit to offer a queen. The only thing that might possibly have met the situation was the beautiful silver and enamel fob-watch her mother had given her and, naturally, she was very reluctant to part with that. At last she decided to ask Miss Birtill's advice, who laughed. Ada need not worry, for what the queen would really like best were potatoes and cabbage from the garden!

On the appointed day a man came from the palace to say the queen was expecting them. The ladies were already dressed with care and Ada eagerly jumped up ready to start at once but she was restrained and told that they must wait, while they sent a messenger to the queen to say that they would be pleased to pay a call. The party then waited for over an hour before setting off. Another messenger walked ahead of them, bearing a large tray with their gifts. Slowly they climbed up the steep hill and stopped to rest and catch their breath by a large *chorten*. They looked down over the town to the Indus valley. From the south gate they could see the mile-long *mani*[12] wall and the *chortens* they had ridden past on their arrival and, at the other end of the plain, the Spitug monastery, perched on its hill like a grim sentinel. Having rested, they climbed up again until they reached a flat place before the great door of the palace. On the door was a great, grotesque mask, with a grinning mouth and, as the door opened in response to their knock, a long, red, wooden tongue clacked out. To the surprised Europeans this was a rude gesture but in Tibet it was considered courteous and right as a greeting and polite welcome.

---

[12]   Mani: stones inscribed with prayers

View of Leh from the hill

Leh palace and gompa

They were led up a great many worn steps, past the empty windows, right up to the top. They knew full well that they had been watched all the way and everyone, including the queen, knew that they had arrived. Nonetheless, their arrival was now ceremoniously announced and, at last, they were ushered into the queen's presence. The First Lady was not sitting on a throne, as Ada had expected, but on a mat on the hearth-stone, looking rather shy and overwhelmed by the three European ladies. It fell to Miss Birtill, who spoke fluent Tibetan, to put her at her ease. Ada and Dr. Kathleen could only nod and smile.

After the first polite exchanges, the queen put her large brass teapot with a dragon handle on the earthen stove in the middle of the floor, and then elegantly poured out butter tea into delicate Chinese cups. With the tea she handed them tiny, hard-baked shortbread cakes, made by herself and stamped with the royal stamp. The newcomers found it very difficult to drink the tea without making a wry face. Tibetan tea was made by breaking off a suitable piece from the tea-brick which was then boiled for hours with salt and soda to extract every scrap of strength from the leaves and, during this process, it became well smoked from the fire. The resulting liquid was poured into a tubular wooden *gur-gur*, or churn, bound with brass top and bottom. Butter was added and, as

Making butter tea

rancid butter was considered a delicacy, the more honoured the guest, the more rancid the butter. The mixture was then thoroughly churned before being poured back into the teapot to be reheated. Ada knew of butter which was forty years old being put into tea for a specially honoured guest. She also saw what happened later! The ladies sat cross-legged on the earthen floor, laid with beautiful rugs, and sipped the tea as slowly as possible, but the cups were never allowed to be emptied and were replenished again and again.

By the window stood another woman, holding a baby, which had a black streak of soot from his forehead to the tip of his little nose, a device to keep away the evil spirits. When he was born it had been publicly announced that the baby was a girl, to fool the spirits, who might have harmed the prince, or even changed him into a girl. This was the queen's grandson, of whom she was naturally very proud. The nursemaid was not allowed to breathe on to the child and so she had a white cloth tied over her mouth. She wore a gorgeous *beragh*, nearly as beautiful as that of the queen herself, which, Ada calculated, must have carried about two hundred large stones.

They did not prolong the call, because of the difficulty of conversation. As they left they pondered on the life of the queen. She hardly ever went out but, from her windows, watched the life of the bazaar and heard any news there was when her husband returned. Ada and Miss Birtill felt it could not be very much fun to be a deposed king and queen.

One of the most interesting patients to visit the doctor at his house was the *Skushog*, or Incarnation, from the monastery at Spitug. The man at the town gate spotted him riding across the plain with two attendants and passed on the news to the loungers sitting nearby in the sun. There was soon a bustle of excitement and pleasure, as all the Buddhists wanted to see the *Skushog*, for he was greatly revered and respected. They stood in a long line, doffed their hats and bowed low to receive a blessing. The *Skushog* held out his hand, in which he held a stick with a tassel on a string, over the waiting people as he passed. One of the lamas rode on to the doctor's house to announce the visitor's arrival. At the Hebers' gate the *Skushog's* wide-toed boots were eased out of his silver stirrups and, as he was a heavy man, he was helped down from his richly ornamented saddle. Before he entered the gate, he untied the yellow ribbon from under his chin and took off his golden hat, handing it to one of his attendants.

Skushog Bakula, to give him his full title, a title peculiar to the Spitug monastery, often thereafter visited the Hebers, who found him an interesting and intelligent guest. He enjoyed listening to their gramophone and examining their European gadgets. He was the seventeenth Incarnation of a line which had continued from the fourteenth century, when the monastery was founded.

Towards the end of the fourteenth century, a lama named Tsongkapa was born in Tibet and became a great reformer. He realised that the Buddhism of Tibet was in a sadly depraved condition, riddled with the superstition and evil retained from the old Bon religion of pre-Buddhist days. He studied the writings of Gautama, the founder of Buddhism, and took the principles incorporated therein as his guide. He determined that the priests should be brought back to a higher standard of belief and conduct, and that they should read and follow religious precepts more closely. He decided too, that some visible difference ought to be made between those lamas who were in earnest about reform and those who were not. In the course of his reading he had found that the early followers of Gautama had chosen yellow as the colour for their dress, while the

Tibetan lamas always wore red, the colour associated with *Bon chos*[13]. The people, accustomed to seeing the red robes of the lamas, were against a change to wearing yellow so a compromise was made, allowing the red dress to be retained but with a yellow cap and scarf.

Tsongkapa sent envoys from Lhasa to all the outlying provinces, including Ladakh, to tell the people of his reforms. At that time Ladakh was ruled by the king Lde, who had strong religious beliefs. He was impressed by the messages sent by Tsongkapa and showed an earnest desire to purify religion in his province. He built the monastery at Spitug, although the records say that it was not built but came into being through a miracle, and the lamas there were instructed to wear the yellow cap and scarf. His attempts to reform the church were not entirely successful, as the people were so afraid of the evil gods and spirits that they dared not take the risk of offending them. For example, public opinion was against the banning of sacrifices, as an inscription carved in a rock at Mulbek records. The Red Cap lamas clung to many of the debased ideas of the old religion of superstition and fear, while the Yellow Caps were more ascetic and strict.

The buildings of the monastery stood on a bluff near the banks of the Indus and wandered down to the foot of the hill. In summer many lovely birds from India, including the hoopoe, golden oriole and bulbul, as well as tits, desert chats and sparrows, frequented the marshy grounds at the base of the monastery, while in winter wild geese, duck and teal flew in from Siberia.

---

[13]   A system of shamanistic and animistic practices that pre-date Buddhism

CHAPTER 4

Life in Leh

The winter in Leh was very cold. The sun disappeared very early in the afternoon and rose late. The temperature would often drop to fourteen degrees (Fahrenheit) below zero (-25C). During the day the sun shone brightly and, in that rarefied atmosphere, the rays seemed to be intensified. Even in the winter they could have a meal out of doors when the sun was shining. They never had to worry whether it would be fine, it always was. The rainfall amounted to no more than two inches a year and Leh itself rarely had snow, although there were heavy falls on the surrounding mountains. The extremely dry atmosphere and the wide range of temperature played havoc with the skin of the Europeans. Their lips became cracked and sore and they developed nasty cracks on their fingers and scaly patches on the skin. Harry suffered very much with his fair complexion.

Early in the month of February there was much coming and going on the hill, as the lamas came in from the surrounding districts to prepare for the annual spring festival of *Dosmoche*. For months past the nuns had been spinning fine wool on their spindles, which the lamas dyed red, yellow, blue and green. The lamas now erected a twenty-foot pole, nailed on a cross-piece two-thirds of the way up and then, with the coloured wools, wove a triangle like a huge spider's web. Below the triangle was another circular web and, lower still, were cylinders of wool, resembling gigantic Chinese crackers. The whole structure, when finished, looked like a set piece for a firework display.

The day of the festival began early, with the lamas blowing on their seven-foot long *shawms*[14] resting on the monastery walls. The sound

---

[14]   Shawm: musical instrument of the woodwind family

echoed and reverberated among the mountains and returned as a whimpering murmur, as if the spirits were complaining at being disturbed. The little shops remained closed. Everybody dressed in their best for the festival and people from nearby villages streamed in through the south gate in a merry holiday mood. Soon everyone in the town could see the procession of lamas and laymen forming above them on the mountain. The band of trumpets, cymbals and long-handled drums struck up and the long column wound snake-like down the hillside from the Red College, perched on its rocky cliff, past the Palace, down and down to the bazaar, which was full of excited men, women and children. Every balcony and window was crammed with spectators. In the centre of the town the procession halted and the band stopped playing as the lamas arranged themselves for the dance. They wore huge, grotesque masks, representing devils in many forms, animal and human.

Dosmoche festival

The dance began in a slow shuffle, the dancers, moving slowly, beginning to enact the flight of birds or the ways of animals according to the type of mask they wore. Some of the lamas carried figures fashioned out of butter, representing men and demons, later to be thrown into a fire in the hope that sickness and other evil disasters might thus be averted. The *dosmo* was held erect by the lamas elected as standard bearers, while the masked dancers twirled and twisted clumsily in their heavy boots to the music of the band. Laughing and clapping, the crowd threw themselves wholeheartedly into the enjoyment of a *ltadmo*, or spectacle. The men, who had by this time drunk plenty of *chang*, were urging the dancers to go faster and faster. The excitement mounted, as the dancers whirled to a frenzy. Then, as the festival finished after the ceremonial burning of the butter images, the *dosmo* was thrown down and there was a scramble to secure a piece of it to bring good luck throughout the year.

Ada had been in Leh only about four months when she first saw the festival and, being somewhat of an innocent, was not aware of the force of superstition among the Tibetans. She was watching with Miss Birtill when a young lama capered almost to their side. As he swung round, the skirt of his

Spectators at the festival

robe swirled up and revealed an extremely dirty pair of bare legs. The two ladies were laughing together and speculating when his legs had last been washed, if ever, when the lama saw them and came dancing back. In his hand he held a small butter goddess about four inches high, dressed as an Indian lady with a piece of white net draped over her head and body, like a sari. Impulsively, Ada held up a four anna piece and indicated that she wanted the image. As he circled round again in the dance, he held it out to her with a grin, so Ada took it and gave him the four annas. Ada was as pleased and interested with the little figure as a child with a new toy and kept admiring it as she carried it about all morning. On reaching home at lunchtime she put it on a bracket in the dining-room. Then, in the afternoon, they went back to watch the feats of horsemanship performed by men of the town, cheered on by the spectators.

Devil dancers

As the year advanced the sun became hotter. An epidemic broke out in the town, which was not unusual as in this town of about three thousand people there were no sanitary arrangements at all. The people were cooped up in their houses for the long winter months and the nearest thing to a modern convenience was provided only in such houses as had stables below. Here a hole was cut in the floor above and the excrement piled up in a corner of the stable. This perhaps was not quite as revolting as it sounds, since everything froze solid in the extreme cold. As soon as a thaw came, the stables were cleaned out and the dung used to manure the fields. However, as the weather became warmer, the whole world was a latrine. Epidemics could spread fast and, in this year, follicular tonsillitis broke out. Several children in the town died and the hospital was crowded with patients. Ada went down with it. She had a raging temperature, which at that altitude caused the doctors great anxiety. Soon the other missionaries were affected too.

The town started whispering, "The little butter figure is still in the miss Sahibs' window. It should have been burned. As it has not been destroyed by fire, disease has stayed in the town. Is it not proof that this is so, since the miss Sahib was the first of the Europeans to become ill and is she not very sick?" A situation such as this worried the missionaries. If they listened to rumour and destroyed the little image, it would seem a capitulation from the Christian teaching. If the image remained and the epidemic became worse, the mood of these friendly people might well change to fear and distrust.

As soon as Ada was well enough to travel, the doctor advised Miss Birtill to take her to a slightly lower altitude to recuperate. They chose a place a few miles away, situated on the banks of the Indus, called Choglamsa, which was a ford. Here a few trees grew beside a long bridge. They packed up their food, cooking utensils, tents and everything else they would need and set out, taking their two servants and three orphan children to give them a treat and a change. It was the month of May and the sun was hot. After the long winter of short days and long, long nights, and the weeks of sickness and anxiety, it was wonderful to be riding out of the town for a holiday. The camp was set up and, before going to bed, they sat outside in the bright moonlight to watch the snowy peaks and the shining river.

The following morning, as they were finishing breakfast, Ada suddenly saw that the desert sand seemed to be swaying and thought for a minute that she must be dizzy. She looked again and was sure the desert was moving, so she called out, "Look, look – over there – it's moving!" The men leapt to their feet shouting, "Water – quick, we must leave!"

There was a hurried scramble to take down the tents, pack up the beds and bedding, clear the table and shift to higher ground. By the time everything was packed up, water was swirling round their feet. The men put the children on their shoulders and waded waist-deep to dry land, while the two women mounted their ponies and rode out. Looking back, it was impossible to see the usual course of the river and the bridge stood isolated and surrounded by water.

Choglamsa (with Mr. Reichel from Khalatse mission)

They saw a young woman coming from Leh. She stopped at the water's edge and gazed in horror at the island bridge. She started to weep as she realised she was stranded then, opening her dress, she squirted milk from her breast to show that she must cross somehow to feed her baby. The men called to her she was not to worry, they would help her. They took off their trousers and tucked up their long robes into their girdles then, taking a tent pole apiece to test the bottom of the river at every step, they each took one of the woman's hands and piloted her through the swirling, icy water, watched breathlessly by the two European women. When they reached the dry land and safety, the young mother fell to her knees and bowed her head before the men, touching her forehead in a salute of respect. She then bowed right down and grasped their feet in humble gratitude, before rising and running home to her child.

When the men came back they had time to explain the cause of the flood. The hot sun had melted the edge of a glacier high up out of their sight and the water rushed down outside of its usual channel, over the cliff, and across the sand to the river. Usually the river bed was deep enough to take the extra water but this year the sun had melted more of the glacier than usual, causing the river to flow over the plain. The irrigation of the fields was dependent on this annual spring flood.

It is difficult to imagine the conditions of a country larger than the whole of the British Isles with no doctors at all. A family distressed by sickness sent for the lamas, a very few of whom had some knowledge of herbal treatment. But, in a barren country like Ladakh, where hardly any wild plants grow, such knowledge was not easy to obtain, or practise.

On arrival at the house of the patient the lamas would sit and drink tea, then read in their chanting manner for hours at a time. Further treatment might be offered in the shape of charms, to scare or appease the evil spirit causing the illness. One device was to sew a charm, or a few coloured rag ribbons, onto the cap, which was always worn, indoors and out. Or a prayer, written on a piece of paper, might be soaked in water and drunk or rolled as a pill and swallowed. In some cases the lama would go to the roof of the house and throw away a *storma*, an arrow with prayer ribbons attached, in the hope that the wind would carry the sickness away. For a wound, bird lime was popular, especially that of the pigeon, or the dried dung of the wild sheep and deer on the mountains was considered very good when mixed with beer. Branding was not uncommon and was one of the treatments used for worms.

Then there was the man who fell from a roof and cut his head severely. The lama who attended him borrowed a thick, home-made needle, threaded it with a fine strip of uncleansed gut, and stitched the wound as best he could. The terrible results may well be imagined.

Aching teeth were removed by the blacksmith's home-made iron tools, or the tooth was fastened by a string to a rock which was carried to the roof top and pushed off. Women in childbirth usually did well, though the unusual did sometimes happen, about which the women had their own ideas.

The Leh hospital was not a modern hospital, even by 1913 standards. It was built, as were the other mission buildings, of mud, with a wide verandah and a flat roof. It had a dispensary, stocked with basic medicines; there was a large room heated by an iron stove and a small inner room, which had to serve as a ward or a theatre. Patients, unless they were desperately sick, camped out in the compound, or in the town, or came from their homes for out-patient treatment.

The hospital in Leh

The day started with a short service to pray for help and guidance in the work of healing. After the service, Dr. Reeve Heber, a
boyish-looking man of about thirty, took his seat at the table to see the
first of his patients. He was a clever young doctor, who had gained a
gold medal at Bristol University, but he chose to devote his skill to the
alleviation of the sufferings of the Ladakhis rather than to set himself up
in a comfortable practice in England. He was extraordinarily kind and
thoughtful, with a lively sense of humour, which quickly endeared him to
the laughter-loving Ladakhis. He and his wife, Dr. Kathleen, had come
to a very practical arrangement. She wanted time to devote to running
her home and learning how to cook, things she had never had time for
as a medical student, and so it was agreed that she would see any special
women patients and be a consultant at any time at the hospital. Ada's
task was to do the dressings, dispense the prescriptions and to help the
doctor in any way she could. She found this absorbingly interesting.
One thing they discovered was that the Tibetans had constitutions like
iron. When it became necessary to prescribe purgatives, which was not
infrequently, they found that ordinary doses had little or no effect; quite
often they had to increase the dosage to poison level for it to react.

Ada with the Hebers

Ada and Zodpel doing dressings

After the morning surgery, Ada would accompany Dr. Heber on his visits in the town, where they found patients lying in the most terrible conditions of dirt and neglect. Whatever they did at the hospital, they had to bear in mind the hostility of the lamas. If they were successful, the people were grateful and spread word of their ability, if they were unsuccessful the lamas made capital out of their failures and whispered fear amongst the people, telling them that the spirits were angry. Naturally, the lamas were not happy if the hospital was successful, because it took business away from them. Dr. Heber, with his kindness, compassion and skill, inspired trust, however, and people travelled long distances to bring patients to him.

One day, two men arrived at the hospital, bringing their aged mother, who was too ill to walk. They had made a stretcher of straw, bound into a thick twist and tied in the shape of a magnet, which they lashed on to the back of a *dzo*. This is a cross between a yak and a cow, a hardy animal which was used for every conceivable purpose from pulling a plough to carrying loads. The old lady was bound on to the improvised stretcher and lay helplessly on her back, gazing into the hot glaring sun, her eyes protected only by a fringe of yak hair. They had travelled for fourteen days over the rough, narrow mountain roads and, although the old woman was very sick and in pain, she never once complained but kept saying how grateful she was for everything that was being done for her.

On another occasion, a Ladakhi brought in a poor woman he had found in one of the huts in the town. She was unconscious and in the most deplorable condition. Her body was covered in terrible sores and her rotting flesh crawled and seethed with maggots. Unfortunately they could not save her.

That year the harvest in Turkestan had been very late. Consequently, many of the merchants had delayed their departure for Mecca until the crops had been safely gathered. But it so happened that that year, too, the winter set in early.

The ancient route, travelled by caravans for centuries, passed through some of the most difficult terrain in the world. The journey from Yarkand to Leh took forty-two days, with very little habitation in between. There was one particularly dangerous pass to cross, called the Sasé, which took two days to traverse and therefore involved one night's camping on the glacier itself. Amongst one of the last caravans to cross that year was a youth of about twenty, whose job it was to look after the horses. The weather became bitterly cold. The boy's boots were torn and ragged after travelling over the rocky, stony road and were no longer adequate protection for his feet in the biting cold, which became severely frostbitten. He struggled in agony to keep up with the party for two days but pain and exhaustion forced him to fall. The rest of the party callously went on and he was left behind. He managed to crawl into a small hut, as he thought to die. He had no food. He was quite alone and the pain was intense. He had little hope that another caravan would travel that way and find him.

A lone traveller, a Tibetan, happened to pass that way and found the boy. Like the Good Samaritan, he made him some tea and shared his food with him, then wrapped up his feet in some rags and put him on to his own pony and brought him to the Mission hospital. Here, when the doctor examined him, he was in a pitiable condition, weak and ill from exposure. His feet, by this time, had become gangrenous and there was only one way to save his life, which was to amputate both feet immediately. The two doctors made the decision, knowing full well the risks they were taking. To begin with, they had no trained anaesthetist. Then, the operating table was an ordinary wooden kitchen table, there was no skilled theatre sister with a staff of nurses, and they had only the most primitive methods for sterilising the instruments. Ada was called in to give the anaesthetic and she ruefully remarked later, "I think I was more of a liability than an asset, because they had to watch me all the time. I was so anxious that the patient should feel no pain that I nearly killed him with an overdose of chloroform. But," she went on, "The doctors were wonderfully calm and brave and did a difficult job well. After it was all over, they were justly proud of the beautiful stumps. Whenever I hear of brave deeds being done, I remember that operation as one of the most courageous things I have ever seen. It was deliberate, calm bravery." The poor boy suffered agony at first but later made a wonderful recovery.

There was a sequel to the story. The doctor was so incensed with the merchant for leaving his servant to die that he reported the case to the British Joint Commissioner. When the merchant returned from Mecca in the summer he was charged with cruelty and fined five hundred rupees, which were given to the crippled boy.

The following spring the doctor arranged a tour of the province to perform the many cataract operations he had promised and to see patients in outlying districts. Harry was to go too to help with the medical work and do his own pastoral work at the same time. First of all, messages had to be sent to the remote valleys to inform people they were coming and tell them to bring the sick to certain centres. These outlying places had no postal service, so when a message had to be sent it was either given to someone from the bazaar to take verbally, or a runner was called to take a written message. The note was written and put into the cleft of a short split stick, the stick was then firmly tied with wool above and below the note and the knots sealed with sealing wax. The man ran off with it in his hand and, if he met a caravan, the animals would be pushed aside on the narrow road to allow him to pass.

When all the messages had been despatched, the two men arranged their caravan. They had to select carefully and pack the necessary medicines, surgical instruments and dressings. They had to take enough food – the village people were so poor and lived so near the subsistence level that travellers could only hope to get a little milk occasionally, or an egg, or maybe, a scrawny fowl. Money would be almost useless, as payment

A cataract operation on the verandah of a Buddhist monastery, Dr. Heber assisted by Harry

was usually made in grain or butter, but silver rupees were sometimes acceptable, as they could be melted down to make jewellery. Bedding, cooking utensils, lamps and fuel all had to be collected and made up into suitable pony-loads.

Dr. Kathleen Heber took over the hospital, assisted by Ada. One morning a man arrived with a message from a small homestead at the foot of the Khardong Pass, which was about 14,000ft. The man said his father was very ill and begged the doctor to go and see him as soon as possible. It seemed urgent, so the two women decided to go as soon as the morning surgery was over. They set off on their ponies, accompanied by Dewazung as escort and interpreter. The road was rough and stony and the ponies had to pick their way carefully. They stumbled occasionally and Ada was, as usual, thrown off. Her tumbles were a constant joke but, as she never seemed to be hurt, she could always join in the laughter.

There seemed to be an unusual stir round the house when it came into sight and they considered what was going on. As they drew near, an infuriated yak charged, head down, right across their path. Like streaks of lightning the women were off their ponies and up on to the roof of the house. When they had recovered their breath a little, they were amused to see the notched tree-trunk which served as the ladder to the roof and could hardly believe that they had shinned up it so quickly. Dr. Kathleen and Ada went in to examine the patient, while the son of the house recaptured the yak and Dewazung caught the frightened ponies and calmed them down. On examination, the patient proved to be a chronic case and really there had been no change in his condition to warrant the urgent call. So they left, saying that they would get the Dr. Sahib to come and look at him when he got back from tour. It so happened that Dr. Reeve returned the following day.

That evening, soon after Dr. Reeve Heber got back, he sent a message to the sisters' house to ask them to go into town to see a patient. He could not go, he said, because his wife had been taken suddenly ill and could not be left. The patient was the wife of an Indian official, who was about to have a baby. Ada knew nothing about babies, having missed that part of her training, and felt rather at a loss, for what use was her knowledge of surgery, dentistry, dispensing and massage at such a time? However,

Miss Birtill's calm common-sense soothed her and they set out. It was a lovely moonlit night and countless stars twinkled in the dusky blue sky. The moon was so bright that they could see clearly, except where the deep shadows fell from the houses. They walked through the quiet bazaar, with all the shopkeepers asleep on their verandahs. The city was dead, except for the occasional pariah dog prowling round, looking for food. The horses in the veterinary hospital rattled their chains as they moved, making an eerie sound. A woman slipped silently past them in the shadows, hiding her face behind her shawl in the hope that they would not recognise her, slinking back from some shady assignment. She was a poor, demented creature of high birth and good family, but the local people said, "What can be done if a devil or an evil spirit enters into someone? She, or her parents, must have committed some fault for her to become so afflicted." So, spurned and helpless, the poor thing had become a harlot to earn a little tea and *tsampa*.

A yak

The guide turned out of the moonlit streets into a long, inky-dark passage. They groped along with arms out-stretched, following the glimmer of the hurricane lamp. At last they saw another light ahead and the guide ushered them into a house. They stepped down into a room and were momentarily dazzled by the brightness of the lamp. As their eyes adjusted themselves they saw a lovely Indian girl lying on a large bed, with a Tibetan woman sitting beside her. Ada examined the patient, who seemed very well and undisturbed and in no pain at all. However, the English women decided they had better wait a little so they sat down on the floor to discuss the situation. After a time, when still nothing seemed to be happening, they began to talk of going home. As they were coming to the decision to leave, the girl beckoned Ada over to the bedside and, to Ada's intense surprise, whispered in perfect English, "Does the other Miss Sahib wear STAYS?" Ada struggled not to burst out laughing. It seemed that the girl had been educated in a Mission School in India. She was lonely and bored with waiting for her baby so she sent for the doctor to introduce a little variety into the proceedings. The baby was not born until a fortnight later.

A most welcome and frequent visitor to the compound was the post-boy. He was about fifteen years of age and intensely interested in everything that was outside his usual experience. He usually walked straight in to the sisters' house and became so interested in his surroundings and their personal possessions that he would have to be reminded why he had come before he produced the precious letters from home and told the local news.

Leh was isolated, high in the mountains. Newspapers and letters from Europe took two to three months on their way and world events seemed unreal and unrelated to the life the missionaries were leading. One day in August, 1914, the sisters were playing games with the children when the postboy arrived and, as usual, had to be reminded of his errand. He opened his bag and produced a telegram from the Commissioner in Kashmir, informing the missionaries that England was at war with Germany. The missionaries in Leh were all of English or Swiss nationality but Herr Reichel, the German missionary who lived at Khalatse with his wife, had to come to Leh to surrender his shot-gun.

In that beautiful land, amid the calm serenity of the mountains, the news came with double shock. It seemed utterly fantastic and unreal that in another part of the world men should be deliberately killing each other. Ada felt sick and forlorn that she could not be at home to share whatever was to come with her own people. When they saw the newspapers with sheet after sheet filled with the names of casualties, it seemed like a nightmare that must soon pass. Instead of going to help, they were told to stay where they were, so they had the repeated agony of waiting until the next mail came in to bring them news of those they loved.

Ada acquired a Tibetan terrier and called him Ishe, declaring that the dog was endowed with greater wisdom than her servant of the same name; she was devoted to the dog and he went everywhere with her. She also bought her own pony, finding it more convenient than to be dependent on ones she could hire. It seemed as if the two animals conspired to throw Ada into Harry's company. The pony, which could be a perverse beast but sometimes showed good sense, refused to walk with any but the padre's pony, and Ishe developed a passion for Harry's bitch, Poppy. Ishe spent a lot of time at Harry's bungalow and frequently had to be recalled or returned. Now Harry had frequent excuses to call at the sisters' bungalow and he would often stay for a chat.

Ada with Ishe

It took some time for Ada to realise that Harry was really coming to see her. She had little confidence in her personal charms and Harry, in his shy way, found it difficult to make advances, especially as they were always strictly chaperoned by Miss Birtill. However, they had their mutual interest in the mission and its work to talk about and they had always enjoyed each other's sense of humour. Slowly it began to dawn on them that their personalities were entirely complementary, but it still came as a complete surprise to Ada when Harry eventually proposed to her. She asked for time to think and pray. In the end she consented.

Harry would not allow his personal life to distract him from his dedication to his mission. His pastoral and evangelical work entailed much travelling and long absences from Leh. He was now looked on as experienced enough to tour on his own but he usually took one of the Ladakhi evangelists with him, or a local guide. The tour he had planned for that autumn was in the remote and bleak Chang Tang – an area few Europeans had ever penetrated. On this occasion he took with him a man who had been in that area before as a guide and helper. On their return, after several weeks away, Harry made his report to Mr. Peter about the work he had been able to do. It was his companion who spread his fame abroad, when he told how Burroughs Sahib had one day gone off on his own and had covered fifty miles, riding at altitudes of 11,500ft to 14,000ft. Everyone acknowledged that this was a remarkable feat of endurance, for both man and horse. The townspeople were also delighted when Harry and Reeve Heber started to play polo (the European version, not the wild local game) and their personal stock rose.

Harry's abilities with horses came from his upbringing in London. He was born and brought up in the Old Kent Road, Walworth, in a house typical for more prosperous working-class families. His father worked for Thomas Tilling, who ran horse-buses in that part of London. Tilling had the business brain, while Burroughs was the expert with horses. When Tilling realised that horses would soon be replaced by petrol, he shrewdly started buying motor-buses. Burroughs would have nothing to do with machines and the association was broken – he died a poor man. However, while Harry was growing up they were comparatively well-off. His mother came from a Kentish farming family. She was a good cook and housekeeper, who created a comfortable and happy home. In summertime she used to take the children for picnics in the country round about Beckenham and Shortlands.

The children grew up playing in and out of the stables situated behind the house and watching the horses being shod at the blacksmith's forge. One of Harry's earliest recollections was how, when he was quite small, he visited the forge and found, to his delight, pieces of what he thought were his favourite 'cokernut'. He would chuckle when he recalled his disappointment and disgust when he discovered that they were not coconut but shavings from the horse's hooves.

On Sundays they went to Sunday school and church. At home they were taught to say their prayers and to be honest, truthful and hardworking. From their father and the other men working in the stables, Harry learnt horse lore; how to buy horses, how to care for them, how to treat them in sickness and handle difficult animals.

At school Harry wrote a good hand and showed an aptitude for figures. He could draw well, was always clean and neat and, though he was lively enough, he rarely misbehaved. When he left school, he easily found a job as a trainee clerk. He started in a railway office, but later went to the City and worked for a tea-merchant in Mincing Lane. He loved the City and in his spare time explored every lane and street and absorbed its history.

It came as a very great shock to his parents when Harry decided to join the army. He wanted, he said, to go to fight in South Africa, and on 31st May, 1900, he enlisted in the Oxfordshire Light Infantry. Before the end of that year he had been made a lance-corporal, but he had not been sent to South Africa. Eventually, in 1903 (the year of Ada's revelation, as she later pointed out), the regiment was posted to India. He spent a greater part of the next four years based at Lucknow where he saw and came under the spell of the Himalayas.

By now he was a sergeant. He enjoyed the professional side of life in the army; he was a first-class shot and had a natural aptitude for games. He took great pride in the execution of the drills and ceremonial, which were part and parcel of army life, but what did not appeal to him were the leisure-time pursuits of his fellow sergeants. He got on well enough with them but he had no desire to drink to excess or gamble; barrack-room talk palled, and 'going out on the town' held no attraction for Harry. He preferred to stay in the mess and practise on his clarinet, read, or study when he could get books. Otherwise, he would read and study his bible and meditate. As his thoughts turned often to the Himalayas so gradually a conviction grew in him that he must carry the Gospel beyond those mountains.

When the regiment returned to England, Harry applied for his discharge and was transferred to the Reserve. He was accepted as an ordination candidate at Clifton, the Moravian Theological College at Bristol. During this period he had to live on his savings, so money was tight and, to save fares, he bought a bicycle and would cycle to and from his home at the beginning and end of the vacations. The Moravians believed that missionaries should live as simply as possible and be as self-sufficient as possible, so their ordination students were also taught manual skills such as carpentry and joinery and basic cookery. After ordination the young men went on to Livingstone College in Highbury for a year, where they undertook a medical course. At thirty years old, Harry Burroughs was a young man of wide experience but such was his reticence and self-effacement that he rarely spoke of his past life or achievements. In years to come he would often amaze his colleagues, his family, and even his parishioners, with some hidden talent or expertise no-one suspected he had.

Now they were engaged, Harry and Ada sometimes wanted to go out on their own so that they could get to know each other better. It was always full daylight when they walked away together from the compound and so, of course, neither they nor the other Europeans thought any more about it. They set off one afternoon for a walk through the

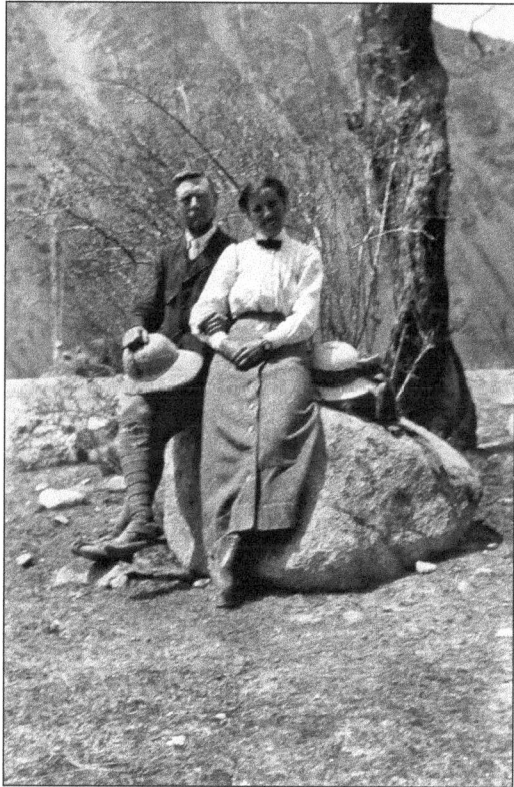

Engaged couple

town, out of the gate and across the plain. Once clear of the town they had a curious sensation of being followed. Looking back they saw Dewazung, their language tutor, a little distance behind. Puzzled, they stopped and waited for him to catch up, thinking one of them was urgently needed. However, Dewazung appeared embarrassed and they had great difficult in eliciting why he was there. Gradually it came out, very apologetically, that he was accompanying them to save them from gossip. It was not the custom of his country that they should go out together without an escort, so he had appointed himself their chaperone. Would they forgive him for his presumption? It was all rather embarrassing, but they had to continue their walk with Dewazung following at a discreet distance.

Another afternoon, Harry invited Ada to accompany him on one of his visits to the leper hospital. Once again, their shadow Dewazung set out faithfully behind, so they waited for him and, once again, he murmured shyly, "It is not our custom that you go out together until you are married". When they arrived at the hospital they saw two of the leper youths locked in combat, wrestling and striking each other with their poor, fingerless hands. They arrived just at the right moment to sep-arate the boys before they did each other serious injury. Looking back over her life, Ada thought this scene was the most pathetic she ever witnessed. The boys, having to live together in isolation and with little occupation, were desperately lonely and bored. There was an older man at the hospital, too, and he was in as sad a state as the boys, but they had their whole life stretching before them. There were not many lepers in Ladakh but

Engaged couple

the missionaries would come across them from time to time. More often than not they would refuse to leave their homes for treatment. There was a woman they knew in one of the villages with leprosy, who had a family of young children, but nothing could persuade her to come to the hospital. Who could blame them?

CHAPTER 5

Marriage and a baby

After a busy winter the missionaries were all ready for a little relaxation and change. It was Ada's birthday on 2nd April so they decided it was a good excuse to go to Choglamsa, down by the river, for a picnic, straight after Easter. Mr. Peter had an appointment with a trader and could not come till later, and Mrs. Peter decided that she had better stay at home with her younger children, but Irmgard, their daughter who was then seven or eight years old, went with the main group. Harry promised he would join the party but would be late as he had a language class. He also intended to call and see the lepers on his way, to make it an occasion for them too.

The Hebers, Miss Birtill, Ada and Irmgard set out soon after lunch, with one of the pony-men carrying the picnic basket and the kettle. It was a perfect day, sunny and warm, with a deep blue sky. As they rode through the bazaar everyone stopped their work to smile and to greet them. When they rode out of the walled town through the gate the gatekeeper ran down the stairs to see if there was anything he could do for them. They passed the flat-roofed houses with their small courtyards where the animals were kept and went out into the desert. The Mohammedan burial ground looked neat and tidy as they passed. Soon they came to the Christian cemetery, where missionaries and their children lay, alongside travellers and explorers who had fallen by the way, or found the thin air of the high mountains too difficult to breath.

As they rode along, Irmgard, who was by Ada's side, suddenly cried, "Tante, look". She pointed to the left where a body was being burned by male relatives and a lama. The corpse, according to custom, had been trussed up as small as possible in order that it might be fitted into one of the local conical baskets to be carried on the back, and then laid on a wooden stand. The flames had burnt the ropes and a hand and arm hung down out of the fire. Ada tried to edge her pony so that Irmgard should not see more of this gruesome sight but Irmgard was all curiosity and not a bit disturbed.

Their way led along the *mani* wall, a mile in length. No Tibetan pony will go on the wrong side of a *mani* wall, no matter how hard you try. Ada did try once and got thrown for her pains. They left Spitug monastery on their right and eventually arrived at the bridge, which the previous year had been isolated by the flood waters. Here they had a very happy picnic, joined by the two latecomers. After tea, the men played ducks and drakes with Irmgard, bouncing stones on to the slabs of ice as they came floating down the river. But the time came all too soon to go home and the tea things were packed up. Mr. Peter and Harry decided they had better get their big horses out of the way. Both men owned beautiful Badakshani pony stallions, bred on the Russian steppes and renowned for their speed and stamina, kept in perfect condition by their owners, who each liked a good horse and who often needed to make long journeys.

Christian cemetery at Leh

As they were mounting, Tommy, Harry's horse, was attacked by Gurang, Mr. Peter's animal. Harry was thrown off and jammed against a rock, with the saddle crushing his chest but Mr. Peter managed to jump clear. The horses fought like demons, rearing on to their hind legs and striking at each other with their forefeet. Tommy pressed Gurang on to the narrow plank bridge, their shoes clanking loudly on the wood as they fought and neither Mr. Peter nor the doctor could get near. The inevitable happened. Both horses crashed through the light railing and into the Indus below, where they lay on their sides in the water, entangled in their reins. Mr. Peter tucked his long Tibetan coat into his belt and waded into the icy water, followed closely by Dr. Heber. After a long struggle they managed to disentangle the horses and bring them to the bank.

It was a sad and dispirited party that rode home. Harry was lifted onto Dr. Heber's horse and taken to their house, where Dr. Kathleen nursed him until he was well again. Mr. Peter was completely silent. He led Gurang as far as the city wall and tied him up, then he borrowed a rifle and went back and shot him dead. No one ever knew whether his beloved Gurang was too badly injured to recover or whether he felt it was unwise to have two stallions on the same compound. The subject was never mentioned again.

Ada wished that she and Harry could spend more time together and she was jealous of the hours he spent studying and meditating. She promised herself that, when they were married, she would cajole Harry into giving some of that time to her. She never succeeded. Indeed, she was known to remark tartly in later life, when Harry retired to his study, "Meditation doesn't get the washing-up done!" She herself was so active and quick that she found it difficult to become reconciled to Harry's contemplative nature. She certainly read her bible every day and prayed night and morning, and in between she frequently chatted to God while she carried out routine tasks, as she would to an old and revered friend, but Harry needed time for prolonged meditation.

As the day of their wedding drew near, everybody, Europeans and Tibetans alike, seemed to want to make it a memorable occasion. It was to take place on the Tuesday after Easter and the keenest interest was taken in the preparations. Ada felt a long way from her own family, but she could not have wished for more help and support than she received from the community in Leh. There had been only one European wedding in the country and the Tibetans were quite as fascinated by the European customs as the missionaries were by theirs.

Harry had written to England, to a cousin of his who was a jeweller, and asked him to make a gold wedding ring. It did not occur to him however, to give his fiancée a locally-made ring for her to wear as an engagement ring, so she took to wearing the gold and turquoise ring her Aunt Annie had given her on the fourth finger of her left hand.

Ada had sent to Calcutta for the conventional white wedding dress and spent some time in suspense wondering whether it would fit when it arrived. All was well and the dress, veil and wreath of orange blossom were just as she might have bought them at home in England. Mrs. Peter volunteered to make the wedding cake. The fruit and other ingredients were hard to get but everyone contributed whatever they had in their store cupboards and they managed to find enough for two tiers. There were anxious moments while it was being baked, for ovens fired by wood can be tricky and more so at an altitude of 11,500ft. But the cake turned out to be a masterpiece and the beautiful white icing was much admired.

All the gardens in the mission compound contributed to Ada's bouquet of carnations, which grew very well in Leh. At the very last moment, Dr. Kathleen found some wide, white ribbon that had not been unfolded for years. It was a beautiful finishing touch and nobody minded the many creases. Irmgard Peter was bridesmaid, decked in a white muslin dress with her *topee*[15] decorated with frilled muslin.

All the Christian congregation assembled at the church, clad in their gayest clothes and jewellery. No one could have wished for a more colourful or resplendent collection of guests. Many of them stopped at the sisters' bungalow on their way to the church to offer Ada some treasure of their own for her to wear. She was deeply touched.

Dr. Heber gave the bride away and he and Ada walked to the church between lines of beaming Tibetan people. Harry was waiting, looking very handsome in his frock coat. For the ceremony, the bride and bridegroom sat on two chairs placed before the Minister, Mr. Peter, who read the service in Tibetan. Ada was concentrating so hard on trying to follow the Tibetan that when the words, "Wilt thou have this woman?" were pronounced in English they came as a distinct shock. All the vows were made in English. Ada said she tried hard to understand the address but

---

[15]   Topee: pith helmet designed to protect from the sun

Wedding photo

most of the Tibetan was beyond her. The golden wedding-ring which Harry had ordered from England had not arrived in time so the one he slipped on to Ada's finger was a silver and turquoise Tibetan ring.

When the service was over, everyone crowded round the newly-married couple, wishing them well in their new life together. It was a fair-sized procession that walked back through a lane of on-lookers to their new home. Some wit had found a 'Burroughs and Wellcome'[16] advertising poster and made the necessary alterations so that it read "Burroughs, Welcome!" – but of course only the English amongst them appreciated the joke.

Now the fun began. A local band had invited itself to the wedding so about eight men sat in a semi-circle on the ground, tapping their drums, blowing flutes and merrily clapping their cymbals.

The bride and groom had been given a magnificent Turki rug as a present and they stood on this to receive their guests. The Tibetans placed traditional *katas*, or scarves made of silk, around their necks, as a mark of honour and many presented silver rings set with turquoises.

---

[16]   Burroughs Wellcome and Co. was a drug manufacturing company set up in 1880

Ada and Harry on the Turki rug

They also received a beautiful silver tea-caddy from the Italian explorer, Filippo de Filippi[17], whom they had met a few months before when he passed through Leh.

The band at the wedding

In the background, huge cauldrons set over wood and dung fires, sent up a delicious steam, promising a feast. The guests duly seated themselves on the ground and the servants circulated, ladling out generous helpings of rice and curry into the guests' own bowls or plates. Ada, too, went round, encouraging the guests to eat. With the tips of their fingers, everyone mixed their rice and meat and started to eat with the utmost delicacy and elegance. Mr. Peter wrote to the Moravian Magazine, saying what an unusual and charming sight it was to see Ada in her wedding gown and veil, carrying round a huge pot of curry and urging the guests to take more. When they had eaten as much as good manners allowed the guests covered the remainder of their food with a clean cloth ready to carry home.

---

[17]   Filippo de Filippi's scientific exploration of the Himalaya was curtailed by the outbreak of the First World War

The wedding feast

Serving-maids next went round, pouring butter tea from shining brass tea-pots, with spouts shaped like dragons, into the guests' own wooden bowls, which were lined with beaten silver. Each guest was urged in highly respectful language to take a little more, and the guests would reply in equally flowery and courteous language. It was an unhurried and graceful ceremony. At last, after many cups, the tea was allowed to become low in the cups and *tsampa* was passed round, which was mixed with the tea into tiny balls and neatly popped into the mouth. The tea-bowl was then licked clean and placed back in the bosom of the owner's dress, ready for next time – a great saving on the washing-up! Tibetans never drank out of a cup other than their own, except when a marriage contract was being made, when the bride and groom shared a cup as part of the ceremonial.

Late in the afternoon, Ada and Harry slipped away to change into riding kit and then took leave of their guests, to a lively accompaniment by the band. They walked out of the compound and through the bazaar, exchanging greetings with the people there, to the spot near the gateway where their ponies were waiting for them. As it was late they rode only five miles across the plain to the rest-house at Spitug for their first night.

Then they travelled on for four days, down the Indus valley, journeying at a leisurely pace, to the mission bungalow at Khalatse which was, at that time, unoccupied. It was a pleasant place, set in a compound of apricot trees and poplars. After recovering from the excitement and bustle of the past few weeks, however, Ada and Harry found it rather dull, as they had nothing to do. They had never been allowed to be by themselves during their courtship, there were no distractions or entertainments, nor books to read, and Ada realised that the man she had married was almost a complete stranger to her. Harry was never very talkative and was inclined to be absent-minded. He would seemingly forget that he had a new bride and would walk out of the house and go visiting in the village, leaving Ada to her own devices.

She became assailed with the most terrible doubts and misgivings. What had she done in marrying this charming but silent man, who seemed to forget that she was there? How on earth was she to penetrate his reserve? She was fired with a tremendous longing to be able to talk to her mother or sister, or a close friend, and confide her worries and difficulties. She realised she was totally ignorant about the physical side of marriage, beyond the basic facts, and was unhappy that her new husband did not seem anxious to consummate the union. She did not feel it was natural, but was herself shy and reticent in such things and had no idea how to overcome what she came to see was Harry's own extreme shyness and reticence.

After a day or two, they decided to ride along a beautiful side valley where the river Indus took a sharp turn to the north on its way to Baltistan. At a village called Skyurbuchan, they set up their tent under some apricot trees in full blossom. Here, in this lovely setting, forced to share a tent, they began to establish a basis of deeper understanding.

With them on this honeymoon trip they had taken two helpers, Chondzin and Madtha. Chondzin was pretty, with long dark plaits and rosy cheeks, who reminded Ada of a picture of a Dutch girl. She and her brother had been orphaned as children so they were brought up by the Mission, where she learnt to become an excellent cook. Madtha was Harry's manservant, who was devoted to his master and nothing was too much trouble for him to undertake on their behalf. However, after the honeymoon was over and they all returned to Leh, Madtha found it difficult to accept his new mistress. He did not like Ada moving into the Padre's house. He had done all the duties for over a year and was determined not to relinquish any part of his office. It was difficult to make him realise that Ada was now responsible for the housekeeping. As she was continuing her work at the hospital, she wanted his help but he took the attitude of all or nothing. It took time to bring him round to seeing that he was still needed and that there was room for them both.

In camp (Madtha is by Harry)

Madtha, which was the Tibetan form of Matthew, had a Buddhist name of Tsodnam Puntsog. He had married a Christian widow and, at about this time, he decided that he wished to become a Christian too. Although there was no hard and fast rule, it was customary for men becoming Christians to cut off their pigtails and wear their hair in a long bob, chiefly because it was thus easier to keep their heads clean and free from lice. Poor Madtha! The making of the decision to cut off his pigtail caused him great agony of mind. Ada frequently surprised him standing in front of their mirror, twisting this way and that, admiring his hair from all angles. He would sigh and walk away sadly, shaking his head. There came a day, however, when he finally made up his mind and went off to the town barber to have his precious pigtail cut off. When he came back, with his long bob reaching nearly to his shoulders, his hair curled at the ends in a most fetching way and Madtha was almost as pleased with it as he had been with his pigtail.

With that anxiety out of the way, he found another hurdle to cross. He wanted to learn to read. He acquired a Tibetan primer, such as the ones made on the Mission printing press, and propped it up on the pile of firewood near the kitchen door. As he chopped, he learned. Whoever went in or out of the house was stopped to tell him what certain letters were. Then he crooned the word and its meaning, as if it were the familiar, 'O mani padme hum' that he knew from childhood. In time he was able to read, not a mean feat for a man of fifty. It was all the more creditable as he had been brought up in the Buddhist tradition that it was unnecessary to learn to read because the lamas did it for you.

One incident particularly endeared Madtha to Ada. She had been looking for him everywhere and although she could hear his voice chanting away, she could not locate him. At long last he heard her calls and came down the ladder from the roof, carrying a broken dinner-plate, "I broke this dinner plate, Memsahib," he said. "It must have cost a lot of money, so I was praying to God that you might not be too sorry about it." Poor Madtha. He knew how costly and difficult it was to get china and was truly upset.

No one was more delighted than Madtha when a son was born to Ada and Harry in February, 1916. They called him Henry Gordon. If the baby was put outside in his pram, all the work would be left while Madtha pushed him backwards and forwards, humming Tibetan songs to him. He knew this was strictly against the rules and that Ada wanted the baby left alone to sleep but, if he thought that Ada was safely out of the way, he always made straight for the pram. It was difficult sometimes to make him understand who had the first right to the child, as he looked on him as his own possession. The pram itself was an added fascination, for there was nothing else on wheels in the country and it was wonderful to him to be able to push it smoothly to and fro.

Childbirth for European women at that high altitude had been the cause in the past of much ill-health, and often mortality, for mother and baby, so that the Missionary Society had laid down very strict rules about the period to be spent in bed before returning to work. Kathleen Heber had already lost one infant, so Reeve Heber was taking no chances with Ada but, despite all his precautions, she took a long time to recuperate. It was not uncommon to find it difficult to sleep at high altitudes. Ada had always been a light, indifferent sleeper and her capacity for excitement seemed to be exaggerated by the altitude too. The thrill and achievement of giving birth to a son seemed to stimulate every fibre of her and her inability to rest seriously affected her health.

Chondzin with Gordon

She was still obsessed by the humiliations and trials of her own childhood and youth. Motherhood seemed to her a tremendous triumph, more so than marriage. She said later that she could hardly believe that she had actually produced a perfect baby and that it had never entered her mind that she could possibly give birth to a son. She now became desperately worried because she had no idea how to dress a boy.

Looking back, one realises that she must have been undergoing a great psychological upheaval but, at the time, she seemed to be suffering from ill-health and malaise. Whether she told the doctor is to be doubted, but she recounted afterwards how the brilliant moon worried her and how she began to imagine all sorts of weird things and worry whether she was going out of her mind. However, the doctor treated her for her physical symptoms and prescribed rest. He specially recommended that she should lie outside in the sunshine and, gradually, her health improved and Ada settled down to a period of quiet content.

CHAPTER 6

Moving house

The quiet period did not last long. Mr. Peter came to the bungalow one day to talk to the Burroughses. He wanted them to take up a new post in a village called Poo, or more accurately Pu, which means a place pushed into a corner. It was aptly named, for Pu, which was in the province of Kunawar, was tucked into a corner at the head of the Sutlej valley, ten miles from the Tibetan frontier. It was the first pure Tibetan-speaking village up the Sutlej.

A quick decision had to be made, since the season for travelling was short. There was a choice of three routes: one was to travel down to Srinagar and Rawalpindi by the road they had come in by, then across to Simla by train and from there by pony up the Hindustan-Tibet road along the Sutlej valley for twenty-one days; the second route was to cross the mountains into the Kulu valley and join the Hindustan-Tibet road there; the third was the most direct but, at the same time, the most difficult route across high passes and rough, sparsely populated country. The last seemed the most feasible for Harry and Ada for various reasons; they could take their own ponies all the way and, for the first fortnight of the journey, their own servants and Ladakhi porters, whom they knew and trusted, would accompany them and they could have the use of the Leh Mission camping equipment. Then they could be met by their new colleague from Pu at the foot of the pass across the Karakorams.

Once they had made their decision Mr. Peter said he would accompany them for the first part of the journey so that he could visit a German couple stationed at Kyelang, a lonely outpost at the foot of the Rotang La. He warned Harry and Ada once again of the difficulties of their chosen route but, being confident and inexperienced, they stuck to their decision.

They had to travel during the month of July, which was the only month in the year when the Parang La could be safely crossed, and then only at full moon, while the snow was frozen. This gave them one month in which to make all arrangements and preparations.

Pony loads

First of all they had to consider how the baby should travel. An ancient *dandy* – a sort of basket-work litter – was decided upon. This could be used as a cot at night by removing the carrying handles from their slots and using them as legs and the basket was big enough to take all the child's immediate needs whilst they were travelling. Mr. Peter recommended that this should be made waterproof, since various rivers had to be forded. Saddlery and harness for the ponies had to be checked and repaired, beds and bedding, cooking pots, lanterns, chairs and tables, indeed all their worldly possessions, had to be packed into suitable pony-loads. Fodder for the animals and food for a month for the travellers had to be bought. The assembling of the caravan was not easy, as villagers usually had only one pony and they needed thirty-eight, so men and ponies had to be hired from outlying villages round Leh. This might seem a staggering number but in fact was exceedingly modest, since each load could be no more than eighty pounds. It was while they were packing up that Ada discovered some watercolours that Harry had painted at Leh. She thought they were very good and looked forward to having them framed. Harry, however, thought otherwise. They did not please him and he tore them up, unbeknownst to his wife.

The time of departure fell at the end of the barley harvest, which varied from village to village, according to the altitude and the aspect of the fields. Some of the men could come as far as the last village in the Indus valley and not across the passes whilst others were prepared to go as far as Korsog on the Rupshu Plain. Yaks had to be arranged to replace the ponies in these places. All the arrangements had to be perfectly coordinated, as a slip-up could mean that men and ponies might be left to starve on the way.

The young people began to realise how valuable Mr. Peter's thirty years' experience was in making all these complicated arrangements and assessing the needs of the whole caravan. He himself always travelled as a Tibetan would, carrying only bedding, and *tsampa* for food. It was quite another matter to move house and cater for a four month old baby however.

During all the hustle and bustle of preparation, Ada had a most unfortunate accident. At the age of eighteen she had decided that her teeth were uneven and ugly and, as she envied the beautifully even teeth of a friend, she went along to the hospital and demanded that all her teeth should be taken out there and then, sound or not. She then had a full set of dentures made. Now, at this difficult moment, her top plate broke clean in half. There was no time to send it down to India to be repaired, or to order a new one, and she worried and puzzled what she could do. In the end she sent for a silversmith and placed her problem before him; after all, she thought, he made very delicate silver ornaments for the people to wear so perhaps he could turn his skill to mending her plate. Ada showed him the denture. After he had recovered from his initial surprise, he became fascinated with the wonder of teeth which could be taken out and put back in again. He took the plate and turned it over, puzzling how to piece it together. He had never seen vulcanite before but, after careful thought, he said he would do his best if she would give him a silver rupee to melt down.

He made a charcoal fire on the ground, took out his few primitive tools from a skin bag and began his task. He placed the coin in a crucible over the fire and heated it until it became molten then drew the molten metal through a plate like a knitting-needle gauge of graduated holes, which he had made for himself, until he had obtained a very fine silver wire. He now faced the problem of piercing holes into the vulcanite, but this he solved by using a red-hot needle to make three holes in each piece. Next, he threaded the wire through the holes and tied the wire tightly into knots and trimmed the ends. The job was done as well as he could do it. Ada was determined to wear the plate but eventually could not endure the way the knots tore her tongue. She had to give in and recalled the silversmith to ask him to make the knots on the upper side of the plate. Although the denture was uncomfortable as it bit into her gum, she got used to it and, in spite of a wobble, she wore the plate like that for over three years, until it was replaced in Simla.

The news of their impending departure quickly spread through the town and they had many invitations to go and drink tea. Madtha was to accompany them on the first half of the journey, but still he insisted that he and his wife must entertain them before they left. He came to them very bashfully one day and asked, since his humble home was not worthy for his master and mistress to enter, would they consent to have the meal prepared and served in their own house? As it made them happier to have it that way Harry and Ada agreed, hoping that their still imperfect use of Tibetan form conveyed their sincere appreciation. On the great day Ada was firmly barred from her own kitchen, while the couple busied themselves from morning to night, shopping and cooking. Nothing but the best would satisfy them. When all was ready, Madtha formally invited them, in highly respectful language, to seat their noble selves so that they could partake of the very poor and unworthy meal, which he and his wife felt was not fit to offer. They replied in a similar vein and truly felt that it was they who were unworthy of such devotion and kindness.

Their plates were heaped with rice and curry but, alas! the meat, which had been bought in the bazaar, was distinctly high, as it was the hot season of the year. Madtha hovered anxiously over them, constantly apologizing for the bad and tasteless food he and his wife had provided for them. It was certainly not tasteless. Ada and Harry tried not to catch each other's eye and insisted, as graciously as they could, that everything was delicious and thanked them again and again for their kindness and generosity, but they were also extremely glad that good manners demanded that they should eat only a little. After the curry, they were given a dish of the excellent dried, sweet apricots of Ladakh, followed by cups of tea. Madtha, ever thoughtful, knew that Europeans found it difficult to like the traditional butter tea and served their own tea.

The following day they were posed with the real problem of how to dispose of the quantities of, by this time, extremely high meat provided for them, without hurting Madtha's feelings. They felt it would be ungracious not to eat the remaining food until all was finished. Surreptitiously and guiltily they extracted the offending meat when Madtha's back was turned, but even Ishe shrunk away from it. Nevertheless, the kindness and generosity of those two simple Tibetans, who gave of their very best, remained as a heart-warming memory throughout the rest of their lives.

The last thing to be done before starting off was to pack food for the journey, which would have to last for a month. All soft provisions, such as *tsampa*, rice, sugar and flour had to be packed into coarse calico bags, to save space and weight. Butter, tea, coffee and all liquids were put into tins or bottles and carefully sealed. There were no luxuries, except a one-pound tin of cheese, six tins of condensed milk, and a tin of honey which a friend had sent from England. Ada also included a tin of Mellins baby food, in case she was unable to satisfy the baby. Bread, biscuits and mutton were cooked to be eaten on the first part of the journey.

Looking back, after many years' experience, Ada shuddered at the thought of how inadequate and meagre were the supplies they took. It did not occur to her at the time what a serious risk she was taking in providing so little for the baby, as she did not consider that she might be unable to breastfeed while travelling at such high altitudes, or when she was thoroughly fatigued. Neither did they realise how seldom they would see a village or encampment where they might buy a few supplements to their diet.

Shortly after dawn on 28th June 1916, the caravan of pack-ponies started winding its way out of the town. At seven o'clock the whole Christian community assembled in the compound and sang a hymn of farewell and all joined in prayers for their safety and well-being, asking for protection and guidance on their hazardous journey. Some then bade them goodbye but the Tibetans had a charming custom of escorting travellers for a few miles on their way, so the party moved off with Dr. Heber riding with them and several of the men walking beside them through the familiar bazaar, leaving the castle and the monastery behind them and out through the south gate, receiving greetings and good wishes all the way. They were escorted across the wide plain of so many memories to where, four miles away, the road divided, going one way down to Srinagar and the other way towards Tibet. Here, with many last words of advice and farewell, their friends turned back and the little party rode away into the unknown, with the words, *"Lam rtampo skyod"*[18] ringing in their ears, and their reply, *"Rtampo zhugs"*[19] echoing behind them.

They were delighted that their very first Ladakhi acquaintance, Pagspa, who by now was an old and trusted friend, was in charge of the *dandy*. He also assumed responsibility for Ada, thinking of innumerable small ways in which he could ease her path. At first the four men carrying the *dandy* found it a difficult load. The two at the back could not see where to place their feet, for the hood, which was necessary to protect the baby from the fierce sun, obscured their view so Pagspa helped them by going in front to set the pace. He urged them to sing and it was not long before the men in front introduced warnings about the path into their song, "Here is a rock, do not stumble,", they would chant. Soon they gained confidence and would strike up cheerily, "This is our little brother, O be careful! He is the son of the Sahib, he is a young prince. We carry our brother." Their voices rang out freely and loudly in the stillness of the desert. The River Indus was in spate, splashing and dashing against the rocks in its path, while overhead a solitary eagle flew, carefully scanning the line of ponies and men for signs of weakness.

All day long the blazing sun shone in a cloudless sky. The heat bounced back off the sandy plain. It was customary, indeed advisable, for the ladies to wear not only tinted glasses but blue veils tied over their faces, but the men had no veils for their protection. During that first day all the Europeans' faces and hands became severely burnt. Harry always

---

[18]   "Go to the empty road"

[19]   "Abide in peace"

suffered agonies from sunburn, even though he had by this time grown a beard, and he used to cover his face liberally with Vaseline. Ada became unbearably hot and slipped off her riding coat. That evening, as she nursed Gordon, he rubbed his little head against her upper arms and tore the great blisters that she did not know were there. She did not leave her coat off again, no matter how hot the sun.

At Sheh, a village about ten miles from Leh, a Christian family welcomed the travellers to their house. They had taken great pains to make it suitable for entertaining guests and their courtesy was charming. A light meal was served on the flat roof and, after the travellers had rested, their hosts requested that a service might be held. All were deeply moved and greatly refreshed by the short service together.

The countryside here was flat and comparatively fertile, being in the flood-plain of the Indus. Their hosts' house was on the extreme edge of the village, surrounded by fields lying along the banks of the river, which at this point was broad and lazy and brown with silt carried down from the mountains. At the eastern end of the village they rounded a spur of mountain. The old summer palace of the Kings of Ladakh was perched above them with many *chortens, mani* walls and prayer masts its commanding view.

The River Indus near Leh

The lamasery of Trigste stood on another hill beyond the Sheh palace, but here the plain was a stony desert beyond the limits of life-giving water from the Indus. The whole area was dotted with *chortens*, containing the relics of the royal household of bygone days, when the god-kings of Ladakh ruled. The lamas welcomed them to the monastery with all their musical instruments, grateful for a diversion from the routine of their lives. Although Harry and Ada and Mr. Peter were welcomed as friends, the performance was not entirely altruistic, since *baksheesh* was expected in return, for the lamas lived in conditions of great poverty.

Trigste lamasery

The party moved on and camped for a night at a village called Upshi, where the village women clustered round the baby, for they had never seen a European child before. They were delighted to find that it was a boy, since every Tibetan woman desires a son. The baby's bath and toilet was of great interest and Ada had to do everything surrounded by an admiring audience. When she finally settled down to nurse Gordon she evoked chortles of surprise, for the women had heard that European women were unlike themselves and were incapable of breast-feeding their children and that all European babies were fed entirely on cow's milk from a bottle. Supper was eaten surrounded by the crowds and, finally, when the time came to go to bed, the onlookers had to be driven away. At dawn they were all back, anxious not to miss any of the baby's routine. Even when all was ready for departure the villagers were reluctant to let them go.

The first few days on the road called for many adjustments and reorganization of their equipment. Some packages were awkward and had to be repacked and to minimise daily packing and unpacking

Chorten and prayer mast

Wayside shrine

loads had to be re-sorted. It was necessary to see that the food and equipment needed to provide meals while they were still travelling were loaded up first, so that that pony could go ahead with the cook, thus wasting the minimum of time when they stopped for rest and refreshment; tents and bedding, too, had to be readily available and conveniently grouped. Ada had to evolve a special routine for herself. While the men were supervising the loads, she had to settle down to the daily washing of napkins and baby-clothes, prepare bottles of boiled water for the following day, and do all the thousand and one things necessary for a small child.

Scenery near Gya

Eventually they crossed the Indus by a bridge and came to the village of Gya, 13,500ft above sea level. The scenery was fantastic. Great mountains had been split by ravages of wind and weather and savagely carved into weird pinnacles and rocks had been sharpened into huge swords or towering steeples. The rest-house in this desolate place was bleak and dirty so the *chowkidar*[20] was set to clean it, but that amounted only to the mud floor being swept with a handful of twigs. All the furniture was turned outside and they unpacked their own camp-beds. They did not use their tents if there was a rest-house in order to save labour, as they could not afford to waste precious time and energy.

---

[20] Chowkidar: watchman

The whole village and all the people were unbelievably dirty. Although Ada described them that way she had great sympathy for them. The smoke from the fires blackened everything but they had neither soap, nor towels, mirrors nor combs, as few travellers went that way with opportunities for trade. The water was icy even in summer, as it came straight from the glacier and, in the winters of intense cold, no water flowed at all and there was everlasting wind. All in all, it was very difficult to wash. They were also very poor. In the summer months the small stony fields were cultivated and sown with barley and field-peas to provide the staple food. The sheep and yaks were driven up the mountain in the spring to a few sheltered spots, where the snow melted early and a little grass grew. They grazed in these summer pastures until after the harvest, when they could be brought down to feed on the stubble. One male member of each family stayed with the flocks to help with the calving and lambing and to fend off marauding wild animals, such as wolves, foxes, and snow leopards, and the huge eagles which would take the lambs, using slings and stones as their chief weapons. The herdsmen milked the animals and made butter by shaking the milk in a goat skin. The buttermilk was fed to the calves and lambs and the butter carefully hoarded against the severe winter months.

The baby seemed a little unwell at Gya. He was very fretful and would not settle down to sleep. Ada did her best to soothe him, but all he wanted was to be nursed and dandled. She was at a loss, for she had all her evening tasks before her. Pagspa came over to her and took the baby in his arms. Although he had been on his feet since dawn he walked up and down, crooning gently, soothing the baby to sleep, so Ada was free to do the daily wash and attend to the food. When at last they settled down to supper, an old man appeared to entertain them while they ate. Accompanying himself on a one-string fiddle, he sang ancient ballads about the glorious days when the kings ruled in Ladakh and it was a great and prosperous kingdom. Gya was the last village in the Indus valley and the following morning many of the men who had come with them thus far had to return. Everyone was saddened by the departure of so many faithful friends. Some of the loads were now lashed on to the backs of yaks and the caravan moved on again.

They soon found the yaks were surprisingly agile. Undeterred by a heavy load on either side, they would scramble up the mountain slopes

The ballad singer

A loaded animal

for an odd tuft of grass or a nibble of a shrub. One yak was carrying the portable harmonium. It was slung on one side of the animal and balanced on the other side by a load of equivalent weight. As he scrambled up an almost vertical bank the harmonium swung over his back, loosening the balancing load so that his feet and legs became entangled in the ropes and he struggled madly to free himself. In his frenzied prancing he put his hoof through the harmonium and the resulting groans and discords enraged him even more. He managed to kick himself free and the instrument bounced, squeaking and rattling, down the hill. While all this was going on, Ada's pony had been lazily deciding whether he should wade through the stream that lay in their path or jump it. The question was precipitately settled when he saw the maddened yak charging towards him. He was over the stream before he knew it, streaking away from the enraged yak.

They came next to a wild, fantastic stretch of country, where the wind howled and whistled, as if it were the habitation of the devil. *Chortens* and prayer-wheels were in profusion and Ada understood then why Tibetan travellers piled up stones and placed prayer flags in prominent positions to please the spirits. The mountains were lashed into strange shapes by the constant wind that blew sand everywhere and which, when there was an occasional lull, left a stillness as of death. Ada hated it and felt she was in some eerie, supernatural place.

Then for a few moments she held her breath with horror, when she thought she saw a whole hillside moving. As they drew nearer she laughed with relief, as what she had thought to be a shifting hillside was the movement of hundreds of marmots. There was a great commotion when they became aware of the travellers, for each marmot evidently had to see the strange intruders for himself. Round heads popped up everywhere out of holes amongst the rocks and stones, each taking a good look with frightened eyes, before popping back into its hole, until curiosity was too much and the animals popped out again, sitting up on their hind-legs. Their look of pained surprise caused great amusement.

The party now left the plain and rode into the foothills of the Saskar Range, which stretches south-eastwards from the Karakorum Range and is sometimes regarded as an extension of the Karakorums. The first pass they had to cross was called Taglang La, a pass of evil repute 17,500ft up. Throughout Ladakh it was notorious for 'pass poison', or mountain sickness, which affected both man and beast. Many a traveller lost his pony here, from the sickness or from starvation, while the man

The road

himself would be left with barely enough strength to stumble back to Gya.

Whilst they were still in Leh a young American had decided to attempt to enter Forbidden Tibet by this route. The missionaries warned him of the dangers but, being young and brave, he wanted to find out for himself. He wore Ladakhi clothing and set off full of confidence. It so happened that, about ten days later, two others were travelling that way and they found the young man lying, almost senseless, in the lee of a prayer-wall. His pony was dead and his food was finished, except for a little sugar. The men carried him along with them, sharing their food and ponies, until they themselves were defeated by the snow on the Baralacha La and had to turn back. They took the young American to the mission hospital in Leh, where the missionaries nursed him back to health. He was lucky, as travellers did not often go that way.

Crossing the Taglang La was an agonising experience, as searing winds beat off the Rupshu plateau, tearing and whipping at anything in their path, lashing dust and grit into eyes and mouths, and stinging every exposed part of the human body, with the force and fury which eroded the mountains and rocks. Entering the pass the travellers were relieved to be sheltered from the fiendish wind but soon the relief turned to distress, for the deep ravine was so enclosed that there seemed no breath of air. The path rose so steeply from a ravine leading from the plateau that they could not ride.

When the Ladakhi men told Ada she must twist her pony's tail round her right arm and let him heave her up, she couldn't believe her ears. Her heart was in her mouth when she ventured to try it but the men assured her that the horses understood and were used to it. The pony half jumped, half scrambled, from rock to rock, taking two or three steps before pausing for breath. Ada could see nothing ahead save for the pony's heaving flanks, but had to be ready to scramble with him. Sometimes sparks struck by the pony's shoes from the rock at the level of her eyes would blind her. Up, and up, and up they went. At times it seemed impossible that the horse could keep his balance and it seemed certain that he would slip and fall backwards. On they struggled, their hearts pounding, gasping for breath, up and up, until at last they reached the top. Here there was a rolling plateau where they flung themselves down to rest, taking in great gulps of air.

That night Ada was overcome by mountain sickness. The whole world seemed to be a heaving sea and she could do nothing but lie on a mattress on the ground. Harry brought the baby to her and propped him against her breast to feed. It was bitterly cold and Harry tenderly wrapped her round with blankets. It was a long while before she could sleep.

How to negotiate a steep road

The next day she felt better and was thankful to be out on the open plateau where she could breathe comparatively freely. It was decided that after the previous day's gruelling journey they should rest, as there was enough *burtse*, or wild sage, and grass for the ponies to graze for a while. During the day they saw a large herd of *rkiang* running at a distance. The rhythm of movement of those Tibetan wild asses was a joy to watch. Mr. Peter gave chase for a time, but his pony couldn't match their speed. It was very exciting, though, to see the flying herd with the horse and rider in hot pursuit.

The following morning they were awakened before dawn by the man in charge of the riding ponies, wanting to borrow Harry's field-glasses. The horses had broken loose and disappeared. When two hours later there was still no sign of them, camp was struck and the two men decided to start walking (they did, in fact, march many miles each day to relieve their stiffness and rest their horses), while Ada was mounted on a yak. This was a new experience and an uncomfortable one. Her mount heaved and rolled like a small boat in a choppy sea. She lolloped along at about two miles an hour all the morning until, at about midday, the ponies were brought up. It seemed that Mr. Peter's pony, Hansel, had travelled that way before but then they had camped at a different spot, where he remembered there was especially good grazing so he had encouraged the other ponies to break loose and follow him for a feast. They had been found there, feeding happily, and were most reluctant to be caught and move on. Ada thankfully exchanged her heaving mount for her pony, Billy.

That afternoon, when they were crossing an easy pass of 18,000 ft which was only a rounded hump, someone suggested that the *dandy* men might be given a rest and that a yak might replace the two men in front. A woman-owner declared that her yak was very docile and he was duly harnessed between the front shafts, with ropes. His owner then walked between him and the litter itself, to urge the beast on when necessary, while the men took turns to walk unimpeded.

The next day they emerged unexpectedly onto a vast plain with a splendid view of the main Karakorum Range, in all its grandeur. Ada started to count the glaciers she could see glittering in the sun but, when she got to forty-six, she lost count. It was only a brief glimpse, for their road turned away up a slope, which, to Ada's astonishment, was of solid ice. It must have been there for centuries, for it was as hard as rock, with the primary colours dull and blurred.

Crossing the Rokshen La, of 18,000ft, one of the pony-men was overcome by mountain sickness. They strapped him on to one of the ponies and carefully brought him into the camp to rest and recover. They had found a pleasant camping-site beside a stream, from which the cook took water to make the tea but, after they had taken a few sips, they noticed that it had a most peculiar taste and was thick and cloudy. They discovered they were sitting by a hot sulphur spring. As luck would have it, someone knocked the vacuum flask, which contained the baby's boiled water, off the camp-table and smashed it to smithereens. There was nothing for it but to boil some of the water from the stream for the baby. Ada left it to settle and decanted off the top, straining it through a handkerchief, and hoped the sulphur would not upset the child.

From the sulphur spring they journeyed on to a rendezvous on the Korsog Plain, where Harry was to deliver a pair of spectacles. Some months before they left Leh, Dr. Heber had operated on an old lama who was blind from cataracts in both eyes. After the operation he could see

A yak helps carry the dandy

again, to the delight both of himself and the young lama who had accompanied him. However, it was essential that he should wear spectacles. These Dr. Heber had had made up in India and, as the party was now travelling near the old man's monastery, he had asked Harry to deliver them and make sure that they were correctly fitted.

As they made their approach to the plain, they ascended a narrow defile. Quite unexpectedly, the loveliest sight they had ever seen lay below them. Rising up into the blue, unclouded sky was a mountain of perfect shape, below which was the Tso Moriri, a lake as blue as the sky above, with the white mountain peak mirrored in its waters. The water was edged around with frills of white, as this was a salt lake, 14,500ft above sea level. It was so unexpected they gasped with pleasure and they were loath to ride on and lose this glorious view.

It was not long before they spotted what looked like a dot on the plain. As they came nearer they could see it was the old lama, sitting quite alone by a small Tibetan table, on which were set a dish of dried apricots and a pot of marigolds. He bowed low in greeting. Everyone was delighted to see this gentle, kindly old man again. Trembling with excitement, he tried his spectacles and, with a mixture of wonder and pure joy, exclaimed at how much better he could see. He was able to point out his lamasery, perched like an eagle's eyrie at the top of a mountain, tucked into a crevice at an altitude of 20,600ft and, below on the plain, a large, low, yak-skin tent, the home of a nomadic family. They must have taken their flocks and herds up the mountainside to graze, for there was no sign of life. It was hard to believe that in the evening the plain, which was so quiet and still, would be covered by bleating sheep, lambs and goats, and that milking would be going ahead at a great pace. The missionaries wished that the doctor could see the old man's happiness. Eventually, after many kindly sentiments had been expressed on both sides, they bade the lama farewell and went on their way.

Eagerly they rode on, contemplating with pleasure camping beside the heavenly lake, a vision of blue paradise in that drab landscape. But it turned out to be a veritable hell for, as they neared the water, they were enveloped in clouds of tiny black flies, which maddened the animals and tormented the human beings. The flies penetrated their eyes, their mouths and nostrils, got into their clothes and into the mosquito nets.

They tortured the baby, who cried and fretted. There was no escape. The lake was twenty-two miles long, which meant camping at either end for two miserable nights and a day riding along the lakeshore. With relief, on the third day, they turned into the gorge of the Parang River, where it became too cold for the flies to follow.

The river flowed straight down from a glacier and was wide and comparatively deep, even at the fording point. Ada now saw the wisdom of having had the *dandy* made waterproof. Pagspa and his men removed their trousers and boots and tucked their gowns high into their *skyaraks* then, raising the *dandy* on their shoulders, they stepped cautiously into the rushing icy water. Harry rode his pony beside them to give a steadying hand. It was a perilous crossing, for the water was swift and the river bed was rocky and uneven, and Ada watched with her heart in her mouth as the men picked their way carefully across. At last they were safely on the other side and it was now Ada's turn. She picked up Ishe and put him across her saddlebow and, with her feet drawn up on the saddle, urged her pony into the water. She, too, made the crossing without mishap.

Beyond the ford they camped on a tiny ledge, just big enough for their tents and animals, including a few goats they had brought from Korsog to supply them with fresh milk. Here they met a pilgrim from Kham, in North Eastern Tibet, who had been travelling alone for many months, visiting shrines and holy places to gain merit. He greeted them in the traditional way, by putting out his tongue and raising his right thumb. He seemed to be short of food and of money, so they gave him *tsampa* and he consented to sell his beautifully chased silver prayer-wheel to them for ten rupees, having first removed from inside the one hundred and eight circlets of prayer sewn into a dirty piece of cloth, which he wanted to keep.

It took another three days to reach the head of the valley. On the third evening Harry and Ada were making their final inspection of the camp before going to bed when they were joined by Mr. Peter. He pointed to the steep, snow-clad mountain towering above them and said, "Do you see our path for tomorrow?" There was a full moon. Here they were at the right place and the right time at the foot of the Parang La but they could see no path, only a white, snowy cliff face. That, Mr. Peter insisted, was the route for the following day. Harry and Ada were incredulous and could only think that they were blind to what his experienced eye could see so clearly.

They went to bed early, for it was essential that they were on the pass before the sun was hot. At half past three in the morning Ada fed the baby and, by half past four, they had struck camp and were on their way. It began to snow a little. After three hours, Ada sat in the lee of a prayer wall covered with prayers and offerings, and nursed Gordon again. Looking around as she sat, at first she could see nothing but snow, then her eye lighted on the skeleton of a pony which had not survived and perched on its haunch-bone was a large carrion crow. Everywhere was desolation itself. Ahead were the pack ponies and it was grievous to see them panting for breath, while the yaks struggled clumsily in the snow.

She settled the baby in the *dandy* with a prayer for his safety and for that of the men who picked up the litter, staggering in the snow as they did so. Harry walked with them to help and encourage wherever he could. Ada mounted her pony on Mr. Peter's insistence but the pony soon began to show signs of distress. She slipped out of the saddle and, as she alighted, the pony collapsed. He was off-saddled and one of the men stayed beside the exhausted animal until he was able to clamber to his feet and continue unloaded. Ishe, Ada's terrier, padded along bravely, leaving a blood-stained track where his pads had been cut by ice.

Much against her will, Ada was remounted on Mr. Peter's Hansel. She implored him to let her walk and spare the animal but he was adamant and said she must think of her child. He himself walked beside her, encouraging the horse. The pony's forefeet sank deep into the snow and Ada was forced to grab his tail to stop herself pitching over his head, then, as he heaved himself out, Ada had to clutch at his mane to prevent slipping off backwards. Foam flecked his mouth and neck and he plunged up and down like a nightmarish rocking-horse, fighting his way up the mountainside. At length Ada could stand it no longer and dismounted to take her chance with the rest.

They had brought a guide with them from Korzok but he seemed to have forgotten his duty for, when they looked up, they saw him far ahead on the skyline, walking unconcernedly with his hands clasped behind his back. Ada dared not look at the *dandy*. It was Mr. Peter who spotted a crevasse across their route and made them turn sharply upwards through fresh snow, towards the neck of the peak.

On and on, gasping for breath, hour after hour, they struggled upwards, until at last they reached the top of the pass and thankfully sank down to rest. As the Tibetans reached the top, they tossed their caps into the air, shouting with joy, *"Lha Gyalo"* (Hail to the gods!). Then each one opened the pouch of his dress and extracted a small offering – a sheep's horn, a prayer-flag, or a tiny clay image. This he reverently placed on the *lhato*, or cairn, which was already covered with similar offerings. Harry stood bareheaded to thank God for his help and goodness to them on the journey, while the Tibetans stood reverently by with bowed heads and their caps in their hands.

They could not rest for long and, having regained breath, they moved on again. Mr. Peter pushed on ahead with Madtha to prepare a meal, for they had had no food or drink since before dawn and Ada had fed the baby twice in between. Now they were on the south side of the pass and the snow turned to rain. There was still no visible path, only huge, wet boulders to scramble round, or over. Before long they came to a cave which would provide some shelter and, miraculously, inside there was a spring of clear water, bubbling out of a rock.

The meal was very welcome, with a cup of hot, reviving tea. Rested a little, they had to move on. Ada always said in later years that the descent of the pass was, to her mind, the worst part of the whole journey. Down, down, down, they scrambled and slithered, watching all the while where to place their feet. This made her dizzy and she had to keep stopping to regain her equilibrium, then down, down again. It had taken them three days to approach and climb the pass and now they were descending the other side as part of a day's march. Pointing her feet so sharply downwards rubbed the skin from Ada's toes, which started to bleed. She sat down to remove her boots and felt in her pockets for something to bind round them. Some tape she found answered the purpose admirably. The descent seemed endless. After about three hours they came to a little sheltered ledge, where shepherds and travellers could make camp. There was plenty of dried sheep dung, so they halted for a while to make some tea. While they sat, an old man with four sheep arrived with bad news. The rain had swollen the river, which was already in spate, so that it now covered the road they had hoped to take. He described an alternative route, which meant climbing the steep mountainside on the other side of the river.

Resting by the road

When everyone was rested, they went on again until they came to the swollen torrent. The trunks of two spindly poplar trees had been placed about twelve feet above the water, which constituted the only bridge. Harry went across first on his hands and knees, followed by the men. Harry then came back to help Ada but, for the first time, her courage failed.

"Come on," said Harry encouragingly, "It's all right. I'll help you."

"No, I can't. I'm not coming."

"But you must. You can't stay here".

Ada paused and looked at those spindly trunks and at the swirling water below. Then she made up her mind, "I'm not going to cross by the bridge, but I will go through the water!" Anything, rather than lie on that narrow bridge, looking down at the rushing water below.

She picked up Ishe and forced her pony into the river. Sometimes they were high out of the water on a rock, sometimes they were wading deep, once or twice there was no footing for the pony at all and he had to swim to find his feet again. All the while the swift current was sweeping them down the river. Harry was rooted to the spot, but the gallant little pony struggled on and, at last, much lower down, they scrambled to the bank, where Mr. Peter, who had run to meet them, helped the pony ashore. He never said a word, but Harry, in reaction and relief, angrily chided his wife for her foolishness.

But the day was not yet done. Mr. Peter pointed above them, "Do you see the way? In Switzerland we call it 'chimney-stack climbing'." Ada gazed up and, far in the distance, high above, she could see the baby's *dandy*, like a tiny speck, with the men struggling up the steep mountain-side. One false step or stumble and the whole group would have plunged helplessly to their deaths. Ada thanked God for the sure-footedness of the Ladakhi bearers.

Once again she had to mount Hansel. It was like climbing up a gigantic uneven staircase, with every step two or three feet high. Mr. Peter and Hansel worked together, the man urging the horse on, "Come, Hansel, hup!" When they reached the top Mr. Peter for the first time showed signs of fatigue and strain and his face had gone quite blue with the effort of climbing and encouraging his horse. There they found Madtha lying on the ground, prostrate with mountain sickness. They did all they could for him and urged him to try and struggle as far as the camp, which was only a little further on, but he only moaned, "Leave me to die. My head swims. I cannot rise again. Leave me to die. I want to die."

Ada was terribly torn but she knew she could not stay, as she had to go and feed the baby. When they were settled in the camp, which Harry and Mr. Peter had gone ahead to prepare, Harry went back, taking Ada's pony, and brought the sick man in. With kindly forethought Mr. Peter had got a dung fire going and a kettle on the boil to make tea for Ada and he had put up a light tent to shelter her and the baby from the rain. He was a wonderful man to travel with on such a journey.

They were all desperately tired so, as soon as they had eaten and done the most essential chores, they all went thankfully to bed. Harry and Ada silently acknowledged to each other that they were glad to be alive, glad to lie on their camp-beds to sleep with their little son in his *dandy* between them.

They had not been asleep long when Ada awoke to hear a cracking sound. She called to her husband.

"Harry, Harry, do you hear that noise?" A grunt was the only reply. "Harry! I think the tent-pole is cracking!"

He stirred and wakened sufficiently to say, "Oh do go to sleep!"

There was another ominous crack. Ada leapt out of bed and picked up the baby. Once more she addressed herself to the slumbering form, "Well, you can stay if you like, but I'm going!"

The words were no sooner out of her mouth than the wet tent collapsed on top of them. The rain had made the canvas too heavy for what proved to be a weak tent-pole. Harry shouted for Puntzog, the head man of the caravan, hoping he would hear his muffled calls. It was one o'clock in the morning and everyone was sleeping the sleep of exhaustion but eventually Puntzog heard and crawled out from his own tent, where he had been sleeping on the ground.

When he saw the heaving, struggling mass of wet tent, he behaved in true Tibetan fashion by shouting with laughter and he called to the others to come and enjoy this comic sight. By that time Harry and Ada, too, were in fits of laughter at their ridiculous position. When everyone had enjoyed the joke, they buckled-to and fixed them up for the rest of the night. What marvellous travelling companions the Ladakhis were, always kind, however weary, and always full of fun. It was fortunate that the tent would not be needed again as all the Ladakhi Mission equipment was being taken back to Leh and Harry and Ada would go on with equipment being brought from Pu.

The next day brought one of the most terrifying experiences of the journey. Ada had been advised to wear Tibetan boots, rather than her leather riding boots, since there was a dangerous section on the road to be negotiated. They came to the place where the track had been obliterated by a landslide and, for two hundred yards, there was nothing but a steep, shingly slope. The *dandy* men, reinforced by others to help, stepped gingerly on to the precarious, shaly surface. The loose stones cascaded away beneath their feet. The men slipped and even fell, but slowly and painfully they inched their way across. Helplessly, Ada and Harry stood and watched and prayed for the safety of their child and the men who carried him.

When it was their turn they started out together, Ada in her clumsy boots to which she was unaccustomed. Suddenly her feet slipped and she felt herself sliding down with the stones towards the roaring Spiti River below. She clutched at Harry, who also fell. Scrabbling wildly to save herself, Ada could gain no handhold, only moving shingle, and she was sure all was lost.

Then she found a foothold! Faithful Madtha had scrambled below her and dug his hand sideways into the shingle to arrest her fall. By that time, Harry was back on his feet again and he helped Ada to hers. Then, step by step, he led her across the rest of the way while Madtha made footholds for her with his hands in the stones.

Safely on the other side Ada started to cry tears of shock and relief from the terrible tension. Determined not to show her feminine weakness, she turned away and put on her dark glasses.

Now they started to look forward to getting into camp in Kyibar in Spiti. There was a general feeling of relief that they had negotiated the most difficult section of the journey and all were looking forward to better food and rest. For days past their food had been poor. They had finished the meat and the bread had gone mouldy before it was all eaten, but they had picked out the mouldy bits rather than throw it all away. Thereafter they had eaten *chapattis*, the local thin unleavened bread baked on a hot stone, and the tin of honey made a welcome addition.

They were in fact a day earlier than they had reckoned and were thinking that they would be able to establish camp before Mr. Marx arrived from Pu to meet them. However, as they rounded the last bend in the road they saw Mr. Marx alighting from his horse. He was a day early too, planning to get food prepared for them! Had they arranged to meet at Victoria Station, it could not have been better timed.

It was wonderful to be able to rest. The tents were soon up and they discussed their plans over hot, smoky tea and *chapattis*. It was decided then that everyone should spend the whole of the following day in camp. There was Mission business to discuss and they all welcomed the chance of exchanging news and comparing notes. Mr. Peter bought a sheep which he killed and he himself cooked the liver and kidneys, which he served hot and sizzling from the pan. It was one of the most welcome and delicious meals they had ever eaten.

When the village women heard of their arrival, they all came to look at the baby, delighted to see that it was a boy. They sat themselves down on a bank opposite the tent door and watched Ada's every movement as she bathed him. They crooned and clucked and waggled their fingers at him and their delight knew no bounds when they won a smile from him. They too had heard that foreign women never nursed their babies but gave them cow's milk from a bottle, so were astonished and pleased to see him breastfed. They were intrigued, too, by his clothes. These Ada had kept to the simplest possible, taking only four flannelette gowns and four vests, which she changed night and morning and washed each night. Napkins were a novel idea. Tibetan babies were placed in a basket with their little bare bottoms resting in dry, finely-powdered deer or sheep dung, which was turned over as the top layer became soiled. The village husbands must have received scant attention that evening, for the women would not go away. When eventually Harry and Ada retired for the night they firmly laced up the tent door, only to find the women peering underneath. Harry had to get quite fierce to drive them away. Back they came at daybreak, staying all day and late into the evening. In a moment of mischief, since they were so inquisitive, Ada took out her teeth. This sent them scattering with shrieks of fright and incredulity, but they soon crept back and implored Ada to let them into the secret of this magic.

Ada and Harry were very sorry to part from the loyal and loving Ladakhis the next day. Pagspa had a long session with the baby, crooning and talking to him in his own language and, when at last he handed him over to Ada, he wept unashamedly. Mr. Peter's farewell to Harry and Ada was characteristically gruff. Although neither Harry nor Ada could warm to the man, they never forgot his moments of brusque kindness. They honoured him for his profound knowledge of the Tibetan peoples and their language, but above all they respected his marvellous skill as a mentor and guide, conducting safely such inexperienced travellers as themselves over some of the most difficult terrain in the world

Mr. Peter was going only part of the way back with the rest of the party, as he was to visit some German colleagues at a place called Kyelang, in Kulu. It was a very lonely place, cut off behind the Rotang La for six months of the year, with no mail or any other form of communication with the outside world. When he arrived at Kyelang, Mr. Peter met the missionaries returning from the little cemetery, where they had just laid their eighteen-month-old child to rest. They were very brave and they felt that it was perhaps God's wisdom, for they had just been instructed to go into a concentration camp until the end of the war because of their nationality.

They were now travelling through the province of Spiti, where the Spiti River in places forms the border between India and Tibet. The countryside was uninspiring. There were a few ancient castles, built in the days when the area had been prosperous, but it was no longer. The people were not gentle and kind like the Ladakhis. In Ladakh no woman was expected to carry a load, unless it was absolutely necessary, but the Spiti men picked the lightest loads for themselves and left the heavier ones for the women. If certain loads could only be carried by men, they threw dice to determine the loser.

The Spiti River was wild, turbulent and very full, owing to the fast-melting snow. In places the road was a frail-looking platform built across the straight face of the cliff. Ada was nervous about the first one they came to but was reassured when she saw the baggage ponies negotiate it safely. At one point they had to cross the river by a rope bridge, where stanchions had been driven into ground high above the river at each side and the bridge hung in a loop between. The footway was made of plaited ropes, about ten inches across, and on either side were hand ropes, tied to the footway by side ropes about three feet apart. Ada had to look down to see where

Rope bridge

to place her feet and could see the river below racing and dashing along at such speed it make her head spin, and at every step the rope gave under her weight before bouncing back. Really, it was easier to fall into the river than not! After leaving the river they started to climb again, having two more mountain ranges to cross where each pass was said to be at least 18,000ft high. They were now only two days' journey from Pu. Up and up they climbed, hanging on to the ponies' tails again, as the way was very steep. Looking back, the previous day's path appeared to be a mere crack in the mountain descending to a sandy floor. It seemed utterly impossible that any human being could descend it safely, but they were living proof it could be done.

The next day was to be the last of the journey – the twenty-eighth day. The thought of reaching their destination spurred them on for yet another steep climb over the Hang-Pu pass. Near the summit, they were delighted to discover some wild flowers –gentians and campanulas – and rare butterflies only to be found at such great heights. Mr. Marx had brought his net with him and tried to catch some of the black and white specimens to send to a collector at home.

Ada sat apart feeding the baby and, while she was sitting quietly by herself, she thought she heard singing. Could she, she wondered, be getting light-headed and imagining things? But when they set off again the singing became clearer and louder and, rounding a bend, they came upon a lively scene of men and maidens dancing. They were formed up in lines facing each other and dancing forwards and backwards, rather as in 'Nuts in May'. The young men swayed and swirled like eagles in flight, with their arms outstretched and holding their sleeves, while the girls swayed to a rhythmic shuffling of their feet, meanwhile making delicate movements with their hands. The corn was green and the moon was full, so the young people from the villages on either side of the pass had met at the top to dance. The dances had some religious significance but the occasion also made a welcome break in routine and a holiday from work.

As they rode over the brow of the hill they saw a brightly-dressed girl of about eighteen awaiting them. She had made a fire and they soon had a delicious meal that Mrs. Marx had sent up from Pu. It was wonderful to have fresh home-made bread and hard-boiled eggs, fresh milk, and butter after weeks of camp food. When they had finished, Mr. Marx tried to point where their future home stood but all they could see was a high range of mountains towering opposite them, divided from the equally high range on which they stood by a deep cleft. They were told that the River Sutlej ran below but it was impossible to see it as its channel ran too deep. A golden spot caught their eye, which was a roof top in the village spread with apricots laid out to dry.

The Tibetan ranges over the Indian frontier looked hard, cruel and aloof. A feeling of deep disappointment swept over Ada. She wanted to run away but there was nowhere to run. There was not a human being within sight or hearing, except for themselves. Dispiritedly, she took the baby to feed and, sitting by herself, it was as if a shutter fell from before her eyes and she saw Piccadilly, with its crowds, hurrying up and down side roads, in buses, cars, or on the underground, ant-like figures all restlessly seeking pastures new. It seemed a hopeless way of living. Then she compared her own position with theirs. She could not go back and she did not want to go forward. Sitting on that lonely crag she might have been the only person on earth, and her heart was as heavy as lead.

'Well, you've really done it this time,' she told herself. 'Just see where you have brought yourself. But,' she thought, 'Have I brought myself?' And her mind went back over the years, how step by step she had timidly tapped on doors, which had opened for her so that she had inexorably arrived at the present. She chided herself for being like the prophet Elijah, who had tried to evade his mission. As she carried her sleeping baby to the *dandy* for the last time, she realised how desperately tired she felt and how thankful she was to have reached the end of the journey. At peace with herself once more, she knew that, whatever the future held in store, this was what she was meant to do.

They gathered up their things and made ready to descend the last pass. The men carrying the *dandy* picked mauve gentians and stuck them jauntily in their caps, pleased to be on the last lap of their journey and looking forward to meeting their friends in Pu. It took four and a half hours to descend the eight thousand feet from the pass at 18,000ft to Pu at 10,000ft, and the rocky going was gruelling and exhausting, but at last they emerged from the defile and saw the village which was to be their future home. Nothing could have looked more pleasant and the villagers turned out in force to welcome them.

Beside their path sparkled the village stream of clear glacier water. At one point it turned the little watermill, and made a shining pool, then it ran past the dancing-ground before falling precipitately over a cliff to the river below. A little further on they came to the mission compound, which had two well-built houses set in their own gardens.

They had arrived at last. No more rising at daybreak to get a meal, or to nurse the baby while the men packed up and loaded the animals. No more bleeding lips and toes, nor stumbling up and down precipitous passes. They were now at their new home and eager to settle in to their new life.

Mr. Peter later wrote an article describing the journey, which was published in the Moravian Mission Magazine in London. In the article he paid tribute to Ada for her fortitude and endurance and claimed for her the honour of being the first European woman to have travelled that route and crossed a pass of reputedly 20,000ft. Gordon must surely be the only European baby ever to have crossed the Parang La. Sir Charles Bell, the great authority at that time on Tibet, wrote to Ada when he heard of the journey and congratulated her on a truly remarkable feat. Dr. Hutchison of Chamba also wrote saying that he had made four expeditions to the Parang La, hoping to cross the Karakorums that way, but each time he had been defeated. It seemed too bad, he went on, that a woman with a four-month-old baby should achieve what he had tried so hard to do.

CHAPTER 7

Pu – and the end of the War

The bungalow was long and low, built of mud bricks, with a covered verandah that ran the whole length of the house. The verandah floor was uneven slabs of stone, laid just as they had been brought from the mountain, with the gaps packed with mud. A railing ran along the open side and in front was a large, flat piece of ground they called the badminton court. Even had the necessary equipment been available, a game would not have been a great success for out-of-court shots would have sent the shuttlecock sailing over the cliff, but it made a good safe place for children to play. The roof was flat and made of mud and straw, packed on top of

Pu costume

twigs and leaves. It sloped slightly at the edges to allow rain and snow to drain off and was reached by means of a thick, notched tree trunk, the Tibetan equivalent of a ladder.

Ada felt rather like Alice in Wonderland when she first stepped inside the house. At one end was the kitchen with a small iron stove, which burned wood and yak dung. Here, waiting to meet them, was Tarchungma, a pretty smiling girl. She wore a dark blue homespun dress, with rows of brightly coloured muslin strips sewn around the bottom. On her head was a little pillbox cap, decorated with strips of muslin to match her dress, with brightly-coloured beads and red berries swinging in a bunch behind. As she was unmarried, her woollen trousers were white. Her shoes were shaped like gondolas, with curled toes and a high curved piece at the heel to protect her feet against the rough stones. She turned out to be a clever, neat and helpful maid and a good cook as well.

The living-room had a round iron stove, about three feet high, with an iron pipe for a chimney. All the plain wooden furniture had been made by the first missionary to Pu, Mr. Pagell. A hand-woven black woollen carpet covered the dusty earthen floor. At the far end of the verandah was a study.

In the bedroom were two low Indian charpoys. Later, they furnished this room with the Venesta packing-cases, converted into three-drawer chests to house their clothes and belongings. There was even a small bathroom,

View from the window at Pu

Villagers at Pu

containing a wooden shelf to hold a wash-bowl and a zinc bath hanging on the wall. A door led outside, so that the bath water could be brought and carried away without passing through the rest of the house, for the rooms all opened off each other. They had everything they could wish for and were very happy.

After their evening meal all Harry and Ada wanted was a long, quiet rest. They had just settled into bed, anticipating deep, untroubled sleep, when a great caterwauling began. It was the call for a village dance and, in no time at all, drums were banging, with loud nasal singing that went on for hours and hours. It was hot; the sandflies came in clouds to bite them and their comfortable, happy feeling of at last being at rest melted away. In desperation, Harry went to the singers and asked them to finish their song and go home to bed, but it was no use. The villagers of Pu were pleased to entertain their neighbours from Hang, across the pass, who had carried the baggage, and they intended to make a night of it. Harry and Ada just had to make the best of it, but they were not feeling very missionary-hearted!

When morning came, however, they were both keen to take a good look around this new place, and Harry was eager to start his new duties.

He was given charge of the hospital and made responsible for the meteorological observations for the Government at Simla.

Pu was a pleasant village, about 1000ft above the River Sutlej, which roared unseen below in its channel. High mountains rose abruptly on the opposite bank of the river and the vista downstream ended with a snowy peak, of perfect shape and great beauty, in the Kailas Range. It was always white and glistening and it was to feature in many of the goodnight stories Ada invented for the children.

Pu village

It was not easy to pick out the houses which straggled up the mountainside for, with their mud walls and flat roofs, they merged into the landscape. The higher up the mountain they lived, the poorer the people seemed to be. High up the cliff, minute and alone, was a hermitage, where a red-capped lama had lived in isolation for many years. The lama who occupied it while Harry and Ada were in Pu had taken a wife, but there were no children. Below the hermitage were a few hovels, built of rough stone with mud walls, where the one room had a large square hole in the ceiling for the smoke to escape. The fireplace was a few stones raised into a ring, where they burned dried dung, roots, and wood when it was

The hospital at Pu

obtainable. There was no water and no sanitation. The people spent most of the time they were at home living out on the flat roof but on winter nights they had to sleep in the house.

The hospital was situated on a terrace below the houses. It had a useful verandah, where the patients could sit out in the sunshine, which in winter had a dazzling view of snowy peaks over the border in Tibet itself. Below the hospital was a well-built house, flanked by a strip of flat land where pony races took place in the winter. The races were organised by man called Chosdar, who was well respected and of high class.

Tibetans were usually very particular about class, rather than caste, according great respect to rank and birth, but not concerned about trade or calling, and it was

The hospital at Pu

interesting to see how the caste system of India had affected these Tibetan highlanders on the border. When water was scarce the landowners could not afford to employ the villagers (as payment was always made in grain), who would spend the winters, usually working as shepherds, on the hills near Simla, where the Indian caste system was observed. As a result, all the weavers, leatherworkers, smiths and shepherds lived in separate clusters, and no caste would eat with another.

Harry's first job of the day was to read the meteorological observations at 8.20, as this time coincided with 8 a.m. in Simla. The details were sent by post every fourth day to Chini, five days' journey away, from where they were telegraphed to Simla, completing their two hundred and forty mile journey from Pu. Mr. Pagell had cut a notch in the verandah railing and, at twelve noon, the sun's light fitted exactly into the centre of the notch, so he always had the correct time for the observations. The instruments were housed in a little thatched shelter in the vegetable garden, where they were shielded from sun and rain. The rain-gauge was nearby and, for most of the year, there was not much rain to record, although the snowfall was heavy in winter. Checking the wind direction was simple too. A Buddhist prayer-flag had been nailed to a large pole and, by looking to see which way the flag stood, it could be seen from which direction the wind blew. The fee paid for doing these meteorological duties was used to help an old man, who was partially blind, and a paralysed idiot who sat in the compound every day.

The banners were a common sight. They had many prayers written on their white cloth, which were carried to the gods by the galloping horses of the wind.

After they had been in Pu a little time the Meteorological Office sent up a beautiful brass sundial to be used instead of Pagell's notch. Harry was delighted by it and treated it with great care. One Saturday he had laid it on the verandah as usual, about five minutes before noon, when Ada called him into the house. He was indoors for precisely three minutes and when he went outside again the sundial had gone. They could scarcely believe their eyes, for very few people went through the compound on Saturdays when the school was closed. It was a mystery but something had to be done quickly so, after consulting with Mr. Marx, Dewa, the headman, was called and told.

He was dumbfounded, for theft was rare. He was a just and sensible man and, when he had thought for a while, he suggested calling from the roof to the upper village to tell everyone what had happened. He climbed up the notched tree-trunk and called to the people to hear him. His voice echoing round the mountainside, he told of the disappearance of the sundial and warned the people that it was Government property and that, if it were not returned at once, every house would be searched. No one came down from the mountain houses and no-one admitted to seeing a stranger about. Then the houses were searched but without result. Reluctantly, the missionaries decided they would have to report the loss to Simla.

One day, after several weeks had gone by, Dewa called to see Mr. Marx and Harry. He asked if they would object to a man called Tsetan becoming devil-possessed, so that the spirits could lead him to the sundial. As Christian missionaries they could not consent to this but Dewa was determined to carry through his plan, whether they agreed or not, as the theft had brought disgrace to his village and to him as headman.

The next morning a call was made from the temple roof. The women were told they must draw their water from the stream early that evening, as the spirits had indicated that no one should be in the vicinity of the temple between sunset and sunrise.

When the sun was low in the sky the women scurried down the hill in timid groups, with their cylindrical water tubs slung on their backs. As they passed the temple wall each woman turned one of the large prayer cylinders with her hand, praying for protection from the spirits. They knelt to scoop up the water with large brass ladles then hurriedly slung the full tubs on to their shoulders and went swiftly up the hill to their homes. The men, too, were afraid. They fed their animals and went inside, barring the doors securely behind them and stuffing rags into the holes that served as windows. From the temple came the sound of beating drums, the lamas drumming the spirits away.

As the sun rose the next morning the call went out that the women could draw water again. They all ran eagerly down the hill, hoping to pick up any news. Dewa was already at Mr. Marx's house, where the Burroughses, too, had been summoned. With him was Tsetan, who was there to report on the success of his spirit-possession. He was not an inhabitant of Pu, though he had relations in the village, but from Dobaling across the river.

The two Tibetans sat on the floor, while Dewa told his story. He described all the circumstances relating to the disappearance of the sundial and how he had decided to ask Tsetan, who occasionally acted as a medium, to help solve the mystery. His choice had been justified, he said, as he drew out the missing sundial from inside his robe and laid it on the floor before the surprised and relieved Europeans. Dewa continued his tale of how at dawn he, accompanied by the village lamas, went with Tsetan to the *chorten*. After incantations, Tsetan had put his hand into a hole where the relics were laid and produced the unharmed sundial. As Dewa finished his story he rose to his feet and motioned Tsetan to stand. He handed the sundial to Mr. Marx then, turning sharply to Tsetan, clapped his hand on his shoulder saying, "Sahib, here is the thief!" It was a dramatic moment, for it was clear that Tsetan had not suspected that he had taken part in a plot to catch him.

Since he could not deny the theft, Tsetan confessed that on the Saturday morning in question he had come to Pu to see his brother and had found him chopping wood for Mr. Marx. As he left there seemed to be no one about, so he thought he would take a short cut through the compound to the upper village. There he saw the sundial gleaming in the sun and, in a moment of impulse, he had picked it up and slipped it into his robe. Back in his own village he had buried his find deep down in a sack of grain. Then he heard that it was Government property and he became afraid. He started looking for an opportunity to return it without being seen and thought his chance had come when Dewa had asked him to consult the spirits. He had hurried back to Dobaling for the sundial which he had then hidden in the *chorten* but he did not know he was being watched.

Dewa took the floor again. Justice must be done, he said. Such things could not be allowed to go unpunished. He had two suggestions to make and, if everyone was agreed, Tsetan could choose his own punishment. Either he could be sent in handcuffs on the five day journey to Chini to be tried by a civil court, or he could be publicly beaten on the village dancing ground in front of the temple. To each of them in the room, Tsetan came to touch their feet and to express his regret. Then, with his hands together, he begged for pardon and accepted the sentence of being beaten by his own people. He was relieved to be let off so lightly.

Life in the remote village of Pu made the war in Europe, on the other side of the world, seem totally unreal. If it had not been for the lists of casualties in the English papers, and the shortage of goods they could import, they would have hardly realised there was a major world war in progress. However, in the autumn of that first year in Pu, the Rajah of Rampur had sent an order to the Mission for one hundred pairs of socks to be knitted. These he was going to send to his Rampuri soldiers, who at that time were fighting in Mesopotamia.

Ada was given the job of organising and supervising this effort. The early missionaries had taught the women to knit and some were very quick and clever. Spinning, of course, every girl learnt from childhood. Ada was shown a room full of small bales of raw wool, straight from the backs of the sheep and goats in nomad encampments. She ruefully realised that she was no good at knitting and she did not know the first thing about spinning.

The 'wool industry'

The women, who were to be paid a small sum for their work, used to come just at sunset to collect the wool to spin, and Ada weighed out ten ounces each. The women would spin as they went about their business.

If they needed to place the spindle on a surface they used little cups made of apricot pulp, which became very hard when dry and almost impossible to break. To create the three-ply wool needed for knitting, the spinner would sit at the edge of the house roof and, having threaded three strands of wool on the spindle, would send it to the ground with a sharp twist of her hands. It was then hauled up and twirled again until the spindle was full, when it was wound off into balls. Some of the women were clever and conscientious, but others used all sorts of tricks to cover up their bad work. Some put well-spun wool on the outside of the ball, with uneven,

Spinning and knitting

knotty wool inside. Some stole part of the wool and replaced it with a small stone or apricot kernel in the centre of the ball to make up the weight. Another ruse was to lay the wool alongside the watercourse so that it would get damp and weigh more. They were all desperately poor at that time and the temptation was strong. Ada did not enjoy overseeing this noble work! The winter evenings were extremely cold in the shed where they met, with a single hurricane lantern supplying their only heat and light. She was always anxious to get home to put her baby to bed, and to let the servants get away before it was too dark.

At last, with the contribution from nuns in a nearby nunnery, who knitted during periods of enforced silence, a hundred pairs of socks were produced. They now had to be washed as the wool was full of natural oil. Fuel for hot water was always scarce and there was no soap. Instead they used soap nuts, from an Indian tree, which were ground to powder between two stones and the big black kernel taken out. Added to hot water, the powder produced quite a good lather. The socks were knitted in two parts which had to be sewn together, before being washed in pairs and dried in the sun. This revealed all the deficiencies in the knitting, where some women had stretched one sock to match the other so that one came out large and the other small. Ada felt she deserved a halo for patience at that time, although she was glad to be making some small contribution to the war effort.

As winter approached Ada became seriously worried, for she realised they had barely enough food to see them through. Their potato crop was poor: they suspected that without supervision their water had been stolen, so that the tubers were very small and they would have to eat potatoes which normally would have gone to the chickens. They had arrived too late to order supplementary stores from India, and in any event there were war-time restrictions on the quantity of rice which could be bought. Their one cow was going dry and it was too late to buy another one. She tentatively went to discuss the situation with Mrs. Marx, who proudly showed Ada her store-cupboard, fully stocked with bottled fruits, butter, jams, rice and loads of vegetables. She gave Ada a long lecture on the virtues of being a good housewife and offered much good advice, but nothing more. Ada did her best to lay-in stocks, with little success and towards the end of the winter the family were in poor straits. Having been once rebuffed, Ada was too proud to throw herself on Mrs. Marx's mercy again and they existed on an almost Tibetan diet of roasted barley meal, made into porridge, and bread with very little butter. The chickens went off lay for lack of sufficient food and the cow produced only just enough milk for Gordon.

That first winter in Pu was very cold and snowy. After a snowfall they had to work quickly to clear the roof. As soon as the first patch of blue sky appeared they called for people to come and scrape off the snow with wooden snow shovels, to prevent the slush and water leaking into the house. Snow fell for days on end then, one night when the family was in bed, a thaw suddenly set in. Ada heard the baby cry and, finding that his cot was wet, she put him into his pram, put up the hood and placed a mackintosh cover over the blankets. Satisfied that he was all right, and thinking that the leak in the roof was in one place only, she went back to bed and was soon asleep again. But later on she woke to find her bed all wet. Hoping for the best, she got into her husband's bed nearer the wall, but that was soon wringing wet too. In the middle of a Himalayan winter's night, they had to scurry the length of the verandah to the study, where they finished the night on the floor. It was dry, but not even an Eskimo could have called it warm!

For about three months, even with intermittent thaws, the snow lay so deep that Ada did not venture beyond the compound, until finally Harry insisted that she must take a walk outside. As she walked in the deep snow under the lee of a terrace wall, everything was strangely silent and she realised that the river no longer roared below, for it was frozen. The silence was eerie and she had the curious sensation of being watched. Looking up she saw that a huge eagle had alighted and was following her with its cruel, greeny-yellow eyes. For a moment or two she hesitated,

Feeding a kid which was saved from an eagle (at Khalatse)

afraid to pass in case he attacked her then, as she pulled herself together
and started forward, he rose, flapped his great wings over her and alighted
on a lower field. She walked right through the deserted, silent village to
the big *chorten*. Here a flock of snow-cock rose up. They, like the eagle,
were desperate for food and hunger had driven them to a lower altitude
than usual, for they are seldom seen below 12,000ft.

At that time the British were still in India and it was their policy to
send what they called 'The British Trade Agency' to Gartok, in western
Tibet. In winter there was no trade and very little for the officials to do
except try and keep warm, which was not easy at that altitude, despite the
houses being built underground. At one time, some of the men had their
wives with them, but they found the cold too severe and the loneliness
terrible and several of them died. Then an arrangement was made for the
men to come and spend the winter just over the frontier at Pu.

One night in May, Ada was woken by her dog barking. A Tibetan
man stood at the door. He begged Harry to go with him at once as the
'Daktor' of the Agency was very ill. Harry was unable to save the man,
who died of opium poisoning. He had taken his own life, unable to face
the loneliness of returning to Tibet.

Instructions came that Harry should conduct a post-mortem examination of the body and remove the internal organs, to be sent for examination
by the Chief Examiner in Lahore. This had to be done immediately and,
as the Marxes were away on holiday in Chini, Harry asked Ada if she
could take over his duties at the hospital. Ada's second baby was due in a
month's time and it was a laborious business climbing the mountain road
up to the hospital. She did what she could for a man with a leg injury,
where the bone was exposed and bare, with a ridge of suppurating flesh
on either side from which the pus had to be drained. Then she toiled
home again and as she rounded the verandah she saw that Gordon had
climbed up the back of a deck chair. Her sudden appearance must have
startled him, for he fell off the chair on to the stone floor. The fall gave
him slight concussion and he had to be put to bed in a darkened room.

When Harry returned, he brought the organs which had to be sent
to Lahore. The problem was how to send them, as they would be carried
on men's backs for nine days under a broiling sun. They had no rectified
spirit so Ada suggested bottling them, as she did her fruit, but leaving out

the water. They sealed the top of the jars with hot mutton fat and finally covered them with a sheep's bladder. The jars were packed into a box, covered with a cotton cloth, addressed and sealed. They received a letter acknowledging the safe arrival of the package in Lahore. Enclosed with the letter was half the fee paid to a surgeon for a post-mortem, as Harry was not a qualified doctor!

That unforgettable day of trouble and upset had not been good for Ada. On 4th June, 1917, she warned Harry that the baby might be coming sooner than they were expecting. She was in the larder measuring out milk for Gordon when she broached the subject.

"Harry," she said, "I think the baby must be coming sooner than we thought."

"Why?" he asked.

"Well, I feel just the same as I did the first time. But I don't really know."

"But it can't come now," he said. "It is not the right time. And the Marxes are not here to help!"

"Yes," she said, "I know all that. But I still think it might come."

He did not want Ada to see that he was worried. "You do imagine things, don't you?" he asked.

"Well, yes! But I think if you were having the baby you might imagine things too".

They decided that it would be best to have breakfast and see how she felt then. After breakfast Ada returned to the attack.

"I still feel odd, Harry. I think I had better start making preparations."

He replied soothingly, "Now, if I were you I'd find a book and lie down and read and forget about it."

"You will come back early from the hospital, won't you?" Ada begged. "And please tell *Abbe* Yangdzom to come down here. I may need her help."

"Why?" asked her absent-minded husband.

When he had gone, Ada prepared the cot, made up her bed, and arranged the meals for the next few days. She knew her time had come, even if it was a month early.

It was past mid-day before Harry returned. He'd had a lot of patients that morning, he said. Ada asked if he had called the midwife.

Again, in his absent-minded way he asked, "Why?" But as soon as he realised Ada was in labour he was alarmed and all action. He went up to the roof of the house and called for Yangdzom, the wall of mountain acting as a sounding board and carrying his voice up to the hospital. Before she arrived, however, the baby was born. Harry and Ada did everything necessary between them and she was very happy that evening with another lovely, healthy boy. He was later christened Ronald Arthur, at Ada's wish, because during the preceding winter she had been reading and re-reading her few books, amongst which were Tennyson's poems and King Arthur's Knights.

There was still something more in store for them, however. As *Abbe* Yangdzom was about to return home she had a slight stroke on the verandah. After acting as doctor and midwife all day, Harry had to attend her and take her home.

The next day the baby and Ada were tormented by sandflies, which were now arriving in droves. They are tiny and can penetrate the finest mesh netting. They are so small that they can bite before they are detected, and bites irritate furiously, although for only a short time. Clearly something had to be done to protect themselves, especially the baby, from this plague, as sandflies also carry dengue fever. They called in a local tailor and had him sit on the bedroom floor, so that Ada could direct him while he took down all her curtains, which were made of fine butter muslin, and made them into nets to go over the beds on wooden frames.

By this time the barley was high in the fields and in the hot sun everything seemed to simmer with pleasantness. The snow was melting on the high mountains, so that it was time for the village men to go over the border to trade. The lamas chose a suitable day on which to start and it was interesting to see the procession of men and ponies assembling. Each man carried a gun, in case he was set upon by robbers, whose busy time it was. They took with them rice from India, thick home-made needles, dried apricots and barley, and brought back salt, butter and raw wool. The women ran alongside saying farewell and giving last instructions to take care, until the men climbed round a bend in the hill and went out of sight. It was autumn before they could return, when those left behind were eager to see them safely home again. As they came into sight, everyone

Ronnie in the pram

Ronnie with his nursemaid

Harry with Ronnie

Ada with Ronnie and Gordon

in the village watched anxiously to see the angle of their caps. If the flaps were down, it was a sign that they had not been successful, or that one of their party had died. It was a joy to see their caps at their usual jaunty angle, with the women and children running to greet husband, father or brother with happy tears of relief on their faces.

One summer morning Ada lay in bed, only half awake, but with the feeling that she was being watched. She opened her eyes and saw a row of men, with their hands shading their eyes, peering into the bedroom. She slipped across the room in her nightie and got dressed round a corner before going out to see who the visitors were.

They were Tibetan nomadic shepherds from across the frontier, who had brought butter for sale. As soon as Harry and Ada went out to them, they put out their long red tongues and held up their right thumbs in polite greeting. They grinned widely as Harry asked questions about their journey and way of life. Their dress took Ada right back to her early dream of coming to Tibet and seeing the people. Each man had his right arm bare and his homespun dress hung over his belt, baggy with all his personal belongings, while a brass ladle for tea, a knife, a spoon, a tinder-box and other essentials hung from his girdle.

Nomads' greeting

From their baskets they produced balls of butter, the size of footballs and wrapped in woollen garments. The balls were covered with black hand-marks as they had been moulded with unwashed hands. Ada brought out a bowl and a large knife and cut through some of the balls to see what they were like inside. One she found had been started round a pad of horse dung. Most of them were streaked with mouldy buttermilk, but from those that were not too bad she bought enough for a year's supply.

The negotiations over, Ada showed the nomads round the house. They were intensely interested in everything, particularly the pram as they had never seen anything on wheels before. They took turns pushing it gingerly along, watching and laughing like children at a fair. They were even more delighted when Ada put the baby in to show what it was used for. The kitchen stove amazed them too, for the only form of heating they knew were dried dung fires on the floor of their houses. They were awed by the height of the chairs, as only people of very high rank had seats so lofty: the height of a man's seat rises from the ground upwards according to his official position. The bedroom amused them and they gave each other furtive nudges and giggled as they looked at the single beds. The Tibetans were charming in their child-like simplicity and Harry and Ada thoroughly enjoyed their visit.

The butter needed to be clarified, so was heated in a large pan. The buttermilk and hair sank to the bottom and the golden butter rose to the top. This was strained through butter-muslin

Tibetan with yak tails

into a paraffin tin, which had been washed then filled with wood ash and left in the sun until the smell evaporated. When the poorer people in the village heard that Ada had bought butter they came and sat along the wall hoping to be given the discarded residues. They were grateful for even the tiny modicum of fat in the dirty sediment which they could put into their tea, gently pushing aside with a finger anything which was not edible.

They lived most of the year preparing for the winter. Grain was of the utmost importance, as they were absolutely dependent on local resources. It was not only the staple of their own diet, but they also had to pay their servants half in grain and half in money. The blacksmith who shoed the ponies, the shoemaker and the weaver, also had to be paid, at least partly, in grain.

After it was cut, the barley was threshed by yaks and *dzos*, ponies and donkeys, harnessed to a pole. They trod out the grain and then it was winnowed by hand. The women tossed the grain in shallow baskets, whistling and singing for the wind to blow away the chaff. Then it was carried to the stream and washed in the shallow basket-work trays which acted as sieves, allowing the dust to filter through. The washed grain was tossed in the sunshine to dry while the women picked out the small stones and solid pieces of debris. Ada enjoyed supervising this process. She spent many happy hours sitting in the warm sunshine, exchanging greetings with the passers-by and watching the ponies unerringly pick their way on the correct side of the *mani* wall.

When the grain was clean it was carried back to the house and spread out on sheets on the flat roof to complete the drying process. A crippled man sat there, banging on an empty tin to scare away the rock pigeons and sparrows. The grain was then stored in large paraffin tins, to be used as currency or to be roasted and ground for porridge. When they needed flour, the grain was taken to the little water-mill, which stood about four feet above the stream. The running water rotated a crossed piece of wood, known as a *babbly*, which in turn moved the millstones. Inside the mill was a large conical basket, with a hole at the base of the cone, into which the grain was poured so that it could trickle through the hole on to the millstone. Any flour which fell to the ground, or stuck on the walls, was carefully scraped up to be used as chicken food.

Ada always derived immense pleasure from the milling of the grain and firmly maintained throughout her life that progress had robbed mankind of some of his deepest satisfactions, by removing the necessity of growing and producing his daily food and laying in store sufficient for the long, cold winter months.

Fields showing irrigation chanels (Khalatse)

All through the summer Ada was kept busy with the two small children to look after, as well as her duties with the Sunday school and the hospital. She was also determined not to be caught again with such meagre food supplies for the winter. They had ordered quantities of vegetable seeds and the plants had to be carefully tended. When it was their day for water, Ada personally watched to see that they got their fair share. She kept a steady vigil, so that no one could surreptitiously block the channel to divert the stream to his own field, for their very lives depended on these summer crops.

Pu was fortunate in that, despite the severity of the winter, it was a comparatively fertile spot. It was sheltered from the worst winds and the rain and snow fall were sufficiently high to produce excellent fruit; not only apricots, which grew in Ladakh, but also peaches. There were some trees in the compound which bore large, luscious fruit. One year there was such a glut that Ada used all her preserving jars and still had a surplus, so she decided to try to raise some money for the mission by selling them at the equivalent of eight peaches for a farthing to the more well-to-do families. The money thus raised would help to buy a few necessities for the really poor and the sick. There were plenty of prospective customers but Ada soon realised that her basic psychology was wrong, for they wanted to beat down the price. She ought to have offered them at eight for a halfpenny to give everyone the satisfaction of making a bargain. In the end, she refused to sell the peaches to the well-to-do and gave them to the poorest families. Her original scheme worked in a rather round-about way, for she found that the families to whom she gave the fruit sold them to her original customers, for the price she had asked. Honour was saved and everyone was happy.

One day, while Harry was away and Ada was working at the hospital, she was brought an unusual patient; a man brought his cow, which had been badly gored down one side. Ada cleaned the wound but thought that, if the animal were to survive, it would have to be protected from dirt and flies, or else the wound would suppurate and the animal die. A cow is a large animal to bandage. She pondered for some time how to find enough material to cover so large a patient. She was reluctant to sacrifice one of her sheets but, in her box, she had a many-frilled petticoat, and this gave her a brain-wave. She decided that frills were really quite superfluous in Pu and she ripped them off, yard by yard. The cow looked a comic sight and gave Ada a lot of amusement whenever she saw it grazing in her petticoat trimmings.

When the shepherds came in to Pu from the plains, the missionaries bought sheep from them to provide wool for clothes, and also as a meat supply. A sheep killed early in the winter would freeze solid and keep for months. There was no need for a deep freeze; it was provided naturally. The offal was used straight away. The skins were cured and used either to make shoe leather or saddlery, or sometimes sold. Every portion of the animal was used with care. With a larger family the Burroughses needed more blankets for the winter months. The wool was clipped from their own sheep, which included a black one and then, when the wool had been spun, a weaver was engaged to make some blankets.

The news of the ending of the First World War took nine days to reach Pu and they were not sure what it meant when they read that an Armistice had been arranged. One evening, Ada was outside the bungalow, enjoying the last of the sun, when an old man came along carrying a bundle of wood on his back and, in his hands, some glowing firesticks. This was an unaccustomed sight, so she called in Tibetan, "Where are you going, *Meme* (Grandad)?"

"*Ri-la* – up the mountain," he grunted in reply.

"Why do you go up the mountain at this time with fire and wood?" she asked.

"Dewa, the headman, ordered me to go."

"But why has he sent you?"

"Who knows?" he answered.

Ada was puzzled. It seemed ridiculous that an old man should be sent to the top of a high mountain to light a fire in the evening. About a month later, when she was reading a copy of the 'Overseas Times', sent from England, she saw that bonfires had been lit all round the world on the borders of the British Empire in celebration of the signing of the Armistice and the return of peace. Here, in this remote outpost, the fire had indeed been lit, but no one had known why.

CHAPTER 8

Difficult times

The mission received their mail every fourth day, it having been brought by a relay of runners the whole two hundred and forty miles from Simla. The usual length of a run was about five miles but the one from Pu to the first hand-over was double the length, as the mountains were upright with no suitable place to build a hut as an exchange point. This stretch of road was like a pencil mark scratched across the face of a vertical cliff.

In the second year, a new post *babu*, or clerk, was sent from Chini. It was his first responsible job and he was keen to do well. Life was lonely for him as he did not know the Tibetan language. Pu was a fairly

The Burroughs and Marx families at Pu

important post office, as it was the beginning of the nine day chain along the Hindustan-Tibet road and, if the mail started late, it meant that several men had to spend many cold and dreary hours alone in the huts by the wayside waiting for it to come in.

It so happened that Ada wanted to send £5, or 75 rupees, to England and, one evening as the postbag was being prepared, she took the money to the post hut in the village. The youth counted it twice, put it into a small leather bag then into another, which

Gyalstan

he sealed, and that went into the bag with the letters. It was so dark in the tiny hut that she did not see Gyalstan, the mail runner, until she was leaving. According to the courteous custom she wished him a good journey in the morning and he left with her to go home to rest, ready for his early start.

When he awoke the next morning thick, blinding snow was falling. It was so bad that his wife implored him with tears not to go, as it was too dangerous. He reassured her that he would not go on that dangerous cliff road that day but it was his duty to report at the post office. The *babu*, however, insisted that the mail could not be delayed and threatened to report Gyalstan for refusing to carry it.

Poor Gyalstan wept as he folded the bag into the shawl, flung it over his shoulder, and went out into the snow. No one else was about and all was deathly still as he made his way through the village. Beyond the *chorten* the road became really dangerous and he kept in by the cliff wall. He became so dazed that his movements became automatic as he could not think and his eyes were inflamed.

When he had trudged for a few miles he came to a well-known danger spot, called Samar (Red Earth). It was probably the old bed of a torrent, as it was very rough and stony, and the path dropped into it to cross. The cliffs overhung, too, where their base had been worn away by water, or men had made holes and small caves wherever they could shelter or sleep.

As Gyalstan stood on the edge of this place he stopped to listen, as he feared that an avalanche might come down. There was no sound but his own laboured breathing, and no movement but that of his breath as it came into the freezing air. As all was still, he timidly stepped down on to the stony bed of the stream and, suddenly, a great avalanche came silently and swiftly sweeping down, carrying him off his feet, down towards the River Sutlej. He was smothering in the snow when he was cast aside from the main fall. He lay shaking and frightened, before fighting free of the snow, thanking God for his safety. His next thought was, "Where is the mail bag?" He lay dazed for a while then struggled to his feet. He looked about and saw nothing but snow and feared that the bag must have gone into the river, a thought that frightened him. He saw that the force of the avalanche had been so great that the snow had gone through the river and was well up the opposite cliff. Slowly and painfully he made his way back to the village.

Gyalstan's wife helped at the mission bungalow. She carried the water, roasted and ground the barley for porridge, and looked after the *dzomo*[21], feeding and milking the animal. Each morning she brought the cooking pot to Ada to receive dried apricots, which were kept in a large bin at the side door. These she boiled, took out the stones when cold, and mixed with barley flour for the *dzomo*. The kernels were dried to make oil for cooking.

That morning she was late because of the snow, so Ada went to the bin to put out the food for her when she was ready. As she looked up she saw Gyalstan returning.

---

[21]   Dzomo: female yak/cattle cross

"Gyalstan!" she said "Why are you here and where is the mail?"

"I've lost it" he said.

He told Ada the story and he wept as he said that he had lost his shawl and his boots. Then he described in detail what had happened. She offered him some tea but he said that he would rather go home, as he felt so tired and dazed. Ada sent Choskyid, his wife, back with him and then went to tell Harry the story. He and Mr. Marx gave Gyalstan a little time to rest and have some food, then they went up to his house to see him. On their return they both said that he was suffering from shock.

The clerk at the post office was almost in a panic, because not only was the mail lost, which contained money, but the whole series of men over the 240 miles to Simla would be awaiting its arrival and the whole line of up and down mail would be disorganised. When he was able to inform the postal officials at Chini by telegraph, they said that Gyalstan's story was a trumped-up lie and that he had hidden the mail and stolen the money. Police came up to Pu for him and led him to Chini, walking the five days with his wrists in handcuffs. As they went through the village the people jeered and called "*Mashukapa*", or "Christian", after him.

Gyalstan had an aged father who lived at Dobaling, across the river on the opposite mountain. For many years he had been a faithful servant of the mission and one of the annual duties he successfully performed was that of going to the bank at Simla, walking twenty-one days each way, to collect silver for wages, as the Tibetans over the border would not take rupee notes of any value. The old man had made that journey successfully for many years and it was his pride that he had never lost a rupee. When he heard of his son's trouble, he came to implore the missionaries to do all they could to help Gyalstan, who was a good and honest man. The father was now old and frail, and his white hair hung in long white strands to his shoulders, but he made a vow that he would live in one of the caves by the avalanche and search for the missing bag. He said that he would keep watch lest anyone should find the bag and steal the contents.

Each day Choskyid came the four miles and back to bring food to Gyalstan's father. Poor Choskyid was jeered at as she passed the houses in the village as the women called out "Christian!" and "Thief!". Each day the old man walked up and down the snow path, digging and looking for the bag, until he began to despair as he thought that the bag must be in

A bridge over the River Sutley

the river. He could see the snow on the lower part of the opposite mountain and watched there to see if he could see the bag. The police came from Chini and dug in the snow and they found Gyalstan's shawl and his shoes. They said that the shawl was folded and his shoes standing side by side, which was proof that the mail was stolen.

Now that the war was over, Mr. Marx was able to take his furlough, which was long overdue. It was suggested that the Burroughses should first take local leave for four months, as they would be left alone then in Pu for four or five years to complete their first period of service of ten years, so they started to make preparations to go down to Simla in May, which was the earliest they could travel. They were very excited to be going and Ada was thrilled with the thought of talking to an Englishwoman again.

They set out from Pu and when they came to Samar, Gylastan's father was still there, waiting and watching for the bag to appear as the snow melted. Snow was still piled so high that where they usually stepped down into the stream bed it was now a climb to get onto it. The Burroughses tried to cheer the old man by telling him that they would be staying with the District Commissioner in Simla and would tell him the story.

People on the streets of Simla turned to look at this queer little party, with their servants in Tibetan dress, riding into the town. They had been invited to stay at the Commissioner's bungalow, where Mr. and Mrs.

Mitchell had kindly offered hospitality. The Mitchells had been to Pu, so understood something of mission life there.

During the first evening, Mr. Mitchell came to Harry and asked if he would restrain Samdan, their Tibetan nurse boy. He had found an electric switch which lit up the grounds of the Commissioner's Residence, all the way down the hillside. When Harry found him, Samdan was standing, enchanted, switching the lights on and off, murmuring happily in Tibetan, "*Skarma tsok dug* – just like stars!" and Harry had not the heart to rebuke him. Ada was rather sorry she had not seen the lights herself. Even to her the civilized arrangements of an English home seemed smooth and easy and a great wonder.

One morning at breakfast Mr. Mitchell gave them the good news that the Pu mailbag had been found intact and Gyalstan had been released. He was reinstated as the mail runner but never received any compensation for the suffering and ignominy of his false accusation.

At last, Ada was able to get her denture renewed, after wearing it for three years in two pieces. The knots of silver wire had arranged a place for themselves in her gum and she had become completely used to it.

This holiday was the first real break in five years and they set off back to Pu greatly refreshed by the company of other people, good and varied food, and the stay at a lower altitude. They broke the journey at

Road (notice the sheep!)

Khotgur, where the Church Missionary Society had a mission in the charge of very kindly and good people. They stayed in the *dak* bungalow, where a dear old man did the cooking. A woman came to look after the children, giving as a recommendation the fact that she was very good at rearing calves, which they accepted with amusement. There was also a sweeper boy, of the lowest caste but of whom they became very fond as he was so kind to the children. This happy relationship with the boy proved of great value years later.

The ride home in the late summer was a happy one. There can be few places on earth which can rival the variety of Himalayan scenery. Below was the fast-flowing Sutlej; between the mountains were little villages with lovely trees around bright cornfields; then higher up the valley grand deodars and cedars, with a background of snow-capped peaks. Nearer the Tibetan frontier were gaunt barren mountains, with their own beauty of grandeur and colour.

Scenery in the Upper Sutlej valley

One can hardly wonder at the fear of spirits in the mountains and rivers. People need not fear their neighbours; it is natural things that can harm them, when the mountains send down rock avalanches, water can sweep all before it and thunder and lightning are surely the wrath of the gods. One day Ada was standing in the compound watching a water-burst from a glacier pour down the mountain face. At first she was not aware that it was water. As she gazed horror-stricken up the mountain, the whole earth seemed to be in motion. A great width of sandy water was sweeping from one side to the other and she knew that if it flowed to the right they would be engulfed and to the left the fields would go. Down dropped a house, like a toy being swept out of the way, and Ada was rooted to the ground with horror. As it happened the last surge fell over the fields, smothering them in mud and stones that rendered them useless for some years.

Mr. Marx was planning to take his family to America, to arrange for his children's schooling. With four children, who had lived in Pu for over ten years and knew no other way of life, there was a lot to organise. He wanted to test his arrangements for mounting the family for the journey to Simla, so had suggested that on Ada's birthday both families should take a picnic to the banks of the Sutlej, which the Burroughses had not yet seen. He knew of a place where a spring bubbled out of rock on a sandy beach by the river. The villagers, when they heard of the plan, came to Mr. Marx and asked him not to go to that particular place because they believed the *lhus*, or water spirits, who dwelt in all springs and wells, would cause harm if they were disturbed. As the missionaries did not believe in *lhus*, or *lhas*, which are the spirits of the earth, they decided to stick with their plan.

Mountain scene

Mr. Marx put his four-year old daughter, Erika, into a ring saddle on his pony and tied Werner, aged six, to the saddle behind his sister, while he walked at the pony's head. Their eldest girl, Ellie, rode the family donkey and Mrs. Marx was on a hired pony with their youngest child. They had a delightful day then, pleasantly tired and happy, the party started for home. At a place where the path widened enough for two ponies to pass easily, Mr. Marx asked them to wait for a few moments while he went to speak to a man who lived in a little house higher up the mountain. He was gone a long time and Ronnie started yelling, so Harry and Samdan, who was carrying the baby, set off ahead as they were on foot. Ada became restive, as she knew that Gordon was also tired and hungry and, as Mrs. Marx was happy to be left, moved to follow her husband.

As she passed the pony with Erika and Werner, it took fright and galloped off along the narrowing, rocky cliff path, with its many bends and steep precipices. Holding the reins in one hand, and with her other arm around her small son, Ada dashed after them. Around the second bend she saw that Erika was lying on the path, screaming with fear. She was wearing a red cloak and, for one terrified moment, Ada thought she was covered in blood. Ada dismounted, awkwardly as she was holding Gordon, to soothe the child and move her to a safer place, but her greatest concern was to stop the runaway horse before he fell over the cliff with the boy, so she quickly mounted again. Then her blood froze, as she saw the horse coming back along the narrow path towards her, dragging Werner behind him and kicking out at the rope entangled in its heels. Ada slid from her pony once more, pushed Gordon against the cliff and held him there with her buttocks. Somehow she had to stop the horse to save Werner from going over the cliff and his sister from being trampled in his path. She grabbed at his bit and held on with her teeth clenched. The roots of her hair burned and tingled, and later she wondered if it had gone white. She saw Werner go over the cliff and thought all was lost, then the horse started forward again and the boy was jerked back by the rope. Again he went over and was jerked back, while Ada hung on and moaned in agony, "God, send help; God, send help".

At last Chotob, the steward, came running round the bend, then Mr. Marx. They managed to free Werner and take the horse from Ada, who was holding her own screaming child and shaking from head to foot. The boy's *topee* was so crushed it looked like a bag of peas, but thankfully he was alive, though unconscious and terribly bruised.

After this incident Ada offered her pony, Billy, for Erika and Werner to ride to Simla, as he was quiet and reliable. Werner had recovered and was no worse for the accident. The departure of the Marx family caused a great stir and many of the men of the village accompanied them part of the way, whilst others went with them to Simla. All in the village felt that they were losing their father and mother.

Ada and Harry moved from their little house into the large, commodious one which Mr. Marx had built so beautifully for himself. Every door and window fitted. There was a sturdy pillar in the middle of each room, as in Tibetan houses, and a verandah with a wonderful view of the great snowy peak which was such a joy to Ada. For the two little boys there was ample room to play.

The bigger bungalow

The badminton court at the upper bungalow, which had seemed such a splendid playground, had become infested with fleas. Ada would spend time in the evenings examining the children's clothes, trying to remove any fleas which they had picked up. Their underwear could be washed every day but the heavy outer woollen garments would never have dried. The beds were meticulously aired and checked each day too and heads were also carefully examined for lice and nits. In a country where life is never taken it is most difficult not to become infested. The local people did not mind these creatures and accepted them as a natural part of life and they could not understand Ada's concern.

In September there was a lot to do to prepare for the winter. Potatoes were dug and sorted, some for food and others for seed for the following year. The small ones went for chicken food, and these were put in bins, or a hole, in an underground cellar. The floor was covered with earth from the garden and vegetables were carefully uprooted with soil attached to the roots and were replanted on the floor, while carrots, turnips and onions were buried in dry sand. In this way they had fresh vegetables all the winter, unharmed by the severe cold.

Ada with the Sunday School, including her two boys

The children, as they learned to talk, spoke in Tibetan. Their parents spoke English to each other and to them, but they always preferred to speak the language everyone else spoke around them. Only when their father and mother insisted would they speak English, lapsing into Tibetan when it became too difficult to think of the English word. They, of course, belonged to the Sunday School, where they learnt all the hymns, as well as the Bible stories and prayers, in Tibetan.

Harry and Ada found the responsibility for the whole mission a heavy one as they were presented with many problems. Several of these were caused by the extreme poverty amongst the people, some of whose fields had been destroyed by the floods. They still carried the responsibility for the hospital as well as shouldering their new tasks. Furthermore, the effects of post-war shortages were being felt, along with the growing unrest in India. The feeling of isolation grew as the autumn came and their connections with the outside world became more tenuous and uncertain.

On the night of 13th November, 1919, their daughter, Monica, was born. They were quite alone in the house, except for the two sleeping children. The room was lit only by a dim oil lamp. What can a man do on such an occasion? Harry lit the fire, prepared the cot and made some tea for Ada. His trousered legs, even covered with a towel, were not much of a place for a new born baby to rest on while having its first wash, so Ada advised rubbing her all over with olive oil and rolling her in a blanket until the morning. She had to have her first wash in the morning, and that was not an easy job. Harry sat on a chair with the yelling infant on his knee and looked so unhappy that Ada begged him to hand her over for her to deal with. When the baby was warm and comfortable, they then had the time to be happy about her arrival.

Three mornings later, two women, mother and daughter, burst into the bedroom just as it was getting light. They were yelling and screaming and tearing at their hair. Harry told them to go and wait in the next room until he was dressed and could attend to them but they would not move and sat themselves on the floor to pour out their trouble. The mother was a Christian widow with two daughters, one of whom was the children's nursemaid, Chungste-ma, a sweet, pretty girl, who was a great favourite with the family. It turned out that she had run away during the night with a Tibetan from over the border and she was wearing her Sunday go-to-church dress, which seemed to worry the mother more than the loss of her daughter.

She opened her own dress and tore at her chest. Harry and Ada knew that chest well, as the owner was very proud of its many scars which the lamas had burnt with hot irons to cure her of worms. She had passed 108 worms, the Buddhist sacred number. Harry at last persuaded the women to leave the bedroom and they became quieter. Eventually they bowed to the ground and asked if the younger girl could now be employed as nursemaid. She knew that she, too, would get good clothes.

After all this excitement, Ada suddenly became very ill, probably as a consequence of giving birth at such high altitude. Harry nursed her as best he could but had no real idea what was wrong. Ada felt herself getting weaker and was sure she was going to die. She made Harry promise that, should she die, he would take the children to the Mortimers, the Salvation Army missionaries at Chini. Then, the thought of leaving the three small children motherless, especially a new-born infant, made her fight for life. She was faced with perhaps the hardest struggle she had yet encountered, but slowly she gained ground. She was exhausted, and very weak, and lay in bed for many days, hardly able to bear the strain of having the children, whom she adored, in the room, but she was out of danger.

Before she was out of bed again, a man came running to Harry one Sunday afternoon asking him to go at once and see his twelve year old son, who had had a serious accident. He said that the boy had been up the mountain with his flocks when a sheep dislodged a rock above where he was sitting, playing his whistle. He heard the stone coming and jumped up but tripped and fell, cracking his skull badly on another sharp-edged rock.

Harry returned after a while with a grave face and looked at his sick wife.

"Do you think you could possibly get up? I need your help."

Ada was still very weak. After some discussion, they agreed that Ada should get up straight away and sit in a chair. The following day she would walk about and rest between-whiles on the sofa. She hoped she would be strong enough in time to save the boy's life.

Two days later the boy was still unconscious. Ada slowly made her way up the mountain to the hospital, resting very often on the way. They felt quite inadequate to tackle an operation of such delicacy, which might have daunted a trained surgeon with all facilities to hand. They also knew that if they failed it might mean that the village would ostracise them. The Christian community in Pu had never been as firmly established as that in Leh and Pu itself was riddled with practices left over from the ancient religion of *Bon chos*. The people were not as kindly as the Ladakhis and were ready to persecute the Christians. Some of the Christians themselves were not as strong in their faith as they should have been, and their undivided support could not be relied upon. Harry searched his medical books for guidance but could not find answers to half the things he wanted to know. As far as they knew, chloroform had not been given in the village before. In fact, they were told later in England that it should not have been necessary to give chloroform in such a case, but who was to tell them?

The boy's father insisted on being in the room. Ada spread an aseptic sheet over the boy but, as she went to his head to administer the anaesthetic, the father half lay across the sheet and would not be moved away. Then Harry asked for silence while he prayed that God would help the operation to be successful and that the boy would recover. A large request it seemed but they believed that God could answer largely in such desperate circumstances. The father prayed his "*O mani padme hum*" ceaselessly during the operation.

The outer cranium was splintered and the inner shelf broken. First, Harry removed the bone splinters. The brain was exposed and they could see it pulsating, so he had to be extremely careful not to injure it. With patience it was all cleaned and Harry was able to raise the bone which was depressing the brain and pack the cavity with sterilized wax. A surgeon may have thought it a poor operation but Harry did his best. Another part of the skull behind the ear was in a pulpy state, but on investigation it was found that the bone was not broken. All this took two and a half hours and then Ada had to leave Harry to finish whilst she went to nurse her baby.

As Ada came down the hill she could see that something was amiss in the compound. She found that Billy, her pony, had arrived back from Simla and was clearly ill. She questioned the two youths who brought him back and eventually they admitted that they had been riding him together over those difficult roads and he was over-ridden. Even the tough little Tibetan ponies have to be carefully treated at those high altitudes and overloading can seriously affect them. His belly was very swollen, so she ordered that a fire of damp straw should be lit underneath him. This is a Tibetan trick. As the warm smoke rises, it tickles the belly and makes the horse pass urine, which helps to relieve him. She sent a man up to the hospital to tell Harry and ask him to bring down a remedy if he had one. He arrived just as Harry was carrying his patient to bed.

She often recalled how funny it was to see Harry come through the compound gate on the upper terrace, still dressed in his white operating coat but with a large, black wine bottle tucked under his arm. He got one of the men to help to open the pony's mouth and emptied the bottle of castor oil down his throat. A few minutes before he had performed a delicate brain operation and now he had to do the work of a vet.

The boy got better without any complications and on the day the Burroughses left Pu he and his father brought them a large dish of apricots as a parting gift. The boy took off his cap for them to see his head. He had a ridge where one part of his scalp was higher than the other but he was well and normal: there were no ill effects, as they had feared, confirming their belief that God helps the ignorant to perform miracles.

There was a good deal of illegitimacy in that district, as a result of the promiscuous behaviour of the young people during the summer orgies, and also a great deal of venereal disease. The local rule about illegitimate children was that the mother should rear them. She must keep the girls until they married, while the father had a right to claim the boys as soon as they came to a useful age, ten or twelve years, when they could go to the hill with the sheep. The poor mother, who would have had a hard time to feed her children, was likely to be deprived of her sons just when she might expect them to contribute to the family.

One woman, who lived in one of the hovels in the low-caste area up the mountain, had two illegitimate sons. She brought them up to be good and honest, and, although they were exceedingly poor, they were a happy, loving family. When the boys were thirteen and eleven years of age their father, from Namgya, came and demanded his sons, so that they could work for him. The poor mother had to let them go and she was left sad and lonely.

In these remote areas taxes were not levied on the people but they were obliged to make up a rota of people from each house to carry the loads of travellers from one village to the next. Early that winter, an Indian official came up to do some survey work in the valley and needed porters. It so happened that it was the turn of the father of the two boys to do this duty and he decided to use his sons to substitute for him on the journey to Dobaling.

The weather was fine and clear but bitterly cold. A considerable amount of snow had already fallen and lay thick on the ground, so the journey took much longer than it might have done. It was getting late by the time they reached the bridge over the river, after which they had to make a stiff climb. When they arrived at Dobaling they were kept hanging about for their eight annas pay and they realised they would never be able to reach their father's house that night, so they decided to go to their mother's house in Pu. They had a small gift of butter for her, tied in their woollen belts with four annas out of their pay.

Dusk fell quickly and they were tired. They missed the pathway and started to wander round a small patch of alfalfa, which grew in amongst the rocks just outside the village of Pu. The older boy put his brother to rest in the cleft of a rock, while he tried to find the path. He stumbled about for a while and realised he too was lost in the darkness, although he knew they were very near home. He cupped his hands and called up the mountainside, "Ama, Ama, ow! – Mother, Mother!" His voice echoed round the rocks. The people in the village heard the cries but, as no one was expected, thought they were the cries of wandering spirits. They were afraid and barred their doors and stuffed rags into the small air holes in the walls of their huts. The boys must have seen the light streaming from the Mission bungalow and tried to make their way towards it but the missionaries, in their securely built house with tightly fitting windows, never heard their cries.

The next morning Dewa came for Harry. The two boys were frozen to death. They had wandered helplessly until they were exhausted; their footprints showed how they had stumbled round. The younger boy was in the rock cleft and his older brother crouched under a wall, yet they were in very sight of their mother's home.

As the winter wore on the great influenza epidemic, which had swept through the world, reached this little Tibetan village. Huge banks of thorns were cut and placed on the road to prevent outsiders from coming and to hinder the evil spirits on their wicked errands. Every day Harry went round the houses caring for the sick, who lay on the earthen floors of their houses on sheepskins. The snow was so deep that it was level with the roof-tops in some places and when the people were too ill to clear it away it was difficult for Harry to reach them. Chotob, their beloved steward, died.

In one home a small child had pneumonia. The Hindu idea of water pollution was strong in the valley and the mother begged Harry to stay out in the snow and she would bring the child outside to him. This he refused to do as the cold air might end the child's life quickly. At last she gave way, but each time he visited the house she had to empty her water pot and refill it as his shadow defiled the water in it.

It seemed as if spring would never come but at last the songs of the women and girls were heard as they carried buckets of manure on their backs to place in piles on the fields. The missionaries called them 'The swallows of spring' and their laughter and merry sounds cheered them. They spread the manure with their hoes and were followed by the ploughmen. Yaks were attached to small wooden ploughs with ropes and all day long in the sunshine the cry of "*O mani padme hum, O mani padme hum*" rang out. Ada made a very rough rag doll for each of her two older children, which became their dearest possessions. Each little boy would play with his doll tied on his back with a shawl, sometimes marching up and down with a piece of wood, chanting, "*O mani padme hum*" while they pretended to plough the fields or sow the barley by scattering imaginary seed. Harry made a little cart for them which they pushed up and down singing snatches of Tibetan songs.

Ada had an overwhelming desire to get away from the village. The mountains were so near and so high that their walls filled the windows. The valley was so enclosed that when outside one had to look straight up to see the sky. Ada longed for the company of another woman of her own kind and begged Harry to let her visit Chini with the children, a village where there was a Salvation Army missionary and his wife. Harry felt he could not leave his patients in the hospital or entrust the meteorological observations to anyone else so Ada would have to go by herself. She stoutly declared that she was also experienced and could manage with servants to help her.

April went by and, as the winter was usually over by then, Ada wanted to set out. Harry asked the old men of the village about the prospect but they shook their heads saying that the last snow had not yet fallen. So far the snow had been crisp and dry and the last fall should be wet, so she decided to wait another fortnight. Then it was May and the first barley was beginning to sprout. They had never had a snowfall as late as that in the years they had been in Pu.

Eventually, in the middle of May, she decided to go. None of the older men was able to accompany her, because this was the busy season when they had water-courses to clear and walls to repair, but she took two youths and two of the maids. Village men, whose rota it was to carry loads, took the bedding and food and the children were carried in baskets on the men's backs, while Ada rode her pony. Harry walked with them for some time, then sent them happily on their way.

The narrow and treacherous road was a shelf cut out of the mountain side. In places were small stone slides which had carried away the path. Between Pu and Shasu, the next village, there were at least twelve spots where a rider had to dismount. Here the pony had to be led by a halter a little way up the cascade of stones and then most carefully across, for with each step his feet would slide with the pebbles. If he slipped below the line of the path he would be lost down the precipice below. One of the party held the rope and it was Ada's job to grip his tail while they went over the landslip. She was always thankful to get over the slide and be safely walking on the path again.

At Shasu the light caught the rocks and sand, causing the barren valley to glow. They could hear the roar of the river, which was still invisible, and there was a little stream by which they camped. A fire was lit and food prepared and Ada felt relaxed and happy. Before she went into the tent to join the sleeping children, she walked round the camp in brilliant moonlight, checking all was well. As she crossed to the fire, where the servants were sitting with the village headman, Ada noticed a ring growing round the moon and she asked them what they thought that meant for the weather. They passed it off lightly, saying it might mean rain or snow, but Ada sensed unease in the headman's manner and felt disquieted. She began to think she had been foolish not to accept the old men's advice.

The following day the road, which Ada knew well, was rough and rocky and led up to a small pass. At the top there was a huge smooth rock to negotiate, which called for both skill and strength on the part of the pony-man. The pony had to take it at the run to gain enough momentum to scramble over the slippery rock. She hated this part as the pony's hooves would strike sparks from the rock at the level of the eyes of the person following. On this occasion, Janphal ran up leading the pony, with Ada behind. For a terrible moment the pony stood erect on hind legs against the skyline, while Janphal hauled on the rope to get him down but did not seem to have the strength or the skill. The women carrying the children huddled against the cliff, calling on the gods to save them, while Ada was rooted to the ground in horror, and again her hair tingled, as it looked as if the pony would fall back and kill them all. After what seemed an age, but could only have been seconds, Janphal got him down and the trembling women scrambled up the rock themselves. Unbidden tears were rolling down their faces as they sat down to recover on the far side of the crest.

They spent that night in a lamasery in a village called Kanam. As in all Tibetan buildings the ground floor was the stable, so they climbed up a wide ladder to a very large room with a boarded floor, where the lamas held their devotions at tiny desks like footstools. In a corner above the stairway was an earthen place where a fire was made on the floor and where the servants cooked their food. In the opposite wall was a door, before which were three stone steps. Each morning at daybreak, and at sunset, a lama came up the stairs carrying a bunch of smoking juniper as incense. He unlocked the door at the top of the steps with a large iron key and went into the little temple, intoning all the time the prayer, *"O mani padme hum"*. Closing the door behind him, he replenished the numerous little brass vessels of grain and oil, which were laid on the altar before the gods, as the mice always disarranged them. All round the walls behind the table were the chief gods. The goddess of mercy had a thousand open hands with an open eye in each palm, and three crowned heads, with a kind expression on her faces. With these eyes she could see the people's needs and sorrows and with those hands she could help. Jamyang, the big horrible one was there, painted black. There were many others, but the main statue was that of Buddha, with his inscrutable gaze, sitting in the centre with crossed legs and a finger touching the earth.

The next day was fine and sunny and everyone was in high spirits. Only one untoward incident occurred. Ronnie was restless in his basket,

Gods and offerings

so Ada took him onto her saddle, holding him with her left arm and with the reins in her right hand. She asked one of the boys to take the leading rein as a precaution against accident. Suddenly, a rock came hurtling down the mountainside, touched a rock, and bounced off again. It flew between the pony and the leading boy. Another step forward or back and it would have struck one or the other of them but they escaped with a mild feeling of shock.

On the fifth day they arrived at their destination, the pleasant village of Chini, which was the centre of administration for the district. The village sprawled down the hillside and above were trees, deodars and firs, which gave them much pleasure as there were none at Pu. Across the valley stood a magnificent range of snowy peaks. They thankfully made their way to the *dak* bungalow, looking forward to a time of rest and peace.

The two youths went straight away to the outside kitchen, which was situated some way behind the bungalow. Here they would cook and sleep. The two maidservants slept on the floor in Ada's room. It interested Ada to see them prepare for bed. They loosened the string of their trousers, pulled their arms out of the sleeves of their gowns, then knelt and leaned forward, pulling the top of their gowns over their heads. They were soon asleep, looking like two large bundles.

Sleep did not last long as soon a first-class storm developed. Thunder, an unknown phenomenon in Pu, started rumbling up the valley and seemed to collide with the mountains, making a terrific noise. Ada had to comfort the servants as well as the children. There was a heavy fall of snow overnight and they were thankful to be at their destination.

However, the following day the sun shone again and they were able to go and call on their friends, Mr. and Mrs. Mortimer. Ada was longing to show off her three beautiful children to another Englishwoman, to hear someone say how charming they were and how like Father (or Mother), for she missed all this more than she would admit. But, while she was fussing over the younger two, to Ada's dismay Gordon stole away with the scissors and chopped a pathway through his hair, from forehead to crown. As she talked with Mrs. Mortimer, however, Ada felt her heart unfreeze as she chatted so kindly and sympathetically with her.

They talked of their way of living and Mrs. Mortimer brought in her new Tilley lamp, with its delicate mantle. Ada was intrigued, as she had not seen one before and Mrs. Mortimer lifted off the lamp-glass to show her

Ada with Mrs. Mortimer and the children

the incandescent burners. At that moment Ronnie, who had been sitting quietly on his mother's knee, leant forward and crushed the mantle in his hand. He was as dismayed as Ada when it disappeared into nothing. Ada consoled herself that Mrs. Mortimer was about to go on furlough, when she could get a replacement, so that the damage was not as bad as it might have been.

Because of the snowfall, Ada's party had to stay at Chini longer than she had intended. Their food was running low, so she wrote to her husband

Chini

asking him to send a man with some bread. Then the kitchen boys came to say that their *tsampa* was almost finished and the people in the tiny bazaar would not sell any. The excuse they made was that Gandhi had said that Europeans should not be helped but turned out of India. Ada also could not persuade them to sell any food, so she decided that they must set off for Pu before they ran out completely.

Then a man whom she knew and trusted arrived from Pu, with a long story but no food. He said that Burroughs Sahib had sent him with bread and *tsampa*, which he had carried in his shawl on his back. On the way he had fallen in with a man who had three donkeys and they had travelled together. As they were crossing the hollow between Jangi and Pangi there was a great landslide, when rocks as big as houses came hurtling down. As he heard the avalanche coming the man loosened his shawl, which was tied at the front, just as a rock struck it behind and he

Chini

just escaped with his life. One of the donkeys was killed and another badly injured.

Ada was disinclined to believe this fantastic story but, as he had not brought food, it did mean that they had to leave for Pangi the following day, in the hope of getting food there. On arrival at the rest-house, the *chowkidar* said he could not help them as it was late spring and the village stocks were low. He also warned them not to travel further because of the landslide between them and Jangi. Early the next morning, as they prepared to leave, the man came again and implored them, on his knees and with clasped hands, not to go lest they should all be killed but Ada told him firmly that if he could not give them food they must go.

When all was ready, she called her frightened servants together and told them about the danger of the road and suggested that as the loose rocks had already fallen there was not much likelihood of more coming down. She was not sure of this at all, but she wanted to inspire confidence. Then, as they were Christians, she said that they must commend themselves to God, who knew the straits they were in, and ask for His help and care. They all knelt amongst the luggage whilst she prayed in the Tibetan language and they all joined in the Lord's Prayer.

It was a lovely morning and they were soon on their way to Jangi, ten miles away. About two miles along the road they climbed up a rocky path and there they saw and smelt a dead donkey. Ada felt very conscious-stricken for not having believed the messenger and told him so. Then they came on to the plain which had been so wide and pleasant on the way down. They could hardly believe their eyes and stood aghast, looking at what was before them. The way was blocked with huge rocks, some as large as cottages, over a length of about five hundred yards. At first Ada wondered if she should accept defeat and return to Pangi, to throw themselves on the charity of the villagers, but decided that as she had publicly asked for God's help she must go forward and believe that He would not fail them.

It would be foolish not to consider that they all might be swept away by another rock-fall, so it was necessary to make a plan for the crossing in case more loose stones came down. The first to go was a man with a load, with another who carried one of the boys. When they were safely across another carried a child and one of the girls accompanied him. Soon all had crossed at intervals, whilst Ada kept an anxious eye on the cliff, glancing occasionally to watch their progress. When all were over, Ada went whilst the rest of the company watched for her. It was impossible to look at the cliff whilst traversing the fall, as it was necessary to pick one's way and scramble through the rocks as best one could.

Feeling thankful they were all safe, they plodded steadily along till they got to Jangi. To Ada's great joy and relief Harry was there. Having heard of all their troubles he had set off to walk until he met them. What a comfort it was to Ada to have someone else to carry responsibility. He had lit a fire and soon they were having a comfortable cup of tea whilst they each related their experiences.

All had not been easy at Pu. There had been a heavy fall of wet snow, which had soaked through the roof before it could be shovelled away, and the house had been flooded. But as they shared their troubles they seemed to lighten and they settled down for a good night's sleep. Ada became aware how much she depended on her husband's quiet reliability, his wisdom and experience as a traveller.

The remainder of the journey was not too bad and nothing untoward occurred until they were near home. Harry was at the front, carrying Monica in her basket, and Ada followed the men who were carrying the two boys. Ronnie was in a basket which was a new design, with a rounded hood made of strong, string-like weed. As they approached a bluff on the edge of a cliff overlooking the Sutlej, Ada heard the man carrying Ronnie cry out in fear. She dashed forward and saw that an up-current of air had got into the hood and the man was being lifted off his feet and was in danger of being carried over the cliff, as if by parachute. It took all Ada's strength to hold him down whilst he manoeuvred himself round so that the air escaped. They were both trembling with fright. On the basis of this experience, Ada gave credence to the theory of man-lifting kites, as described in 'The Third Eye' by Lobsang Rampa. Once safely at home, Ada vowed that she would always listen to what the local people said about the weather in future and not trust her own judgement.

CHAPTER 9

Life goes on

The barley ripened and was harvested and the fields were re-sown with millet or buckwheat and a few with turnips and peas. The buckwheat soon sprang up and flowered, clothing the fields in brilliant patches of red against the drab hillsides, with snowy peaks behind and clear blue sky above. As the apricots ripened they were picked and Ada preserved as many as she could. She could not spare much sugar for jam but made some to enliven their winter diet. The rest of the fruit was stoned and laid out on the roof to dry.

Women sat in the sunshine and cracked the stones. The shells were put to one side to dry for fuel while the kernels were placed on a large stone slab with a hollow at one end. Another, rounded, stone was taken and the kernels were pressed and rolled until all the oil was squeezed out. Every child was told the story of the maid-servant who worked and worked and could not get the oil to run. 'The sun was high in the sky and she had produced nothing. Despairing, she started to cry and, as her tears fell on the stone, the oil began to come; so always remember to put a drop of water on the kernels before you start pressing.' The oil was carefully collected and stored. Ada used hers mainly for cooking and gave some as gifts to her servants. The residual pulp was boiled to dispel the prussic acid before it could be used to make cakes for winter cattle food. This was a task the women hated, for it gave them a headache. Once, one of the cows had escaped and eaten some of the apricot pulp before it was treated and it died an agonizing death from prussic acid poisoning.

Now there was great excitement in the village, for there was to be a wedding. The bride was the daughter of Chosdar, who was called Drohma, after one of the goddesses. This would be a grand occasion for they were a well-to-do family and Drohma's mother, Barma, was a capable woman. The bride was fourteen years of age and it was high time she was married, since she was the daughter of high-class parents. Some years before, a promise of marriage had been made according to the custom; the day of the ceremony had now been fixed. There was only one suitable period for weddings and that was a full moon after the harvest, when there was a lull in the work. The moon would light the dancing-ground for the revels and the weather had not yet turned too cold. The bride's family were thrown into a whirl of activity.

The weaver was called in with his loom to weave cloth for new clothes. The men mostly wore undyed cloth but the women of Pu traditionally made their dresses from cloth dyed with indigo, which was imported from India. The dye was fixed by soaking the newly-dyed cloth in matured cows' urine, which was a very valuable commodity, and all the clothes retained a curious smell. The stable and cow-shed at the Mission bungalow had to be securely fastened to prevent people sneaking in and worrying the cow in order to get the urine. They were more interested in the urine than the milk but, if the cows were interfered with too much, the milk yield went down.

Weaver (the loom is typical but the people are not)

When the cloth was woven and dyed the tailor was called in to make the dresses. Each dress had a simple top, fastened on one shoulder, but the skirt was full and flared, made of fifteen narrow panels gathered at the waist. Then, all round the border, gay strips of muslin were stitched. The whole garment finally weighed about five pounds. Trousers, which were long and tight, were tied over the hips. The bride must now have black trousers to show her married status.

The silversmith, too, was summoned. Earrings and bracelets, necklaces and head ornaments were ordered, and rings in plenty. Quantities of oil had to be pressed for the wedding feast; to fry the delicious oil cakes or *khurahs*, to dress the women's hair and to fill the little stone lamps.

Smith

Drohma was happy and excited as all the preparations were made. The invitations went out. To the missionaries a polite little deputation came saying that, as much as they would like to invite them, it was against the custom and their presence would be an embarrassment. The missionaries thanked the messengers for their courtesy and apology, which was quite unnecessary, since they understood perfectly. They felt a twinge of regret, but thought it kind of Chosdar and Barma to explain their predicament.

When the day of the wedding came, Harry and Ada stood outside in their garden watching the distant procession of yaks come lumbering down the pass, bringing gifts and guests to the wedding. Suddenly Barma, the bride's mother, burst upon them and demanded angrily, "Where is Drohma? The ungrateful hussy has disappeared." Barma raved and fumed and said she hoped the devils had taken the good-for-nothing trollop and that her corpse would never be found. Ada and Harry were very shocked and tried to soothe the frenzied mother, who would hardly let them get in a word of comfort or help. She stormed off, raving and shouting to the devils to get her daughter, and, if they did not, what she would do to the girl if she found her.

It would take the procession about four hours to make its way to Pu, surely enough time for Drohma to be found. Chosdar mounted his pony and rode to Namgyar, where they had relatives, to see if the girl had taken refuge with them. There he found Drohma, shy and bashful.

Meanwhile, the bridegroom's party arrived at the house. Barma met them, tearing her hair and calling her daughter every shocking name she could put her tongue to. An hour or so later, Chosdar arrived back with his daughter, the bride, riding pillion behind him. As soon as they arrived

Smith

Drohma ran into the house, covering her face, and hid. The relatives and friends went to her and eventually persuaded her to come and meet her future husband.

Harry and Ada were still anxious and concerned, for they were a nice family and they hated to see Barma so upset. They need not have worried! It was the custom for the bride to appear shy and reluctant. Barma and Drohma had put up a particularly fine show and Barma's acting was highly praised, but Harry and Ada had been the only ones taken in. They now appreciated that Barma had included them in the drama.

A bride

After the ceremonies were over the procession of yaks and ponies wound back up the pass, this time with the bride, who rode with her face veiled by a white cloth until such time as she would reach her new home and the further rituals were completed.

Earlier in the year, Harry had decided that now the war was over he ought to take an extended tour through Spiti and he reckoned that he would be away about six weeks. Ada had become accustomed to his absences so had raised no objection but when the time came for him to go she began to feel uneasy. She knew that the journey Harry was undertaking was hazardous and difficult but she also knew that he was well experienced and that if he felt it was his duty he would go, despite protests from her. But she had a premonition and begged him not to, thinking of a case of amoebic dysentery in the village and a thousand other trivial

A bridge in Spiti

Harry on tour

excuses to persuade him to stay. In the end Harry agreed, reluctantly, to shorten his tour, but he was puzzled and said to Ada "You've never minded before, or tried to stop me. What *is* worrying you?"

Ada realised she was being unreasonable, but still she kept saying, "I do wish you wouldn't go."

However, the revised tour did not look too bad and, before he left, Harry made up many different packets of medicine for Ada in different coloured papers, including some for dysentery, although there was only the one isolated case. He knew Ada was quite capable of dealing with almost any situation and his faith in her was absolute.

Ada and the children accompanied Harry to the foot of the pass and watched him ride out of sight. Ada turned back home, feeling terribly lonely and uneasy. She now had sole charge of the hospital and had to cope with all the Mission business, as well as her household and the children. She reminded herself firmly that she was a missionary in her own right and was proud of it, so she should not succumb to depending too much on her husband, much less hamper his work.

Harry had only been gone a day to two when Gordon started to run a very high fever and was restless and fretful. Ronnie was his usual wriggling self, always into mischief and needing little sleep, which did not help when there was a very sick child and an infant to look after. The maids went home at sunset, leaving Ada completely alone. Then Ada fell ill, her temperature soared to 104°F and she could hardly attend to the children in the night. Ronnie, too, succumbed and they all lay weak and depressed in the one room.

While Ada was lying there, a man from across the border in Tibet arrived to repay a debt to the Mission. She knew that he had travelled many days and that he had a long journey home, so she must try to deal with him. She staggered from her bed and, with the help of the maid on one side and wall on the other, she managed to shuffle along to the study. The high altitude always seemed to exaggerate the effects of fever. Ada thought she was suffering from dengue, or sandfly fever, which has the most debilitating effect, making one feel completely weak and helpless. Once in the study, the man fumbled to produce the money. He had the rupees in a long knitted string purse, only wide enough to take one rupee, and he had this sausage-shaped roll knotted round his waist very securely. Ada waited patiently while he fumbled and fiddled with the knots, wondering if she could hold up. Finally, he produced the rupees, one by one with agonizing slowness. Ada counted and recounted the money but could not

Harry with Billy

Missionary at work

get it right. She kept losing count but in the end she gave up and decided to take the risk. She smeared his thumb with ink and he countersigned the entry in the book by making his thumbprint.

After a few days the fever subsided and Ada felt much better. Thankfully, the children too were quite well again. A woman came to her with a message from the house of the richest man in the village to say that the little daughter of the house, who was nine years old, was ill. Ada knew the child well. She was a dear little girl, already promised as a nun, but waiting until she was old enough to enter the nunnery. Ada questioned the woman as to the nature of the child's illness and suspected that it might be dysentery. She changed into her nurse's dress, sleeves, and apron and hurried to the house. The child was clearly very ill, with a high fever. Ada bathed her hands and face and gave instructions as to how she was to be cared for and said she would send medicine, which must be administered exactly as she prescribed. She was sure now it was amoebic dysentery. As soon as she left the house she rinsed her hands in the swiftly-flowing stream and, before she entered her own house, she took off her sleeves, apron and cap, then changed the rest of her clothes immediately, putting them to be washed and hung in the sun. She scrubbed her hands and gave strict orders to the servants to be meticulous in washing their hands before handling food or touching the children.

No sooner had she done this than a man came, saying that his friend had been injured in a quarrel; his eye was badly cut and it was bleeding profusely. Would she go with him and see the friend? Ada packed her bag with dressings, a sterile needle, and gut, in case stitches were needed, and set off to the village once more. When they got to the house the man was sitting there, looking a terrible sight with blood trickling down his face. Ada opened her bag and made preparations to clean him up, so that she could see the real extent of the damage. But the man would not let her touch him. He was talking excitedly and had obviously been drinking. Ada got annoyed and asked why she had been summoned when he did not want treatment. Out of a jumbled torrent of words, Ada made out that he wanted her to give him a *rappatt* (report) to take to the police in Chini, to show what injuries he had suffered. Ada smiled to herself when she realised of course he did not want the blood wiped off his face but would keep it there as evidence! She declined to write a *rappatt*. She said she was prepared to try to heal his wound but not to take sides in a quarrel; neither would she be prepared to act as a witness in a police court. He got very annoyed and refused any medical assistance, so Ada shut her bag and left.

The following morning she went round early to see the little girl, who was a favourite pupil of hers. When she reached the house she was greeted with the doleful news that the child had died in the night. Ada turned away with a heavy heart and climbed up to the hospital.

Three days later Monica started to become fretful and unwell. Ada had taken every precaution. None of the children had been in the village, but it soon became apparent that she too was suffering from dysentery and was very ill. She did not respond to the medicine Harry had made up and became steadily worse. Ada searched the medical books for help.

'Complete starvation and the medicine. Albumen water might be of benefit.' Albumen water – what was that? She searched the books again but found no clue on how to make albumen water. She searched her cookery books, without success. She tried to experiment with egg-white, but it did not look right. Ada felt alone and helpless – suppose she got dysentery too? She sent a runner with a message to Harry imploring him to return, not only for Monica's sake but for the other children and everyone in the village.

Still there was no improvement in the child. Her bowel was exposed and she lost consciousness. Ada was desperate. She sent for Gyalstan, the postman, to come. He had just returned from a twenty-mile run with the mail but, when Ada told him how worried she was, he agreed to set off as soon as he had had some food and short rest, to take an even more urgent message to Harry. Ada said she was deeply grateful and was there anything she could give him? He shyly asked if she had any *gharrum*, a kind of dried molasses which was sold in the Indian bazaars in large balls, and she was pleased because she did have some. Gyalstan went home to have his meal and rest and promised to return for the message when the moon was up. Ada put the two little boys to bed. Monica still lay silent and still. She had been unconscious for twenty-four hours.

Ada went to the store-room to get the sugar ball and break it into pieces for Gyalstan. First she tried with a large knife, but it was too hard, so she fetched a chopper. She was not a very good shot and the ball rolled across the kitchen floor. Next time she got in a good blow but found that the chopper had stuck and she had to struggle to release it. She tried to chip bits off the outside, but the ball kept rolling away. Suddenly Ada saw herself crawling round the kitchen floor with tears rolling down her cheeks, chasing a ball of sugar with a chopper, and through her tears she started to laugh at the ridiculous scene. At last she succeeded in chopping up the *gharrum*. It was not long before Gyalstan reappeared and took the note in his cleft stick. He gratefully accepted the sugar, which he said he would chew as he ran and that it would help to keep him going.

Sadly Ada went back to the bedroom, where the child lay completely still. She wondered if she had missed anything in the medical books; she searched through them again but found nothing new. There was nothing she could do except moisten the baby's lips every now and then and wait.

Earlier that evening Paulu, the schoolmaster, had come. He had agreed to help Ada keep the meteorological records and now he came with the thermometers for her to check, but as he had wrapped them in a shawl she wondered if they were correct, and she asked him to come again next morning and bring them unwrapped. Then she said, "Please can you come very early? My little daughter is very ill and I do not know if she will live through the night. If she dies, I must ask you to arrange for her funeral".

She went back to the child and gently wet her lips with a few drops of boiled water. Then Dewa's wife came. She knelt on the floor and said, "I have come, Memsahib, to see if I can help. May I give you some advice? Please do as I ask you. Take a little *tsampa* and sieve it very, very fine and then mix it with some warm water to a thin gruel and give it to the child. Do do as I say, Memsahib, you have always been kind to us and now I want to help you!" Ada was so touched by this that she started to cry. Dewa's wife tried to comfort her, but she too was crying. Eventually she left and Ada was on her own once more.

She paced the floor. Should she try the local remedy? The medical books firmly said 'No food', but should she try something new, since the child had not responded to treatment? In the end she felt she must obey the books. How otherwise could she justify herself if the child died?

The evening was very hot and close and the bedroom seemed stuffy, so Ada tenderly picked up the child and nursed her, walking up and down, up and down, crooning to her. Then she laid her back in the crib and prayed. Restlessly she wandered about. If only there were something she could do! She became angry and stamped up and down the room, asking God how He could let this happen when they were doing their best to serve Him. She said, "I would not treat one of my servants in this way, so how can You, the God of Mercy, take my precious child away from me?"

Anger exhausted, she picked the child up again and carried her out to the cool night air. The moon was bright now and as she stood in the doorway she could see the little graveyard above, where children of other missionaries were buried, and she felt deep remorse at having railed against God. Calm and chastened, she looked down at the child in her arms and saw the tiniest flicker of one eyelid. It was the first sign of life for two days and nights and she knew then that the child would live and God had not forgotten.

At dawn, Ada went outside again and found that Paulu was there. He had, he said, stayed near the house all night in case she needed him. He asked if he could borrow the binoculars, because he thought he could see a red horse at the top of the pass, which might be the Sahib. He took the glasses and confirmed that it was the Sahib. Four hours later Harry stumbled into the house, utterly exhausted.

Ada told him she thought the child would live. She made him some tea and then he lay fully clothed on the bed and fell asleep. He had walked and ridden for thirty hours, without rest or food, crossing two high-altitude passes to get back. When he woke, Ada prepared some food for him and they looked at Monica, who was still barely conscious. Harry examined her and said he would have to repair the ruptured bowel straightaway. Ada thankfully handed over the medical treatment to him and went to rest herself.

All during this time there were disturbing undercurrents reaching the village from the political unrest in India. Parcels sent from England frequently arrived empty, all the contents having been stolen en route and the wrappings neatly stuck together again. When one parcel arrived intact from some kind friend in England, who had sent a box of Woolworth's toys out for distribution to the children, it was an occasion worthy of celebration. They hit on the plan of holding a *lgol-lgol*, which literally translates as a madness, but in English would mean a sort of picnic party. Chosdar told them of a place in the mountains where shepherds congregated which was flat and grassy.

On the day, all the children gathered in the compound very early. Quite small children were carrying even smaller ones tied on to their backs with a shawl. Everyone was noisy and excited. They set off, scrambling up a stony gully, the boys carrying the cooking pots and food and the mysterious box. The children leapt and scrambled up the rocky hillside, as sure-footed and agile as young goats. At the picnic place, the boys busied themselves making a fire, collecting roots and dried sheep's dung and anything else that would burn, while the girls played with the babies and looked after the younger children. Chosdar had agreed to come with them to cook the food and make the tea, because he was of sufficiently high caste for none to be offended.

Places were arranged for all the different castes: high-class, farmers, carpenters, weavers, leather-workers, and Christians. The Christians were allotted the lowest place. As soon as the food was ready, all sat down to eat, producing their own bowls and cups. After the meal Harry played ball-games with the boys and Ada played with the girls and the little ones with their accustomed playthings, stones and dried balls of sheep dung, making patterns and villages while they told stories.

When it was nearly time to go home, all the children gathered round, sitting cross-legged on the ground. Harry and Ada made a great ceremony of opening the mysterious box. They distributed whistles and drums and trumpets to the boys, while beads and coloured wools were for the girls. The girls examined the beads with interest and then handed them back, saying, "No thank you, they are not real stones." However they liked the brightly-coloured wool. Then they formed a procession. Trumpets and whistles led the way, followed by the drums. Those carrying pans beat them on the lids. Imagining they were lamas, they set off, dancing and singing, down the hill. The mountains echoed with the din and any lurking spirits must have fled in terror.

When they reached the Mission bungalow there was a message waiting for Harry, saying that the cook's mother, who had been ill, was much worse and please could he go and see her. He set off straight away with his bag. When he reached the house he realised that there was nothing he could do, for she was dying, but he stayed with her and tried to bring her comfort.

The funeral, according to custom and necessity, had to be the next day. Rigdzin, the cook, came to Ada and requested that she would give her a nightdress to dress her mother in for the funeral, as she had done for two other Christians. Ada said she would see what she could do, as she did not think she could spare another nightdress. She turned her box over, looking for something. All she felt she could spare was a pair of white cotton combinations, with a frill round the neck and round the legs, but they had no sleeves, so she added a striped blouse for form's sake. She took these up to the house and helped to prepare the corpse. She could not help giggling to herself at the strange outfit, but the daughters were most impressed. They felt it was so splendid that she must be buried in the European style in a *bakus*, or box, rare and precious in those parts. All Ada and Harry's travelling boxes were used as furniture; however Harry found two rather small half boxes and took them to the house. They were delighted. Soon the undertakers came for the corpse. First they put string through the rings on her fingers and pulled them off. Next, to Ada's horror, they broke both her legs so that she would fit into the improvised coffin. The family were completely unmoved.

The next day, about half an hour before the funeral, Gyalstan arrived with a cablegram from England to Harry, bringing the news that Harry's mother had died. This was a severe blow to him, as he adored his mother and he had always been her favourite son. Ada, who had never met her mother-in-law, felt that it was cruel turn of fate that he should receive the news at that moment. They silently turned to go to the funeral of Rigdzin's mother. When Harry read the funeral service it was as if he were conducting it for his own dearly-loved mother, and tears poured down his cheeks. The tension and solemnity of the occasion were almost unbearable as the 'coffin' was lowered into the grave. But the tense atmosphere was shattered by Rigdzin and Tarchungma, as they shrieked hysterically and flung themselves into the grave wailing and tearing their hair, showing their grief in the traditional fashion. They had now captured the scene and Ada was relieved for Harry's sake.

As time passed, the Burroughses found that their nerves were being frayed. The altitude was beginning to tell and the monotonous and frugal diet took its toll. Minor incidents seemed to swell out of proportion; they became sensitive to gossip and minor failures. Harry became restless and craved the companionship of other men, while Ada longed to talk to another European woman.

One day a British Forest Officer made a detour to come and see them and they were thrilled at the thought. They were just sitting down to have some tea when Ada remarked that they had been puzzled by a mysterious red glow in the sky since the previous day. The Forest Officer sprang to his feet.

"Where?" They pointed in the direction from which he had come.

"My God, my forests!" he shouted.

Immediately he called for his horse to be saddled and, hardly stopping to drink his tea, he gave a hurried explanation – Gandhi's followers were setting fire to the great forests all over the country as a political protest and he must try to save as much timber as he could. Sadly Harry and Ada watched him ride away.

Another day Gordon was playing outside when he screamed. Harry rushed out of the study, Ada from the kitchen. Harry got there first and, when Ada arrived, cried, "Quickly, hold the child's thumb tight!" He dashed indoors and came out with a scalpel with which he made an incision, then started sucking the thumb. When all the commotion had died down and the child was soothed, he explained, "He was stung by one of the biggest scorpions I've ever seen. I killed it with my heel. It was lucky we were on the spot, he could have died within minutes."

They used to get snakes occasionally, after the sparrows and their nests. They found one or two dead sparrows on the verandah and wondered why they had died but suspected snake poison. Then one day Ada found Ishe eating one of the dead birds. She scolded him and, to her surprise, he growled menacingly at her.

Later that day Harry had gone to the village and Ada was resting in the house with the children. The servants had gone home for their dinner and had not returned. Suddenly Ada heard Ishe barking hysterically, which was unlike him, and she went out to see what was the matter. The dog was racing round and round in circles, barking in a high unnatural manner. She thought for a moment he had been stung, but as he became wilder she realised he had gone mad. She ran back into the house and shut the children in the bedroom.

At that moment Harry came in and asked, "What's the matter with that animal?" Ada told him that Ishe had earlier eaten a poisoned sparrow and she feared it might have affected his brain.

"I'll have to shoot him. You go inside and don't come out until it's all over." Harry knew that it would be a great blow to Ada to lose her pet but he went away to the study and loaded his rifle.

CHAPTER 10

Isolation and a sad story

Friends and relations, particularly Ada's sister Mary, wrote to them regularly and sent copies of various newspapers but Harry and Ada found it increasingly difficult to relate to what they read. The world as they knew it in 1913 was, in 1920, a different place. Women of thirty or over had the vote and there was a woman in the House of Commons. Motor vehicles had become a commonplace. Pictures of modern fashions and hairstyles for women and reports of new social mores seemed to them rather shocking. They felt cut off from the mainstream of their generation.

In India the political unrest made disturbing news. Young men discharged from the Rajah of Rampur's army returned to their villages and the harsh conditions of subsistence farming, where they eagerly took up Gandhi's Quit India movement. The new discontent developed into the whispering campaign which, since Harry and Ada were the only two Britishers within range, became directed against them. One young man swaggered into the Mission compound surrounded by a group of girls. Ada spotted him from the window picking her precious chrysanthemums and presenting them to his companions. When she demanded to know what he thought he was doing, he replied that this was their country so the land was theirs and the British would soon be kicked out. Harry arrived at that point and, hearing this, told the youth not to be impertinent and to get out of the garden, whereupon the youth made the girls giggle with some rude comment. Harry lost his temper and slapped his face.

Following this incident there was a lot of murmuring behind their backs. Walking through the village was no longer a pleasure. The people they met still greeted them but they were sure others scuttled into doorways at their approach and avoided any contact.

In the Mission itself there were also problems. For some time Harry had had doubts about the sincerity of some members of the Christian community, and indeed he had written a report to the Mission Board which was published in part in the Moravian Messenger in February 1918. In this report he had suggested that a long period of probation should be served before candidates were accepted as fully baptised members of the Church. He felt that sometimes in the past people had presented themselves for baptism for the wrong reasons and were not as staunch in their new faith as they should have been. The congregation in Pu consisted of twenty-one baptised adults and thirteen full communicants. These thirty-four people had divided themselves into two factions, *nangphas* and *phipas*, insiders and outsiders. Harry and Ada had never been able to discover what the basis of this division was but they suspected it was something to do with caste. Harry wrote again to the Mission Board asking if they had any information in their records which might help him to get to the root of the problem. The reply he eventually received was of little help, however, it did say that Bishop Ward would be making a pastoral visit to all the mission stations in Western Tibet sometime in the near future and they could discuss the matter then.

They looked forward to the Bishop's visit. The prospect of discussing the work of the Mission, to perhaps receiving a little encouragement and some spiritual refreshment, and to conversing with someone from the outside world buoyed up their spirits. In the event it was a disaster for them.

The Bishop did not appear impartial and preached a most untactful sermon. To their dying day the memory of Bishop Ward's visit gave them pain and neither of them would talk about it, Ada only saying, "I do not want any discredit to fall on anyone, least of all the Mission."

Winter set in again and the Burroughses had nothing to do except sit and brood during the long dark evenings. Their Christmas was marred for much of their mail was lost and, worst of all, they heard from the Mission Board that Bishop Ward had put in an unfavourable report about the Mission at Pu.

Harry now became increasingly restless and he would pace up and down, saying, "I must get out of this place!" He felt imprisoned. From the windows of their bungalow they could see nothing but the mountainsides, their tops towering out of sight. Ada was listless; she cried easily and seemed to succumb to every minor ailment. She complained of increasing dizziness.

The drumming of the lamas through the dark nights kept them from sleep. The dancing orgies at full moon, which went on all night, seemed to bring evil to their very doorstep. Harry, never a talkative man, became more and more silent; he hardly ever spoke. Ada focussed all her attention on the children, whom she felt were her only companionship and solace.

One night, as they were sitting alone after Rigdzin and Tarchungma had gone home and the children were asleep in bed, Harry seemed unusually restless. He was not quietly studying his Bible or his medical books, or his Tibetan grammar. Ada sensed that something was preying on his mind and after a while he told her what was troubling him.

He had gone off late that autumn on one of his lonely tours, accompanied by one man, as was his custom. They had come to a small village far off the beaten track and, as it was too cold to pitch the tent they carried, they had asked for shelter in one of the houses. But they were poor, miserable hovels and the headman found it difficult. In the end he had come to Harry and explained his problem; the houses were small and over-crowded and he could not think that they would be suitable but there was a small hut a little way outside the village, consisting of just one room, which was sometimes used by shepherds or travellers. This they would gladly let him use, if Harry were willing. Harry was tired, cold, and hungry and welcomed any shelter. The villagers did their best and swept out the little hovel. It was a small mud hut with a rough stone roof, too low for Harry to stand upright, but it was reasonably clean and with a fire would be warmer than a tent. Harry and his companion, Puntzog, settled in for the night.

After they had eaten a simple meal of tea, according to their taste, and porridge made from *tsampa*, they went to sleep. Harry decided it was too cold to undress properly so he merely took off his riding boots and breeches and wrapped himself in his Tibetan gown and his blankets. When they awoke the following morning, deep snow had fallen and they found they were completely cut off, even from the village. However,

Harry in Central Tibet

there was plenty of fuel and they had sufficient food. They were stuck for three days. They had nothing to do but sit and talk. Harry was intensely interested in the old religion of the country, *Bon chos*, and he started questioning his companion, trying to find out how much it still persisted, for he knew that sacrifices were still being made despite Buddhism being opposed to killing.

Puntzog characteristically did not give a direct answer. Instead he launched into the following tale, "You may remember that we once went to a village where I took you to see an old man called Stopgyas, who always sat on the roof gazing across the valley? He hardly spoke. He hardly ever does. He just sits and remembers. You see, it was like this."

"When Stopgyas was a little boy, he was the apple of his parents' eye and, as they were well-to-do people, he did not have to go out into the fields with his mother. He was rather a lonely little chap but he was always happy and greatly loved by everyone. Now, when he was about five years old, a brother was born and Stopgyas was delighted. He immediately called the baby Trashi, which means 'happy'. As Trashi grew, Stopgyas carried him round in a shawl on his back and wandered over the mountainside. They were inseparable and Trashi followed Stopgyas everywhere. Once, when they were on the mountain with the shepherd boys, they decided to devise a private signal, so that they could call each other from even quite long distances. They practised until they found that a queer sort of howl, like that of a wolf, seemed to carry best."

"Trashi, of course, being the second son, had to become a lama and, from quite an early age, he had worn a little pointed hat and was dressed like a lama. When he was eight years old he had to go to the lamasery to start his education."

"The two brothers were very sad at the thought of being parted, but they knew they would see each other sometimes and they made a pact. Stopgyas said that if he were on the mountain he would build a little cairn of quartz stones, which would glint in the sun, and Trashi would be able to see it from the high lamasery, where he was. Trashi never failed to go to the roof each day and the brothers called to each other."

"Trashi was a clever boy and learned his lessons very easily. He also endeared himself to all the other lamas and postulants. He was singled out as being a particularly apt pupil and was brought to the notice of the Abbot. One year, a great calamity befell the village when an epidemic of smallpox struck them. The lamas kept up constant prayers and

Harry in Tibetan dress, with his horse

incantations and did all in their power to drive the evil spirits away, but still many people died. When eventually the sickness abated, the people realised that they had no prayer-wall at the entrance of the village to protect them and they bewailed their lack of devotion. A council of elders gathered and decided that they must go to the Abbot and ask permission to build a wall to placate the gods. It would have to be done quickly before it was time to till the fields and sow the crops. After due consideration, the Abbot granted their request and sent some of his lamas, who were specialists in this work, to direct the operations. Men, women and children all took part. Some dug the foundations and carried rocks and stones from the mountainside, while others knapped the stones to make a good wall. Everyone sang as they worked. In the lamasery, suitable flat stones were being carved by lamas recruited from other monasteries, the prayer, 'O *mani padme hum*' being cut out in Tibetan and in Sanskrit."

Harry was very interested in this detailed description of the building of a *mani* wall and pressed his companion to continue.

"When the wall was finished by the masons, the artists added their work. The sides of the wall were whitewashed, then a border of black circles was painted to represent watchful eyes. At the four corners red paint was splashed, representing spilt blood to frighten away the spirits. Poles were erected, each carrying a black yak's tail. All was now ready for the dedication. There was an air of expectancy in the monastery, for they knew that a very solemn ceremony was approaching. The lamas wondered why their Abbot looked troubled while everyone else was gay."

"The Abbot sent out a decree that all the members of the monastery were to assemble in the great meeting-room. They gathered, murmuring amongst themselves as they seated themselves in close rows, leaving a passage-way for the Abbot and his procession. As the procession approached, they all knelt and bowed themselves to the ground, only rising again when the Abbot was seated. Slowly he began to speak."

"'My sons, this is a very solemn occasion, but how solemn I do not think you understand. When the great sickness ravaged our village, the people felt they had neglected their duty and the gods were angry. They petitioned me for permission to build the *mani* wall, which is now complete. While you have all been labouring, I too have been busy, searching through the holy books to learn what we must do to dedicate this wall of stones, for stones are nothing. No details must be forgotten or overlooked, if such a disaster is not to befall us again. I found in my searching that I alone cannot conduct these solemn rituals and it has been my humble duty to beg for the holy presence of the Incarnation, the *Skushog*. He has condescended to honour us.'"

"The lamas were awed by this announcement. The Abbot went on, speaking very quietly and slowly, 'My sons, from what I have just told you, you understand that this is an occasion of great solemnity, otherwise His Holiness would not come to such a poor monastery as this, but you do not understand – you cannot contemplate – what else we have to do.' The old man's voice trembled, but he steadied himself and went on. 'As I studied the holy books I found that, when a wall such as we have just made is built in expiation of past neglect and sin, and when the people seek protection from plague or sickness and other evils, the spirits are not content with stones and prayers. We have to make a sacrifice, a costly sacrifice.' He paused and almost whispered, 'The gods decree that this sacrifice must be one of us.'"

"Looking around the room, the Abbot continued, 'I have decided that we will draw lots. Spaldan has come from another community and he holds the bundle of sticks. Each one of us will draw a stick and no one must open his hand until I give the word.'"

"The strange lama moved round the room with his bundle. Each lama and each boy drew his stick with a sinking heart; some snatched quickly, others seemed paralysed and could hardly move their arm."

"The Abbot gave the signal. Each man opened his hand and, seeing his own stick, quickly looked at his neighbour's to see if the lengths were equal, and sighs of relief went up. But who was the victim? They gazed round the room and all saw Trashi sitting gazing at the short stick lying in his palm."

"The Abbot rose to his feet and the lamas recovered themselves sufficiently to bow to the ground. The old man moved across to Trashi and said quietly, 'Come, my son,' and the youth got up, as if in a trance, and followed his superior from the room."

"That night, when Stopgyas called from the house roof, there was no reply."

"Trashi sat in a quiet cell with his prayer-wheel and rosary, to spend his last days in prayer and meditation. The village soon heard

Tibetan with human thigh bone trumpet

the dreaded news. There was no singing now and everyone went about their work with down-cast eyes and heavy hearts."

"The *Skushog* arrived with his procession and the people prostrated themselves before him. When he reached the monastery and blessed the prayer-stones, villagers climbed up the hill to carry the stones down to the wall. They walked solemnly and almost furtively, as if they were guilty of some awful deed. Young lamas followed them down and arranged the stones on the top of the wall."

"The following day, the women were up before sunrise, fetching water from the stream. There was no chatter or chaff on this day. Fearfully, they hurried home and kept the children indoors. When the animals were fed the shepherd boys were told to take them to faraway pastures."

"Soon, some of the women slipped quietly into the house of Trashi's mother, sitting heart-broken in a darkened room. Each woman who came to mourn brought a pot of butter tea, which she set by the hearth, and a dish of traditional oil cakes. Then they started to lament."

" 'Trashi is the flower of the village, chosen to wither and die before his time' 'He was the child of the gods, with a heart like snow; it was melted by the sickness and the sorrows of his friends and he vanished away.' So they mourned, each contributing her piece and the mother sometimes chanted too and sometimes wept silently. The father sat on the roof alone. Stopgyas was nowhere to be found."

"Suddenly the silence in the village was shattered by the sounding of the long *shawms* from the monastery, and then of the smaller trumpets with bells and drums, the sound echoing round and back from the hillsides. The women huddled together on their rooftops, curious and yet afraid. Children, sensing the fear in the air, hid themselves in their mothers' skirts. The men recognised the signal and made their way to the foot of the hill, where the procession would pass."

"The lamas, wearing the ceremonial cockscomb hats, were gathered, waiting for the procession to move. The drummers, carrying their long-handled drums, beating them with long curved sticks, led the way. Then came the trumpeters, with their slender trumpets, and finally the lamas, who walked in front, banging cymbals. The rest of the community, some carrying baskets full of holy books, followed the band."

"Then came the *Skushog* wearing a golden hat, riding on a white pony and surrounded by his attendants and, walking on either side of him, were the Abbot and Trashi."

Skushog of Hemis in his dress of human bones, used in the Mystery Play

"As they moved down the hill, the men could see Trashi more clearly. He walked with his shaven head bowed; his lips moved as he nervously fingered his rosary. They murmured to each other, 'How young he looks – it seems only yesterday that he was with us in the hills.' The procession moved on to the plain and the villagers joined on. They wanted to run away, but dared not. The *Skushog* was lifted from his pony when he reached the head of the wall, and Trashi stood with him. An old lama took the cover off one of the books and handed round sheets; men began to read and chant, while others rang bells and clashed silver cymbals at specified intervals. A necklace of prayers, bound in small coloured packets strung together, was hung round Trashi's neck. He looked as if he were in a dream."

"The procession formed again and then processed round the wall, always leaving it on their right. The Abbot dipped a peacock's feather into a vessel of holy water held by a high-ranking lama and sprinkled holy water on to the prayer-stones. When they arrived at the head of the wall again, the Abbot took Trashi's hand and turned with him to face the *Skushog*, who blessed him and then shouted in a ringing tone, 'Today Trashi becomes a god!' He bade him step towards the wall. For a moment Trashi raised his eyes towards his father's house, then he turned and stepped forward and the executioner stepped after him."

"Trashi motioned him to wait a moment. He looked up to the mountain pastures to where a glint of quartz caught his eye and he threw back his head, emitting the strange wolf-call. Then, in the deep silence after his call had echoed away, came the reply. Trashi knelt down with a bowed head and the axe fell."

The implications of this story did nothing to cheer the Burroughses. If centuries of Buddhist teaching had failed to eradicate the worst evils of *Bon chos*, what hope had two lone and rather tired missionaries of making any lasting impact? Try as they would, they could not shake off the black depression that had settled on them, despite the kindnesses of their friends, who sensed their unhappiness.

CHAPTER 11

Going Home is hard

When Ada was walking through the village one day with Monica, Dewa's wife beckoned to her. As Ada went across to the house the woman conspiratorially drew her inside and said, "Memsahib, I have a favour to ask of you."

Ada wondered what was coming next. Dewa went on, "Please, Memsahib, I beg of you, do let me into the secret of your little daughter's hair."

"Why, what do you mean?" Ada asked.

"Oh, Memsahib, don't be bashful. Please tell me what dye you use, for her hair is like the colour of sunset."

Ada was rather taken aback because, although she was proud of her daughter's red-gold hair, it had never occurred to her that anyone would think it was anything but natural, especially as her father had fair hair. She replied as best she could, "I do not do anything to it, except wash it and brush it."

The headman's wife nudged her playfully and said, "Oh go on, do tell me. I promise I won't tell anyone else your secret."

This was difficult, for Ada knew no way to express in Tibetan 'it is natural', so she said, "It is her kind". Then she realised that what she had said could just as well be interpreted, 'It is her high caste', and felt very uncomfortable. She tried to cover up by pointing out that the colour was not unlike Harry's.

But the woman was much too impressed by the high caste and went on, "Ah, yes, we know she is very special, otherwise she would not have a squint, which sets her apart, and with that hair as well she must be very,

very special indeed." (A squint was normally regarded in Tibet as an indication of a reincarnation of the Buddha or a holy person.)

Ada felt embarrassed and made an excuse to go on her way. She also felt her worst fears were confirmed, that the child had a distinct squint, which was definitely not special in England.

It so happened that one of the Indian Government doctors was touring and when the Burroughses heard that he was to visit Chini, they sent a message saying that they would be grateful if he would come and visit them. He agreed and when he came they found him a delightful man. He listened enthralled to their experiences and was impressed by what Harry had done in his little hospital. When they asked him about Monica's squint, he said he thought it was lazy-eye but that they must take her to an eye-specialist as soon as possible.

Then he turned to Ada and said, "Mrs. Burroughs, I do not think you are looking at all well. I think you had better let me examine you." He questioned her thoroughly and gave her a careful examination.

Afterwards he spoke with Harry and said, "I think it is absolutely imperative that you get your wife away from here as soon as you can. She is a very sick woman. I am not sure what the cause of her illness is, but I cannot be answerable for her if she stays here much longer. I will write a report for you to send to your mission, if you like – better still, I will send it direct from Simla. It will be quicker that way." He looked at Harry and went on, "I don't think it would do you any harm to have some furlough either."

Surprisingly soon afterwards they received a letter from the Mission Board telling them to proceed on furlough as soon as possible. They were to wind up the Mission business and close the station down, as there was no relief to send at that time and in any case the future of the mission was under review. They were, as far as possible, to appoint leaders from amongst the local Christians and instruct them to carry on.

Some of the villagers looked smug when they heard the news of their departure. Others showed concern and distress, especially when they learned that no one would take their place, not for a while anyway. Pu had earned the reputation of being a well-administered village and many attributed this to the influence of the missionaries. Winding up the mission business was not an easy task; there were debts to collect, officers to appoint, property to dispose of, the hospital to close, and a thousand details to settle. Then they had to think of their own affairs.

Ada had knitted vests and combinations for the children during the winter and had pyjamas and knickerbocker suits made from locally-woven cloth. She had knitted them long stockings, but she realised that their wardrobes were by no means adequate. Harry wanted to take a very special present back for his brother, so he commissioned the weaver to weave the finest cloth he could and went to great trouble to get him to make it into a sort of herringbone tweed, using the wool from their own grey sheep. When it was finished, both Harry and Ada thought it was really beautiful and were very proud of it.

They sent a messenger ahead to arrange the journey for them and to warn the village headmen that they would need ponies for riding and baggage, and men to carry the two younger children. Harry had been teaching Gordon to ride on the faithful Billy and he was confident that the child could manage the journey on horseback.

They had to dispose of their animals, the sheep and goats, the cow and the poultry and they had to pack up their few possessions ready to go. Ada felt terribly excited and thrilled to be going home and tried to tell

Gordon, Ronnie and Monica with the maids

On the road to Simla

the children what England was like but they showed no interest in that strange, faraway place. She tried to explain what rain was, for the children had never seen rain, and what buses and trains were like. The only things on wheels they had ever known were the pram and the little cart Harry had made for them. The sea was incomprehensible, since they had only seen the village stream and, occasionally, the River Sutlej.

They decided to take their two maids with them as far as Simla, partly to help and also as a reward for their faithful service.

When all was ready, they set off from Pu with all the traditional farewells from the accompanying villagers. Now that they were actually leaving, everyone seemed sorry to see them go.

As they got further away from Pu, they found the atmosphere quite different from that which they had experienced when they had last travelled this road. The porters and the pony-men were sullen and uncooperative, the *chowkidars* at the *dak* bungalows were not helpful and, the nearer they approached to Simla, the worse things became.

As Gordon rode Billy, Ada was dependent on hired ponies and the two younger children had to be carried on porters' backs. Daily it became more difficult to arrange for porters. Then they reached Khotgur. Here the headman came and said that in no circumstances would he arrange for his men to carry children of the British Imperialists. They pleaded and argued but it was to no avail.

They had already reduced the porters and pony-men to the absolute minimum because of the difficulty of hiring them and, although their two maids offered to do all they could by helping to carry the children, Harry and Ada knew it was out of the question. Gloomily they sat on the verandah, wondering what to do but, as they always did when their problems seemed insuperable, they prayed and asked God for help.

After a while they saw an old man coming towards them. He came and made his greetings and then said he had been made very sad to hear that they were in difficulty and that the people were not being helpful. However, he remembered that they had been very kind to his son, who had worked as a sweeper when they had stayed at Khotgur before, and therefore he had come to offer his services and those of his son for as long as they needed them.

They could have wept for joy. They could not help but admire the old man for his loyalty and character, because they knew he would have to face ostracism and petty persecution from his fellows. When they asked him if it was too much of a risk for him to help them, he dismissed the idea scornfully by saying that he might only be an outcast but he believed that he should stick by his friends. With much dignity he said goodnight and promised to be there in the morning with his son; and he was.

Once again, when they arrived in Simla, all heads turned as their quaint-looking party rode through the streets. The two Pu girls in their attractive costume excited interest, but Harry and Ada came in for supercilious smirks from the European population, as did the children. They were dusty and travel-worn and Ada and Harry looked thin and ill. The girls kept getting left behind as they gazed at some new wonder: bicycles, *tongas*, *gharris*, motor-cars – indeed everything on wheels to them was a miracle. But they were not the only ones who were bewildered. Harry and Ada felt lost in this busy town. Ada said she felt like Rip Van Winkle awakening in a strange place.

The children, awed at first by all the strange new sights, soon showed signs of fright and clung to Rigdzin and Tarchungma, who themselves were afraid. Ada had to try to reassure them, though she herself felt anything but confident. The worst shock of all was to see European women brazenly going about in short skirts, with their hair cut short and wearing lipstick – and even smoking cigarettes! They were appalled! The Tibetan women, too, were deeply shocked and came to Ada for an explanation, which she could not give. When Ada herself went out she was conscious that people stared at her as if she were odd, and indeed she must have looked strange in her 1913 clothes, for this was 1921. Harry, too, looked peculiar in his old-fashioned suit and with his fine beard amongst the men who were now mostly clean-shaven.

They stayed in Simla only long enough to make arrangements for the next part of the journey. They were booked to sail on the SS *Egypt* from Bombay. First, they had to arrange for the train journey across India. Then all their luggage had to be sorted and re-packed into suitable boxes for the long journey home. They had to arrange for the return journey to Pu by Rigdzin and Tarchungma with the man who had accompanied them down. Billy, their faithful little pony, and Harry's horse had to be sold.

Eventually, all the arrangements were made, the heavy baggage was sent off and they were ready to go. When they got to the station, Rigdzin and Tarchungma clung to the children, crying and wailing at the thought of parting, but when they saw the train their sorrow turned to terror at this huge monster, like a dragon, with fire in its belly, that was going to swallow up their master and mistress and the children. As the train whistled and started to move, Harry and Ada, who were leaning out of the window, saw Tarchungma run wildly down the platform towards the engine and they yelled at her to stop and go back, for they feared she might, in sheer panic, throw herself under the train. Fortunately some railway officials grabbed her and held her, struggling and screaming.

The train soon plunged into a tunnel and the children were petrified with fright. Thus began a nightmarish journey. They managed to explain to the two boys and calm them down, but Monica, who was only just over a year and a half old, was not to be reasoned with. In that mountainous country there were innumerable tunnels and she screamed through every one.

During the first part of the journey, to Amritsar, they had, as was customary, a compartment to themselves, which by night could be converted into a sleeper and, they had easy access to a bathroom and lavatory. They reached Amritsar in the middle of the night, where they had to change into one of the big trans-India expresses. The train into which they had to change was already at the station. In their ignorance and naïveté they had not thought to reserve a compartment for this section of the journey.

Ada carried Monica, while the two little boys clung to her skirts. Harry tried to deal with their baggage. All around were milling throngs, fruit-sellers, sweet-sellers, beggars and porters, all pestering and importuning. Everyone tried to attract the children's attention, who cowered into their mother's skirts, frightened and sleepy. They were, as missionaries, travelling second-class. When they got to the train, every carriage was shuttered and locked. They banged on several doors and asked to be let in but loud European voices shouted at them, "*Jao* – go away!" They pleaded to be let in, but no one would unlock their door. Frantically they went up and down the train but the carriages were either full, or barred. They were desperate. At long last, as the whistles were being blown, a kindly Hindu gentleman, who had a compartment to himself, opened his door and let them in.

This experience was a bitter one, to be spurned by their own people. They were deeply grateful to the Indian gentleman, but the arrangement was by no means ideal. He was some sort of holy man and, all through the remainder of the night and through the following day, he would retire to the bathroom and perform his ritual ablutions. As a result the place was occupied for a great part of the time. When it was unoccupied, the whole floor was awash with the water he had poured over his head. Every time one of the children had to be taken to the bathroom, which was very often, Ada had to trail her sweeping Edwardian skirt through the swill which, with the swaying of the train, lapped round her feet. She became somewhat bedraggled. Towards evening, however, a lot of people got out of the train and they were able to re-establish themselves more comfortably and relax.

When they finally got to Bombay, they were reluctant to leave the security of their railway compartment, but they were cheered to find that a missionary and his wife had come to meet them. They quickly took the Burroughses under their wing, dealing wonderfully and easily with porters and pedlars as they guided them through all the horrors and complexity of an Indian railway station. They were taking them to their home for a few days, until it was time to board the ship.

The children settled down happily but Ada said that she spent most of her time in the bathroom, where the boys were fascinated and charmed by the W.C. – for them a totally new experience and a great delight. The Burroughses had reckoned they would only need to stay a day or two but the ship was undergoing repairs and refitting in Bombay docks, where there had been labour troubles and political strikes, so she was not ready.

At long last work on the ship was completed and they thankfully went on board; their friends, equally thankfully, saw them go. They had now been travelling for more than two months.

The ship, SS *Egypt*, was not a happy one. In the first place, she had been lying in the docks for months and was full of mosquitoes; secondly, she had been repainted and reeked of new paint and, even more disconcerting, they found that the wire cages which were used to hold the life-belts had been painted and the pins which held the lid in place were immovable. Try as they would, they could not move them to get the life-belts out.

The first boat-drill, unannounced, was held on the first evening. Ada had all three children in the bath, so she clutched the youngest and wrapped her in a towel and found a steward. She explained her dilemma and he told her not to worry and carry on – it was only a drill.

The first disaster on that fateful voyage happened the second night out, when the ship's doctor committed suicide by throwing himself overboard. Soon afterwards, the carpenter slipped and broke his leg. As there was no doctor on board, Harry volunteered his services and set the leg in splints and, for the rest of the voyage, he acted as unofficial ship's doctor. The sea was fairly rough and Ada, who was never a good sailor, began to feel ill. Although Harry was heartily sea-sick to begin with he soon recovered whilst Ada continued to feel awful and had a raging head.

One day a middle-aged, rather brusque lady came over and spoke to Ada, who warmed because someone had bothered to notice her and speak to her. After a few minutes' chat the lady said, "We have been wondering why you don't do something about your elder boy's hair?" Ada was stunned. She tried to explain that it was stiff and wiry and would not lie down, but the woman cut her short and asked, "Have you tried brushing it?" and walked back to her gossiping group, who tittered admiringly. Not unnaturally Ada, although deeply hurt, was furious. Her opinion of her compatriots sank even lower. Not long after this incident Ada felt very ill, with a swimming head and a high fever. The brusque lady came over to her again and said, "Mrs. Burroughs, where is your husband? Why doesn't he help you with the children? I'm going to fetch him". She fetched Harry and gave him a thorough dressing-down for neglecting his family and leaving his wife to struggle alone, while he sat on deck talking. Ada knew Harry needed rest and relaxation as much as she did and had not told him she felt ill, and it had not occurred to her she could have asked for help from the stewardess.

The ship had sailed late from Bombay and now they were delayed by a severe storm in the Mediterranean; then there was a fire in the engine-room. When they reached Marseilles, many of the passengers decided to leave the ship and join those who had already planned to do so, as they could no longer stand this miserable voyage. The SS *Egypt* sank on its next voyage, on its way back to India with a cargo of bullion. Harry and Ada often wondered if the life-belts were still painted in.

The Burroughses intended to disembark at Plymouth, where friends would meet them and take them to stay at Exeter. They had sent a cable from Marseilles, explaining that the ship was late but, at the last moment, as the ship entered the English Channel, it was announced that they were going straight through to Tilbury and not stopping at Plymouth. All their careful plans were ruined. They were desperately worried. Where were they to go? Harry's mother was dead and his father had moved into lodgings. They realised that they were hopelessly out of touch with everything. They had no idea how to set about life in England. They had lost all confidence in themselves and their fellow-countrymen.

Miserably, they disembarked at Tilbury on a grey, rainy day. Diffidently they hung back, while others pushed forward and passed the customs with brisk efficiency, and they were about the last to leave the customs shed. They stood together in an unhappy little group wondering what to do next, when suddenly they saw someone waving frantically. At first they ignored the man but it became plain that the man was waving at them and they went to meet him. They were overjoyed to find it was an old friend of Harry's, Ernest Richardson, who had heard from their Plymouth friends that the ship was not stopping there and had come to meet them. He hustled them into the boat-train.

After a week with the Richardsons, it was decided they should stay with the Setchells near Exeter, the friends who were to have met them at Plymouth. Harry had at one time been very fond of their daughter, Hilda, who had died. But before they left London, Harry went to see his father and brother. He proudly took his piece of tweed along as a gift. He was mortally offended when his brother burst out laughing and said, "What do you take me for? I wouldn't wear that!" Harry was so hurt that he hardly ever saw his brother again.

When they got to Exeter, their friends made them most welcome. Mrs. Setchell had had the house newly papered and decorated before they arrived. She had also laid in quantities of food. She and Mr. Setchell did everything in their power to make the Burroughs family feel happy and comfortable but the children were unsettled and were shy and difficult. It was worst for Gordon, who, being the eldest, was more conscious of the recent upheavals and he seemed overcome with shyness. He spent much of his time quietly sitting in a corner, twisting his hair and making a slight ticking noise with his tongue – a habit which persisted for years. He would not speak to anyone or even look at them. Wallpaper, however, was a novelty and one night he discovered a loose corner and was fascinated as it tore off in a most satisfying strip.

This was the last straw. The Setchells were kind and understanding, but Harry and Ada decided they must move on and get the family settled as soon as possible. Harry had to go back to London on Mission business at the headquarters in Fetter Lane, and Ada was naturally anxious to go and visit her friends and relations in Scarborough, so it was decided that she should stay at Douglas House for a while until such time as she could find a house to rent.

Once in Scarborough, Ada's sister Mary decided to take her in hand. She declared, "Ada, you really cannot go around looking as you do. You must get some new clothes. No one wears long sweeping dresses any more. And the children! No children wear stockings over their knees any more – and those funny knickerbockers! Everyone will laugh at them."

The only house Ada felt they could afford to rent was in a rather slummy terrace, with only a tiny backyard in which the children could play and an outside lavatory. Mary came to help Ada unpack. When she saw the clothes that Ada had so painstakingly knitted for the children, the combinations and the stockings, pairs and pairs of them, she said, "I think you'd better let me pack those up and send them to the Russians!" and she firmly took them away.

The two boys started to attend the local elementary school in Gladstone Road. Ronnie, who was a happy-go-lucky child, settled down quickly, but Gordon was still painfully shy with strangers. By now both children were chattering away happily in English, their Tibetan all but forgotten. One day Ronnie came home from school saying that he had been called out in front of the class by the teacher to talk to the others in Tibetan.

Ada smiled to herself, "What did you say?"

"Oh, I told them about our chickens and things."

"Well, you tell me how you said it in Tibetan."

Unabashed Ronnie launched into a stream of twaddle, spattered here and there with a Tibetan word. Ada laughed and said, "But that's not Tibetan!"

Ronnie grinned and said, "I know, but they didn't."

In the garden of Scarborough

They hated that little house. Everyone was miserable at being cramped in such close quarters. Ada must have said one day that there was not room to swing a cat, because she found the boys in the backyard experimentally swinging the cat round by the tail.

She told her friend at Holy Trinity how unhappy they were and a miracle happened. Some kindly people, called Mr. and Mrs. Bakewell, had a large house and garden in one of the nicest parts of Scarborough, at the head of the Valley in St. James Road. They offered half the house to the Burroughses at a very reasonable rent. It was like heaven after St. John's Road. Now, at last, they began to feel they could relax a little.

Ada had been to see various doctors, but, where all agreed that she was badly run down, they could not find the cause of her giddy spells and severe headaches and she was sent to a specialist. He said, after he had examined her carefully, that she was suffering from nothing more or less than starvation. She was tall and she weighed only seven and a half stone. She had breast-fed three children on a very frugal diet. The very things she needed, such as milk, eggs, meat and cheese, were the things which had been scarcest and she had put her husband and children before herself. She simply had not had enough to eat those five years in Pu. Good food and rest were what the doctor recommended. Food she could get but rest was impossible.

Harry was away a great deal on his deputation work. Mary had persuaded him to shave off his beard and he looked younger and more handsome than ever. Ada's meetings were usually local, so that she did not have to stay away but, on one occasion, it could not be avoided. She had been invited to address the Harrogate Convention, a huge annual gathering where people from all over the country gathered to discuss the work of their congregations and also to learn more of Mission work. There was an exhibition of curios and things relevant to the various Missions represented, who usually sent their top speakers.

She donned her Pu costume. Everyone lent all the curios they had and the Mission sent more. There were only three speakers at this final meeting of the Convention and she was to speak last, by far the most honoured position. She was terribly nervous as she sat on the platform in the huge marquee, which was packed to capacity, with people standing,

Ada, wearing her Pu costume, at the Harrogate convention

and she knew there were seats for 4,000. She said she was barely conscious of what the other speakers were saying her heart was pounding so.

When it was her turn to speak, she stood and quite simply told the story of their past few years. Suddenly it struck her that she had the whole audience in the palm of her hand. In a heady moment she realised she could do what she liked with them, she could make them laugh one minute and cry the next. When the bell rang to warn her that her time was up, she finished rapidly. As she did so, she became conscious that she was shaking from head to foot. After a moment's complete silence, the audience went wild. They clapped and cheered.

When the meeting was over, people clustered round her, pushing cash and cheques into her hand as contributions to the Mission she was representing. Ada was so overwhelmed that she passed the money straight to a Board member who was present, without counting it. She was surprised to read in a report afterwards that the Moravian Missions received a comparatively small sum from the collection and wondered what had happened to all the money which had been pressed on her.

Harry, in the meantime, had stayed at home to look after the family. At dinner time he let the potatoes boil dry and they were rather scorched.

Cheerfully he told the children to eat them up, as it would make their hair curl. Monica, whose hair was quite straight, for years afterwards used hopefully to examine her hair for signs of curls.

After eighteen months, the Burroughs's furlough was nearly over and they had to start planning for their return, not to Pu, but back to Ladakh, to Khalatse this time. The children were oblivious of the heartaches suffered by their parents, who knew they could not take the two boys with them. They started to make enquiries about suitable guardians for them, as none of their relatives was able to take on two extra children.

One of Ronnie's godfathers wrote to say that he knew of someone who would make an ideal guardian for the boys – a Miss Hilda Warne, who was a kindergarten teacher. She was presently working at a school owned by her uncle at Kingston-on-Thames, called The Grange: it might be possible for the boys to board there under her care. For the holidays, she owned a charming cottage in the Wye Valley. They arranged to go to London to meet Mr. Warne and his niece, but the boys, who were primarily concerned, did not go with them. It was satisfactorily settled that Gordon and Ronnie should start at The Grange the following September, but first they would spend the summer at Miss Warne's cottage at Brockweir, which lay on the opposite bank of the Wye to Tintern.

Rosewell was a pretty little cottage set in a beautiful situation. Miss Warne had the reputation of being an excellent teacher with much experience, especially with young children, Harry and Ada felt that they had been fortunate in finding her. Ada handed over new school outfits and suggested that the boys might wear out their babyish pyjamas, combinations and knitted jerseys and shorts in the holidays. Little did she realise that Miss Warne, with a misguided idea of economy, was to send those poor children to boarding school in their babyish clothes, where they were teased unmercifully about them.

The night before their departure, Ada hardly slept as she was crying her heart out. Gordon said that he, too, lay awake that night in an agony of apprehension and that he could hear his mother sobbing in the room next door.

The next morning they all went to Tintern station together. Just as the train came into sight, Harry and Ada produced the two most wonderful toys the boys had ever seen; one was a clockwork model of the liner *Majestic*, which was one of the best-known ships of the time, and the other was a fine set of bows and arrows. As intended, these toys distracted the children while final goodbyes were being said. As the train moved out of the station, Ada leant out of the window and the children waved their toys happily. She stayed leaning out of the window until she could no longer see them, when she flopped on to the seat and wept as if her heart would break. Harry took her hand and quoted gently, "There is no man that hath left brethren, or sisters, or mother, or wife, or children, or lands for my sake and the Gospel's, but he shall receive an hundred-fold now in this time." Ada nodded dumbly: she knew, but her heart ached for her boys.

A few days later Harry, Ada and Monica sailed from Tilbury.

CHAPTER 12

A new beginning in Khalatse

When they reached Rawalpindi, they found that the journey to Srinagar was no longer done by *tonga*, but in a lorry, and only took one day, with first-class passengers in front, second-class on a wooden bench behind and the luggage in the rear. The drivers, however, had not changed their characteristics; they drove the lorries just as furiously as they had driven their *tongas*. They now had klaxons instead of little boys with hunting-horns. Vehicles still met head-on and all the old arguments ensued, despite the fact that vehicles going up were supposed to have the right of way. It was hair-raising to watch the drivers reversing their vehicles into the passing bays, for they seemed oblivious to the fact that another lorry might be coming around a blind corner.

Once again they were struck by the beauty of Kashmir. The distant snow-peaks, the serenity of the lakes, the glory of the trees and flowers and the picturesque wooden houses built on stilts at the water's edge made a breathtakingly beautiful picture. Few tourists, however, realised the terrible sufferings endured in those pretty houses. The Muslim women and girls, who lived in strict purdah, rarely enjoyed the sunshine. Even if they went out of doors they were heavily shrouded in veils; they lived in semi-darkness. Through lack of light and sunshine they were prone to tuberculosis and rheumatic diseases, particularly osteomyelitis. The agonies of many of these women, especially in childbirth, because they were crippled or deformed, were unbelievable. Girls were married when they were mere children, often to elderly husbands, and became mothers pitifully young.

Two splendid people, Miss Mallinson and Doctor Neave, worked tirelessly at the Zenana Mission Hospital to try to help their less fortunate sisters. They had trained a team of nurses and midwives who looked after the women in their own homes, for the husbands rarely allowed them to go into hospital. Denyed, who had worked for Ada and Miss Birtill in Leh, had done her training and was now a senior member of the team of nurses. Ada was overjoyed to see her sweet, smiling face once more and, remembering the way Denyed had mothered her, she felt sure she must have brought comfort to many a poor patient.

Once they had gathered their stores, Harry and Ada set off on the road for Khalatse, riding

Houses and chortens, Khalatse

hired ponies and with Monica in a *dandy*. However, when they reached Kargil, Harry bought a horse for himself and a handsome little pony called Kim for Ada and Monica. Ada took an instant dislike to the animal and very rarely rode him, so it became Monica's pony.

The last stage of their journey, from Lamayuru to Khalatse, was not a long one, but the first part was unpleasant. The road dropped into a deep gorge, sunless and cold. At the bottom the travellers had to zigzag across the rocky stream, where sometimes there was a bridge and sometimes they had to ride through the water. Then the road climbed, a narrow path which had been hacked out of a rocky ledge, with the mountain rising sheer above and a sharp drop to the stream below.

Eventually they emerged from this valley of shadow into a wider, sunnier valley, and then went over a steep and narrow little pass, from the top of which they could see the Indus winding its way far below.

The gate to the compound

Beyond the river, in the far distance, they could see a patch of green at the end of a barren plain. Their hearts lurched, for this green oasis was the Mission Compound at Khalatse. They were nearly home

They found that they had an unusual house, for it had two storeys. There were two bedrooms built over the living-room and the downstairs bedroom, and these opened out onto the flat roof of the church, where Harry and Monica sometimes slept in the hot weather. Ada did not like sleeping out of doors because the moonlight worried her. The staircase to these bedrooms went up from the end of the long narrow passage, or *rhol*, which divided the house from the church and dispensary. An arched gateway from the road opened onto a pathway through the apricot orchard, across the watercourse to the house. Another path led to a side gate, beyond which lay a rocky patch. The path meandered across this to the fields, making a short cut to the village.

Two smiling Ladakhi women and an untidy young man, grinning broadly, were waiting to greet them. These were Tsering Yangzdom, the cook; Elisabet, the housemaid, and Tsodnam, the gardener, groom and handyman.

Elisabet was a tall, rather gaunt girl, the daughter of the evangelist Chospel. She was unhappy and rarely smiled and she was not easily likeable. Her chief enemy on the compound was a black ram. It was an amusing animal with a black, curly coat and down-curving horns and it

The house in Khalatse

The orchard

had its very definite likes and dislikes. Monica could do anything with him; he followed her about, rather like Mary's lamb. He never bothered Tsering, or Harry or Ada, but had to be shut up when the school children were about. Every now and then he would playfully chase and butt Tsodnam, but he attacked Elisabet every time he saw her. He had to be shut up each time she came and went.

Ada and Harry with Tsodnam

One day Harry and Ada decided to give a *dron* or feast. Cauldrons of curry with meat and small potatoes had been cooked and all the guests were seated in groups on the ground. Elisabet was busy carrying pans of curry and rice from one group to another. Suddenly Monica, who was sitting with a group of children, shouted, "*Kabbadar* – look out!" for she saw the ram stalking Elisabet; but it was too late and, as Elisabet bent to ladle out the curry, the ram butted her from behind. Elisabet dropped the pan and fled, with the ram in hot pursuit, while the children rolled on the ground in agonies of mirth. Ada tried to keep a straight face and show concern for Elisabet, who, unlike most Ladakhis, could not see the joke while Harry caught the ram and locked him up. His face was suspiciously red as he returned, mopping his eyes.

Unfortunately, it was not very long after this incident that Elisabet was caught red-handed stealing grain. Stealing was considered a very serious offence in Tibet and a thief could be sentenced to having his right hand cut off. Elisabet had been suspected for some time and had been warned. Now Harry felt he had to dismiss her. They were sad for Chospel's sake, especially as he had a large family to maintain and his evangelist's pay was not very big.

Tsering used to fetch the drinking-water every afternoon. She put a large earthen pot into her *tsepo* on her back and climbed down a steep little path nearly a mile to the river's edge, where a fresh spring bubbled with pure water. She ladled the water into her pot and toiled back up the hill. As she walked, she usually sang one of the strange, plaintive songs of the country, at the same time busily spinning, teasing the wool with her left hand while she twisted the spindle in her right.

Ada had her daily housekeeping to do. She always received the milk when it was brought in, scalded it and set it in a bowl to cool for the cream to rise. She skimmed off any cream and collected it until there was sufficient to make a little butter. She measured out the food for the animals and the barley for Tsering to roast for their daily *ngampae*. She used to buy coffee beans direct from the coffee gardens in the Nilgiri hills, a year's supply at a time, and Tsering would roast these too, and the roasted beans were sealed into a kerosene tin.

Washday

She grew a few flowers, especially sunflowers, the seeds of which made a useful addition to the chicken food, but the vegetables she left to Tsodnam. In the spring, she picked wild caper buds for pickling, from plants which grew on the mountainside outside the gate. At first she thought that it was the seeds that were used but discovered that the seeds were tiny and she learnt from a German colleague to use the buds.

School sports

Ada ran the Sunday School and she sometimes had a class for girls after day school was over, when she endeavoured to teach them to knit. While they were knitting, she tried to teach them such things as elementary hygiene and child care. What she enjoyed most was playing with the children. She taught them some English games, such as Poor Jenny sits A-weeping, Nuts in May, or In and Out the Windows, when everyone wound in and out of the apricot trees in the orchard. But the children also taught her some of their Tibetan games. One of these was played as follows:

The children stood or sat in a circle with their hands held out in front of them, fists closed, palms down, while a child in the middle of the circle chanted a rhyme:

"Tsikaling, mikiling,
Tsik shamo
Darko, larko,
Somani andro,
Lahak nang, tukang,
Tre, be, kulik!"

On the word *kulik*, which means open or unlock, all the hands were opened and turned palms up. The child in the middle made a great play of pretending to swoop like an eagle. Hands were snatched away and put behind the back but eventually he caught the wrist of a child who was not quick enough. He then asked if anyone had a knife to cut off the hand, but in the end pretended to produce one from his own belt and started to chop at the wrist with the side of his hand until the victim let his hand flop. He then asked, "Will you have meat or butter?" If meat was the answer, the executioner pretended to cut off a lump of flesh; if butter was the reply, he answered, "Well, you will have to go to the Mons' *decho*[22] for it," which made everyone shriek with laughter. (The Mons were the

Ada with the kindergarten. In the background is a nun with goitre, who attended the dispensary for treatment

---

[22]   Decho: latrine

gypsies of Ladakh and the butt of many of their jokes.) Sometimes the question was, "Which will you have – *tsikim* (fine silk thread) or thick wool for a dress?" If the reply was *tsikim*, a tiny piece of skin was nipped until it hurt; if it was thick wool, lumps of flesh were pinched up and down the arm in the manner of spinning coarse wool.

Harry was the Superintendent and pastor of the mission. He was assisted by Elisha, the schoolmaster; Chospel the evangelist; and Lobsang, an assistant evangelist. Later on, their old friend and tutor Dewazung, who had been ordained, joined him as assistant pastor. In addition, of course, he ran the dispensary with Ada's help.

Khalatse Mission Day School

Chospel was unprepossessing to look at, small and skinny with a swivelling eye. He reminded one of a Tibetan dragon, his skin was so wrinkled and scarred. He had been educated as a lama and, being exceptionally intelligent, he had been sent to a seminary near Lhasa. While he was there he began to question the dogma, so he went on a pilgrimage to try to resolve his problems. On his journey he heard of the Christian missionaries and decided to study their teachings. After years of inward conflict, he relinquished Buddhism and was expelled from his monastery. He went to Leh and had further instruction in the Christian faith but, before he was accepted for baptism, he was told to go home and live according to the Christian rule.

Chospel preaching

He was rejected by his family and everywhere he went he was persecuted by the lamas because of his defection. He was considered particularly dangerous and reprehensible because he had been admitted to many secret rites. For three or four years he lived as a mendicant, preaching his new-found faith, but eventually he was able to return to Leh to be baptised. He was then sent to Khalatse in the hope that his persecutors would leave him alone. Chospel travelled widely, preaching and teaching, and he was often beaten and spat upon, but nothing would deflect him from his mission.

The first Christmas they spent in Khalatse was a sad one for Harry and Ada, as there was no Christmas mail from England. They felt completely cut off from their two little boys, spending their first Christmas away from home, and the parents had not even a card or a letter to console them. It seemed that, being Christmas time, there was an unusual volume of mail with several parcels, which were too heavy for the mail-runner, so a pony was used. The mail runner had fallen in with a caravan crossing the Zoji. The caravan completely disappeared when the string of ponies and the men were swept away in an avalanche. When the spring sun melted the snow, there was still no trace of anyone – no cap, no shawl, no shoes – no trace of anyone or anything. It remained a mystery for years.

Harry and Ada tried to make Christmas a happy time for Monica and for their Christian family. Ada found some small things for Monica's stocking, including a treasured tin of chocolate fingers. She could have found nothing more thrilling for the child, who was quite unused to sweets of any kind. Harry constructed a Christmas tree by drilling holes into a wooden pole at intervals and into these holes they stuck branches of *shukpa* (mountain fir), which he had sent a man up the mountain to get. It made a very passable tree. They had some candles and a few baubles Ada had brought with her. She found a few goodies to give the children when they came round on Christmas Eve to sing carols. As they came into the lighted room their eyes widened as they saw the candlelit tree. Most of them were only clad in rags and tatters and were barefoot, even in the extreme cold of a winter night. They sang the old German carols in Tibetan and they understood far better than any child in Europe could what it meant to be rejected by the rich; what they did find difficult to understand was why anyone should bother to give up all heaven for the poor and lonely.

The candles soon burnt dim and the children had to go. Just as they were singing their last carol a candle guttered and the tree caught fire. With great presence of mind, Tsodnam seized the branch and rushed outside with it. Everyone in the room was almost choked with the smoke and doors and windows had to be flung open to let in the fresh, but icily cold, night air.

CHAPTER 13

Festivals and an accident

The Buddhist year has thirteen lunar months. The reckoning of time is made in twelve- and sixty-year cycles of Jupiter and is a combination of the Western and Chinese systems. There are twelve zodiacal beasts and five elements. Each element is given a pair of animals: the first animal is considered to be male and the second female. The New Year starts from the new moon of the first month, but the festival of *Lotsar* starts at the full moon of the thirteenth month and reaches a climax with the appearance of the new moon, after which the festivities continue for a further seven days.

For weeks beforehand the older children collected branches of resinous woods, juniper and mountain fir, to be used as torches, and any other wood they could find they piled up ready for the festivities. Excitement was intense. On the night of the full moon, instead of the children being sent to bed after their evening meal, they were allowed out. Two processions formed, one at the top of the village and one at the lower end. Each child carried a torch, which scented the chill night air.

With shouts and laughter and waving torches, the two processions wound their way through the village until they met on a large field where two trees grew, the traditional festival field. By now the torches were burning a little low, so they were tossed into a pile and blown up to make one last finger-warming blaze, around which the children danced and played until the fire burned down and they scampered home to bed, happy and excited.

The women had much to do. They had to make dozens of little cakes out of barley-flour, butter and water and fashion them into the shape of an ibex. The children's eyes sparkled with anticipation as they watched. Once made, the cakes were set on every available ledge and shelf to dry and anyone who visited the house during the festive season was given one. Oil-cakes had to be made and fired and *baba*[23] fashioned into a cake, tiered like a wedding cake. There was butter to dye red, yellow, and green, to decorate the beer pots and the cake.

Festival with baba cake

Every female member of the household had to wash and re-do her hair. It was a whole day's task for a woman to do her hair, with the help of friends. The numerous plaits were undone and the hair washed and combed and oiled (a few of the lice were killed in this process but most escaped) then the hair was re-plaited with new wool and thread. They brushed and cleaned their lambskin earflaps and re-attached them to their plaits. They cleaned their jewellery by dipping it into the juice of stewed dried apricots. The men, too, washed and combed their hair and their sheepskin caps were brushed and cleaned. In addition men had the important task of brewing the *chang*.

The following day was spent feasting. Relatives called at each other's houses, carrying with them cakes of *baba*. Everyone broke off and ate a

---

23   Baba: a form of bread

small piece of the cake offered to them. Early in the day all the ponies, mules, and donkeys were brushed clean and their harnesses were cleaned and polished, with particular attention being paid to the collar of bells that the ponies usually wore. Then every animal was given an especially good feed; the cows, *dzos*, horses, donkeys, mules, dogs, cats and fowls were all well fed, for it was said that if they were not satisfied on this day they would never be satisfied again.

When *Lotsar* was over, the two young men who had been elected as clowns for the period of the festival went to every house carrying horns. They went inside and scratched on the stove chanting, "*Zam bile, mizam bile.*" This seemed to have no meaning, but rhymed nicely. Then they said, "*Jomo dranak jomo* (which referred to the Abi Jomo, a sacred rock in this village) *kyorarji, zukspo la nad, jodna, ahag, yod no uhreg jodna, chu nugsa, ngima laga sa, kryer at, rang di la, trashi shik, gym lak shik.*" And having said this, they ran away fast.

One year Harry went off on his usual winter tour and did not return before *Lotsar*. Ada was sitting in the house alone with Monica, who was asleep. In the distance she could hear the noise and the drumming but all else was still. Suddenly she heard angry men's voices coming towards the

Women dressed for a festival

house. She got up and went outside, where three or four men loomed out of the darkness. She spoke sharply to them and told them to be quiet and not waken the child. As they came onto the verandah she lit a hurricane lamp and held it high. She could see that they were very drunk, and they all reeked of *chang*. She recognised Tsodnam and his elder brother, Ngorrub, and two other villagers, who were all covered in blood.

She ushered them into the living-room, where they sat on the floor in the light of the oil lamp and Ada inspected their wounds while she listened to what they had to say. It appeared that the two brothers had got into a drunken brawl with the other two men. She picked up the hurricane lamp and went through the dark church to the dispensary, where she collected some dressings, then along the dark hall to the kitchen for some warm water to bathe the wounds. She thought one or two of the men would need stitches, but as soon as she started cleaning the first wound, the man protested indignantly.

Monica woke up and peered round the bedroom door. Ada saw her and ordered her back to bed and the child could see that her mother was angry. She was indeed angry, particularly with Tsodnam, who ought to have known better, she said, than to try and involve her in a drunken quarrel. She made it plain that if they wanted medical help she would give it but otherwise they must go and take their squabbles to the *Dragchos* (headman). The men became argumentative, so Ada turned on her heel and went out of the room, returning a minute later dressed in her outdoor cloak and woollen cap. With the hurricane lamp in her hand, she announced tersely that she was going to the *Dragchos* to lodge a complaint, as they had disturbed her and refused to leave her house. Ada swept out of the room but paused on the verandah, ostentatiously fiddling with the wick of the lantern.

Sheepishly Tsodnam got up and gestured to the others to follow him outside. Tempers had cooled by now and Ada persuaded them to let her dress their wounds. While she swabbed and stitched, she chided them as if they were children. When all was done, they got up to go, bowed their thanks and left amicably together.

The first winter in Khalatse was unusually severe. There had been an early fall of snow which had subsequently thawed and left a lake of water outside the side-gate of the compound, which then froze solid. Harry found an old sledge, which he managed to repair. He wrapped rags round the hooves of one of the ponies and harnessed him to the sledge, which Tsodnam then drove round the frozen lake. It was much too cold to ride, except in the case of utmost necessity, so this was an excellent way of exercising the horses as well as giving Monica some amusement.

The cold weather gripped the country. Deer and wild sheep came down from the mountains in search of food. One day Ada spotted a snow leopard chasing a deer on

Winter in Khalatse

the mountain-side across the valley and called to Harry to bring his field glasses. They had not seen a snow leopard before. Foxes and wolves became bold with hunger. Tsering came in with tales of how this household or that had had a donkey killed, or a goat, usually just at dusk. The servants were anxious to be away before darkness fell. At night in the mission house the howling of wolves sounded uncomfortably close.

One morning, after a fresh fall of snow, they found wolf prints, not only round the stables and byre as formerly, but on the kitchen doorstep. They no longer dared to go across the bridge to the outside lavatory after dark. The villagers became more and more afraid and Tsering asked that Tsodnam should accompany her to the spring to fetch the water after she found spoor on the path.

Harry decided that he had better try to shoot the marauders. He waited until full moon. They killed a goat and he arranged for some youths to drag the entrails from the spring up to the side-gate, and then leave the carcase on the frozen lake as bait. He and Tsodnam established themselves in the *chaksar*[24] by the gate, which made a good vantage point. Tsering decided to stay the night, so she, Ada and Monica sat in the living-room playing Snap, waiting for the report of Harry's rifle. It was bitterly cold. Time dragged on, but there was no shot. Monica was nearly asleep. After several hours of anxious waiting, the silence was suddenly shattered by three shots and then shouting. It seemed an age before the men approached the house and Tsering had blown up the kitchen fire ready to make hot drinks for them.

When Harry came in he was very downcast. Tsodnam followed, carrying three dead foxes. It seemed that Harry had been so numb with cold that his aim was bad and he had only wounded two animals but had managed to kill the third outright. He had climbed down from the tower with the intention of finishing off the two wounded foxes and in the excitement had clubbed them with the butt of his rifle and broken it. He was furious with himself for having botched the job and disappointed that his bag was only foxes, not the wolves he was really after.

There was very little work that could be done in the winter and early spring, so naturally other diversions had become traditional. One night during February the drums played all night, because that was the night that all the insects were supposed to move their heads in preparation for waking up in the spring.

Then there was an arrow shooting competition, which lasted three days. A mound of mud was raised on which the target was fixed. This was made from a skin, stretched on a willow frame and painted black with a mixture of soot and oil, with a whitewashed centre, or bull. The competitors sat in a semi-circle. Each man built up a small pile of earth in front of him, into which he stuck his arrows. Every competitor had to provide at least two arrows but, if he had no bow, he might borrow. The lamas were first to take aim, then the *Dragchos*, while the rest were divided into teams. A referee was appointed and his judgement was final. Each time a bull was scored there was a great noise; drums beat, pipes played and there were shouts of triumph. The team which was finally

---

[24]   Chaksar: watch tower

declared winner was given beer and they had the privilege of leading the ensuing dance.

Arrow shooting

Women produced food and in between competitions there was dancing, eating and drinking and general merry-making. At the end of the day there was a special feast, after which the women were invited by the men to perform their particular dances. At the end of the festival there were quite a few drunken men and the inevitable brawls and quarrels broke out, but on the whole it was a merry and entertaining few days.

For Ada and Harry the festivals, especially the religious ones, were difficult periods. They never felt they could watch, except from a distance, as their presence would have been an embarrassment. They could not countenance the drunkenness and the subsequent bad behaviour and, of course, they found the rites so often associated with the festivals distressing, based as many were on the superstitions of the old religion.

If it was difficult for them it was infinitely more difficult for the Tibetan Christians. They were deprived to a great extent of their traditional fun, although they did participate in things like the arrow shooting, if they wanted to, but so much was bound up with the religion they had renounced. It speaks very highly of their staunchness to their faith that they managed to forgo so many of the traditional pleasures. It must have been very hard on the young people.

Whenever possible, the missionaries tried to provide some counter-attraction, but during this period of feasting and merry-making the Christians were observing Lent, with penance and fasting. The radiance of their faces on Easter Sunday morning in the little graveyard service indicated, however, how deeply and truly happy they were. The Resurrection of Jesus Christ meant far, far more to them than the occasional merry-making, for behind the Tibetans' gaiety there was always fear: fear of evil spirits, fear of not finding the road after death, fear of being reincarnated in a lower form of life. The fear of spirits was in everything – there were spirits in the rocks, the springs, the passes; there were spirits of the dead; of the winds, thunder, lightning and hail; of disease; of fire – everything animate and inanimate had its own spirit, which could be propitiated or angered. If one was poor, one had small hope of gaining sufficient merit to be reincarnated in a higher form in order eventually to be released from the wheel of life, for one had little time to turn prayer-wheels or to go on pilgrimages, prostrating oneself full-length and measuring one's length for miles before a shrine. There was hopelessness in the religion. Whatever the Christians may have missed, they had abundant hope.

When the first signs of spring were apparent, the fields were blessed. Early in the morning the Mons processed to the *gompa*, or monastery, playing and drumming. The men and women followed and received the holy books into their *tsepos*. They then processed behind the musicians. Children ran behind carrying smoking *pok* (juniper) like incense sticks, so that the sweet smell pleased the spirits. The children made a special point of going all round their own fields, hoping that the incense would keep away insects and blight.

Two years in succession in Khalatse this ceremony was greatly magnified. One household, in the hope that a son might be born into the house, had imported many borrowed books, indeed the whole *Kangyur*[25], from a large neighbouring monastery, and also many lamas to read the one

---

[25]   Kangyur: sacred texts

hundred and eight volumes. The reading took two years. While all the lamas and the *Kangyur* were in the village, the opportunity was taken of having an extra special Blessing.

Everyone turned out dressed in their best, with their hair done and all their best jewellery and ornaments put on. The lamas processed in front, playing their special instruments, the long trumpets, short trumpets, long-handled drums, and cymbals. Harry and Ada were rather amused, because the whole procession was headed by someone carrying a flag, an obvious approximation of the British Union flag. Behind the lamas, the precious books were carried and everyone hoped for especially good crops. All this was thirsty work, of course, and after the fields had been blessed they gathered under a walnut-tree and slaked their thirst with *chang*. The ceremony was called *Zheepal Chosnga*.

Ploughing with dzos

The date for ploughing in Khalatse was fixed by the sun. When the sun fitted into a certain niche in the black rock hill in the village, it was time to plough. About six days before this, three men assembled on the *Dragchos's* field: the *Dragchos* himself, carrying a handful of seed, a man with a plough and a man carrying a branch of burning *shukpa*. The man with the plough drove a small furrow and the *Dragchos* cast in his handful of grain, while the man with the *shukpa* waved the incense over it.

The women now started carrying the winter manure onto the fields in their *tsepos*, while the men started to repair the drystone walls and clear the watercourses. Everyone sang as they worked. They were glad that winter was past and that spring was with them again. The animals were released from the stables and the children scampered about collecting their droppings. No self-respecting Ladakhi would ever pass a pile of dung on the road without stooping to collect it in the corner of his or her dress. The corner of a woman's dress had universal use, from collecting dung or firewood to wiping the children's noses or polishing up a cup for a visitor. Harry and Ada had learnt always to carry their own cup, in the local fashion!

Threshing with yaks

Harry decided to go on tour again and he suggested that it might make a nice change for Ada and Monica if they went too and camped by the river near Skyarbuchan, while he went further afield.

Everyone was delighted to be having an outing and the caravan set off in high spirits. Harry went ahead on his horse, then followed the pack-ponies carrying the tents, food and bedding, then Ada on a hired pony and lastly Monica, in a new ring-saddle on Kim, being led by a reliable man. They rode over the plain to where the road forked by a pool

Monica on her pony Kim, at Khalatse with Tsodnam

The ring saddle

of brackish water, and took the way following the Indus valley. It was a very ordinary sort of road, wide enough for only one pony and covered with loose shale and rocks, with a steep drop of several hundred feet to the river and a steep slope up the mountain on the other side. A man, on foot and carrying a rolled umbrella, met Harry and greeted him and then, as the rest of the caravan came up, he courteously climbed a little way up the hillside to allow it to pass. He greeted all the pony-men and Ada and all was well until he met Kim. All the other horses and ponies had passed him calmly enough but the fiendish Kim shied.

First he tried to bolt up the mountainside and overtake Ada but was hauled down by the leading-rope. He started to rear and plunge. He twisted and bucked and kicked, all the time being held on the rope, the man fighting to keep him down. Eventually, he became giddy and slipped over the edge of the *kud* and fell on his side, slithering down the shaly cliff. The pony-man clung on with all his strength, twisting the rope round his arm and bracing himself against a rock to stop the horse and child falling to almost certain death. Ada was off her horse in an instant and slithered and slid to where the pony was lying with Monica's leg trapped beneath him. Harry heard the commotion and galloped back, and he and the other men scrambled down. Harry promptly sat on Kim's head, while the others lifted the pony sufficiently to release Monica from the ring-saddle, which thankfully had held her securely. The child was sobbing with fright.

Ada carried her to the shelter of a rock and found that fortunately she was not hurt, beyond a few bruises and grazes. The poor man with the leading-rope was the most hurt; his arm was lacerated and bruised where the rope had cut him and Ada did what she could to ease the pain. The men got Kim back on to the road, where Harry ran his hands over him looking for injuries. His own horse had bolted for home, so Harry borrowed a saddle and mounted Kim to follow him back to Khalatse. Everyone stood aghast because he took his whip and thrashed him. He had never been known to thrash a horse before, but he was now red with anger and rode off at a furious pace.

After Monica had been comforted and the caravan got back into order, Ada and she walked a little way but Monica's little legs did not cover the ground very fast and eventually Ada coaxed her to mount the hired pony while she walked close by, since she wanted above all to restore the child's confidence. When they eventually reached the camping place by the river they found that the tents had been put up on a grassy spot under some apricot trees in blossom. The fire was going and the kettle boiling, while *chapattis* were cooking under the ashes. After an exciting morning and a long trudge in the afternoon, *chapattis* with apricot jam, washed down by smoky tea, was like the food of the gods.

After they were refreshed, the men took *Nomo-le*, as they called Monica, and showed her how to make *chapattis* for her father. She took a ball of dough and worked it flat between the palms of her hands, patting it to and fro until a uniform thickness was obtained and it looked rather like a pancake. A selected stone from the river was placed at the side of the fire, where it was heated through and the *chapatti* laid on it and covered with hot ashes until it was cooked. The child became so absorbed in her cooking that the frightening happening of the morning was erased from her mind.

CHAPTER 14

Two babies

In a Ladakhi household it was customary for the eldest brother to take a wife, who became the common wife for all the brothers. Ada once enquired whether this arrangement did not lead to difficulty and jealousy between the brothers, but Tsering reassured her that it usually worked well. All children were automatically regarded as the sons and daughters of the eldest brother. It was also customary for the second, and sometimes the third, son to enter monasteries at an early age and, if there were any other brothers, one spent several months every year travelling and trading, while the youngest was usually sent up to the summer grazing ground, or *drogs*, for a month or two. The eldest brother remained at home and attended to the fields and other family affairs. Despite Tsering's assurances that polyandry worked well, the

Lamas at Khalatse

Lama and his attendant. His hair shows he has meditated in a cell for many years. This particular one had power over demons in springs and wells

missionaries knew that there was quite a lot of promiscuity and venereal disease was rife.

At the beginning of the summer the younger brothers prepared for their trading journeys. Ada pored over the catalogues from the stores in Calcutta and made her annual shopping list – rice, sugar, sago, lentils, soap and tins of kerosene as well as stationery, needles and thread, elastic and buttons, lamp-wicks, toothbrushes and other toilet articles. She allowed herself a few luxuries, such as biscuits, cheese and tinned goods, to make a little variety in their diet, but these had to be severely restricted. Harry made up his orders for money, medicines and cartridges. He used to send down his collection of butterflies, which were caught by the children or Monica, or even Harry himself, to be sold to a dealer in Srinagar. He also sent down his three fox skins. These sales brought in small sums that helped to feed an old leper woman who came daily to the gate for food and treatment.

Visitors from outside the country also travelled between May and September. Only eleven permits a year were issued to foreigners, most of whom were young British army officers, who travelled light and speedily in order to reach the shooting grounds beyond Leh and bag the heads of

Lama performing the rites for a dead person

Argali sheep, or whatever other animal they had permits to shoot, and get back to their regiments before their leave expired. The British Resident, or his assistant, and his entourage took residence in Leh for one month each year. The party sometimes spent the night on the way at the *dak* bungalow in Khalatse and if they did, they invited Harry and Ada to dinner, for whom it was a memorable occasion. They always hoped that travellers would call and were most disappointed if they did not. If any visitors stayed at the *dak* bungalow, either Harry or Ada would go and offer any assistance.

One year two American ladies, Mrs. and Miss Abbott from Massachusetts, came to the house and asked if they might pitch their tents in the orchard. Of course, the Burroughses were delighted, more so when the ladies decided to spend a few days there. Mary Abbott, the daughter, astounded everyone by shoeing her own horse. When they departed, the Americans left behind as a gift some tins of food, which were very much appreciated by the Burroughs family. Ada corresponded with them for very many years afterwards.

Another interesting visitor was an Italian countess. Excited rumours preceded her arrival. It was said that a princess was coming, and imagination ran riot about the size of her caravan, the magnificence of her tents and equipment and the number of people in her entourage. Of course, she travelled in the same manner as any other visitor. When she arrived in Khalatse, she stayed at the *dak* bungalow for several days. She was most interested in anything Harry and Ada could tell her about the country and she was particularly interested in their journey to Pu, because she was hoping to reach Lhasa by that route. They did their best to try to dissuade

Officer's shooting expedition

Mrs. and Miss Abbott

With the Italian countess

her from attempting the journey. In the meantime, she was happy to investigate some of the aspects of life in the village, assisted by Ada, who took her to call on the wife of the *Dragchos*. According to local custom, she sent a messenger ahead to announce that they would be pleased to make a call. When they got to the house however, the old lady had done absolutely nothing to tidy herself up; her face and hands were filthy and all the time they were talking she scratched her head with her dirty thumb-nail. The countess was the wife of one of Mussolini's closest associates, but she held her title in her own right and was obviously a very wealthy, as well as intelligent, woman. She did not get very far beyond Leh. When she returned to Italy she sent Ada and Monica exquisite sets of underwear, which had been handmade and embroidered by nuns.

One year there was a tragedy. There was an old man of the village by the name of Drambuchan. He was a very poor man and a widower with only one son. Because Drambuchan was poor, his son had not much choice in brides. The girl he had married was pretty and healthy, but she had one great fault – she had smelly feet. One might wonder how this could possibly matter when everybody stank anyway, but it did, because it was thought that anyone who had strong body odours was possessed of an evil spirit. However, she was a good, hardworking girl, who looked after her husband and father-in-law well.

As was the custom, she joined the other young women on their annual jaunt to the mountain pastures but, as she was pregnant and near her time, she did not stay with the others but set out to return to the village by herself. No-one knew what happened next, but the following day Drambuchan found his daughter-in-law dead on the mountain-side, having given birth to a daughter. The baby was still just alive.

The poor old *meme* (grandfather) cut the umbilical cord and wrapped the infant in a sheepskin.

With the Italian countess

Tearfully he killed a kid and tried to make a primitive feeding bottle of its stomach but the baby was too weak to suck. He was alone and was afraid to leave his few animals, but he decided that he must run as fast as he could to the mission as he desperately wanted to save the baby's life. When he arrived at the bungalow, tears coursed down his dirty, wrinkled face as he handed over the baby and begged Ada to try and save its life for him – his only grandchild.

Ada reassured the old man and invited him to sit down and rest and take some tea while she attended to the infant. She bathed it, rubbed it with oil, retied the umbilicus and then dressed the child in some of her own baby-clothes. She found a feeding bottle and coaxed the poor mite to suck. She told Drambuchan that she thought the baby would live and persuaded him to go home and return the next day. She prepared a linen-basket and laid the baby in it.

That night she thought over the problem. It was unlikely that Drambuchan's son would find another wife, as he had married a girl possessed of an evil spirit, and in any case he was too poor to be able to afford another wedding so soon. It would be unfair to all of them if she offered to bring up the child, who would become divorced from her own environment. Drambuchan and his son needed a girl who would grow up to look after them.

Drambuchan and his grandchild

In the end she decided to tell the old man that she would look after the baby until it was well and strong, on condition that he came each day and learnt how to care for her himself. Drambuchan was pathetically pleased and promised faithfully to come. The first day he watched while Ada bathed and dressed the child. When the baby had taken most of her bottle, Ada handed her over to the old man to feed. He gradually gained confidence and, after about two months, Ada suggested that the time had come for him to take his grand-daughter home. He was so happy that he danced and wept at the same time. The child thrived.

A young officer, who had called in at the mission bungalow on his way up to Leh several weeks earlier, decided to call in again on the way down. He saw Drambuchan's baby asleep in the linen-basket and, at the same time, he kept casting furtive and puzzled glances at the obviously pregnant Ada. Ada intercepted one of these looks and burst out laughing and explained the whole story.

The following spring it was announced that the Hebers would, at last, be going home in the late summer. This caused Harry and Ada some anxious thought, because they wondered whether they should send Monica home. If they did not, they could not see the prospect of anyone else being able to escort her, and they were concerned partly about her education and partly about her health. The missionaries were advised not to keep their children at such a high altitude after the age of about six and Monica would be nearly six when the Hebers left. In the end they decided to keep her with them for a little longer.

Ada's baby was due in June and she hoped that Dr. Heber would be able to deliver it but with his impending departure he was far too busy to leave Leh. However he heard that two English nurses were spending their leave travelling up to Ladakh and he wrote to one of them, whom he knew slightly, and asked her if she would be kind enough to help Ada. Miss Ferguson and her companion arrived in Khalatse at the beginning of June, about the time the baby was due. They agreed that the companion should continue her tour while Miss Ferguson stayed behind. Not unnaturally, she was very impatient at having to hang about awaiting the baby, but she took complete charge and bossed poor Harry about so much that he did his best to keep out of her way and Monica used to slink after him.

At last the baby was born, in the early hours of 15th June, 1925. Monica's cot was moved out of the bedroom and put into the living-room but there was so much coming and going that next it was put into the passage and finally ended up in the church.

As Ada lay in bed for the prescribed three weeks, she had nothing to do. She had read every book in the house several times and she had not had any new ones for some time. She lay watching wasps building a nest on the frame of the bedroom window and, as she watched, she thought about her little boys so far away in England.

Gordon was now nine. The Grange had closed down and Miss Warne had retired to Brockweir so Gordon had gone to the Moravian school at Fulneck when he was eight, while Ronnie had spent a year at

Ada comforts the baby

Monica with Geoffrey and the staff

Brockweir under Miss Warne's tuition. She thought of how Gordon had had to undertake the complicated journey from Tintern to Leeds completely on his own, with two changes of train. When he got to Leeds, he had to change stations. No-one had escorted him, even the first time he went to the new and unseen school. Ronnie followed him when he was eight. Ada's heart ached for her children.

In due course the baby was baptized by his father in the church in the presence of the Christian community of Khalatse and other members of the congregation, who had not finally committed themselves to Christianity. One regular member of the congregation was an old woman who attended every service. She had never been formally admitted to the Church, but she insisted on standing up with the Christians to say the creed. When she first started to do this, the non-believers were embarrassed and tried to prevent her, but she shook them off and repeated the Apostles' Creed in an unwavering voice. The baby was named Geoffrey David.

CHAPTER 15

Enough is enough

The first half of the year 1926 passed uneventfully. Days plodded slowly, one after the other, like a string of pack-ponies, each carrying its special burden along a well-known road. Then, early in the summer, a seemingly unremarkable event dramatically changed the lives of the whole Burroughs family.

Among the first visitors to come to Ladakh that year were two single ladies, Miss Wingate and Miss Rudd. Miss Wingate, whose family had strong connections with the East, worked in India, but her friend, Miss Rudd, had taken an extended holiday from her post as Principal of a home for girls in Cockermouth in order to fulfil an ambition to travel in the Himalayas. They stayed for a few days at the mission bungalow. As they talked, Harry and Ada showed their anxiety about Monica's future. They thought she ought to go home. It transpired that Miss Wingate had hoped to travel beyond Leh but was curtailing her trip in order to escort her less experienced friend back to Kashmir. Miss Rudd then offered to take Monica as far as London, if her parents could make the necessary arrangements within a week, when she would be returning from Leh. The decision was made and cables were despatched to Miss Warne and friends in London, asking them to take responsibility for the child in England.

Ada decided that she would travel down to Srinagar too, so that she could help Miss Rudd and equip Monica with clothes and procure a passport for her. She tried to persuade Harry to come for a holiday but he thought it would be better for him to stay in Khalatse with Geoffrey and thus leave Ada free to see to Monica's affairs. They asked Chondzin, who had looked after the Heber children, to come from Leh and take charge of Geoffrey.

As soon as the news got round the village that *Nomo-le* was going back to England, everyone assumed that she was going to be married and nothing would persuade them that this was not so.

Monica certainly knew the bride's song, as did all the little girls in the village, and she often sang it as she played, but Ada had to insist that she would not be singing it when she left. A bride usually sang a farewell to each member of her family, her friends, her home,

Nomo-le (Monica in Tibetan dress)

Monica's playmates

and her village when she left for her bridegroom's home. On the day of departure nearly the whole village was waiting outside the compound gate to say goodbye. They had brought gifts such as dried apricots and jewellery but, as she was not a bride, Ada had schooled Monica to touch each present graciously and return it with a gesture.

Miss Rudd, Monica and Ada on the way to Kashmir

They took the journey slowly, covering only ten or fifteen miles a day, but even so it meant being on the road as soon as it was light. Each morning Ada rose and dressed while it was still dark, then busied herself supervising the preparation of picnic food to be eaten during the day and checking the loads for the hired ponies. When the porridge for breakfast was cooked and the kettle was nearly boiling, she roused Monica, who whimpered and implored her mother to let her sleep. While they breakfasted, their tent was struck and loaded, the fire was stamped out and the cooking-pots were packed up so that the cook could go ahead and make preparations for their evening meal. They reached the next camping spot, or rest-house, about four o'clock. A cup of tea, followed by a little exercise to stretch saddle-stiffened legs, then supper and bed were the order of the day.

There was still a lot of snow on the Zoji. They crossed the remains of fifteen avalanches and twenty-seven snow-bridges. Ada spotted three huge vultures sitting on the crags above and she gazed around to see where there was a dead animal. Then, as they rounded a small bend, a frieze of animals and men plastered into the mountainside across the river confronted them. The avalanche which had struck them had been so swift and violent that the ponies had not even raised their heads. It was this caravan, Ada discovered later, which had been carrying their Christmas mail three years earlier; it had been immured until that day in snow and ice in a perfect state of preservation.

Ada thought it would be fun to stay on a houseboat during her sojourn in Srinagar. She had just negotiated the hire of a boat when Denyed came hurrying along and, quite firmly, said she could not allow her Memsahib to do such a thing; unaccompanied women who hired houseboats, she said, had very dubious reputations. The houseboat owner was rather annoyed but Denyed brushed his protests aside and swept Ada and Monica off to stay with Miss Churchill-Taylor. Auntie Churchie, as she was known, was an elderly lady of some means, who gave her services to the Church Missionary Society and at the same time kept a large house going, to

Descending the Zoji-la. Monica is being carried on a man's back

Snow bridge, coming down the Zoji-la

which she welcomed other missionaries who needed a holiday or, like Ada, temporary hospitality. Staying with her at that time was her older sister, Mrs. Rudduck, who had come to Kashmir on an extended visit after her husband's death. She and her doctor husband had themselves been honorary missionaries in Morocco, Syria and the Lebanon. She was well over seventy and rather eccentric, with a formidable presence which masked a kind and generous nature. She was a scholarly woman who spoke several languages, including Arabic, and she occupied her days in Srinagar taking Urdu lessons. She and Ada enjoyed each other's company and they became firm friends, each respecting the qualities of the other.

Ada had expected to spend about three weeks in Srinagar but her return to Khalatse was delayed by Miss Rudd's illness with dysentery and then Monica was unwell for a few days. It was almost a relief when the day came when Monica and her guardian boarded the lorry for Rawalpindi and the agony of parting could be forgotten in activity. Besides, Ada had been anxious for her new baby. Ada's former travelling companions had had to return without her and now she could only find a man whom she neither liked nor trusted, but he was prepared to leave immediately and travel fast, so a contract was made.

They had been on the road for a while when Ada became suspicious that the ponies were overloaded. Her loads had been weighed under her supervision and the appropriate number of ponies had been hired. She called a halt and inspected the baggage. As she had feared, the man had introduced his own packages, not just his travelling necessities and the odd bag of rice for his own use, but many bags of rice, which he had obviously intended to sell. The man was very angry when Ada insisted that he hired a pony on his own account or abandon his goods. After this episode, she took to riding ahead of the baggage-train. She had never travelled quite alone before, responsible only for herself, and she began to understand her husband's passion for touring.

The moon was nearly full and rode high in the sky, so she rose each morning very early and covered many miles before dawn in the cool. One morning she had got well ahead of the pack-ponies and thought she ought to let them catch her up – she still did not entirely trust the pony-man. At the top of a small pass she dismounted and sat on a rock. The moon had set but the stars were still brilliant in the dark sky. As she watched, the stars went out one by one and sky brightened with the dawn. She could see no living thing except her pony. She thought, "If I disappear now, no one would ever know what had happened, my bones would be picked clean by vultures and jackals and there would be no trace at all." Just then she heard the jingling of the bells on the ponies' harnesses as they came up the pass and the sun rose over the mountain, so the thought vanished as quickly as it came, but the memory of that moment of utter solitude remained with her for ever.

It was wonderful to be home again in Khalatse. Her anxiety about Geoffrey had been unnecessary as he had flourished in Chondzin's care. Harry was overjoyed to see her back and talked happily about all that had been happening in her absence and he was interested in all that she had to tell about her experiences. But all too soon there seemed to be very little to talk about and the house seemed quiet without Monica's chatter. Harry withdrew into himself and they both began to dread the long winter nights when the sun set at three o'clock and did not rise again until ten in the morning. They heard that Monica had arrived safely in England and that their friends, the Richardsons, had taken her to Brockweir by car. The gap of separation was very wide.

Harry had made it his custom to go to the village in the afternoon about the time that the people were returning home after their day's work in the fields, or with the animals at the grazing grounds. He found it a good time to have a chat and perhaps to do a little pastoral work. Each afternoon, after Tsering returned from the spring with the daily supply of water, she would prepare the evening meal and then, as the sun dipped behind the peak across the valley, she would take glowing embers from the kitchen range and carry them in her hands, tossing them from palm to palm as she hurried down the corridor to the living room. Here she would place the fire in the iron stove and blow it to a blaze. When it was burning satisfactorily she would sit on the floor to wait for Harry's return, while Ada encouraged her to talk about local customs, taboos and ceremonies. But Tsering would become impatient when Harry delayed his return from the village and he was becoming increasingly dilatory.

As the autumn progressed Harry became run-down and morose. His wife noticed that he frequently examined his thumb. She asked him about it and he told her that he had accidentally punctured his own hand when he had been giving an injection to a leper-woman and he feared he had become infected. Ada examined the thumb but could see no sign of infection. Then he had a number of cases of venereal disease to treat, which depressed and worried him. Ada tried to divert him and she wished that Geoffrey were old enough to go out with him in the evenings, as Monica had done.

A letter arrived from the Richardsons. They had had slight misgivings about leaving Monica with Miss Warne when they had first taken her down to Brockweir. The boys had already gone back to Fulneck, so they could not talk to them, but somehow the atmosphere was not right. They had decided to pay a surprise visit after Monica had had time to settle in, after which they wrote guardedly, but it was plain that they did not consider Miss Warne the ideal person to be taking care of the children. Worriedly, the parents discussed what to do. Should Ada return to England and leave Harry by himself? Ought they both to go? They prayed for guidance as to where their duty lay.

They decided to go down to Srinagar for a holiday and to consult a doctor while they were there. Harry by this time had not had any sort of a holiday for three years. The doctor was emphatic that Harry should not return to live in Khalatse alone. He recommended that both Harry and Ada should return to England, as he was of the opinion that the altitude was seriously affecting both of them. His report was cabled to the Mission Board, who ordered them both to come home. Harry set off at once to go back to Khalatse to pack up their possessions and hand over the mission to Dewazung. There were only about three weeks left before the first snows were likely to fall on Zoji so Harry rode double, sometimes treble, stages to make the journey in time.

The people of Khalatse were shocked to hear that Harry was leaving them. Dewazung, their old friend and mentor, wept. Chospel and Lobsang, the evangelists, and Elisha, the schoolmaster, expressed their deep sorrow, but Tsering and Tsodnam were perhaps the most upset. Many villagers came to wish him goodbye and some touched his feet and brought gifts of respect and gratitude. He sold a number of things, including, to Ada's sorrow, the Turki rug which they had received as a wedding-gift. Other things he gave away and the remainder was packed. Even now he could not believe that he would never return to this fascinating, sometimes cruel land, whose people were merry, loyal and kind, despite the harshness of their existence and the fear which dominated every aspect of their lives.

When he reached Srinagar once more, they sorted out the pony-loads into boxes for transport by rail and sea. They had to discard many things for which they would find no use in England and, while they were doing so, they selected gifts for the pony-men. Dorje, the headman, came with a special request – could he please have the tea-cosy – a hideous confection knitted by Ada's great-aunt Jane in scarlet and emerald, with finishing touches of red and green bows. Early the next day the men came to bid them farewell.

It was almost exactly thirteen years ago that they had set out on the road to Ladakh, young and eager to meet every challenge. Now they watched the pony-train wend its way out of sight with tears streaming down their faces. A brilliant splash of scarlet and emerald caught their eyes as Dorje's head bobbed along at the tail of the procession. The looked at each other and tears of laughter mingled with their tears of sorrow.

They turned away together, at the end of a chapter in their lives. Now they had to set out into the unknown future, possessing little except humour and courage and, above all, an unwavering Faith.

CHAPTER 16

What happened next

They arrived in England in time to spend Christmas with the children in Brockweir. They were shocked at their first meeting to find Monica dressed in an extraordinary collection of cast-off garments and a pair of shoes from Miss Warne's childhood, (although she said she normally wore her brothers' cast-off boots). The chicken on the table for Christmas lunch was only partly cooked, which gave Harry an upset stomach, and it was obvious they would have to make new arrangements for the family without delay.

It was doubtful that Harry and Ada would ever be fit enough for missionary work again, so Harry decided he would seek to re-join the Church of England. He went to discuss his future with the Bishop of Lichfield, who suggested that Harry should do a year's refresher course at theological college before he would ordain him and help to find him a curacy. It was arranged that Harry should spend one year at the London College of Divinity.

In the meantime the family had to live. The Moravian Mission Board was generous enough to agree to keep the boys on at their school, Fulneck, until the end of the school year, spending the Easter holiday with Miss Warne. Monica also had to stay with Miss Warne, while Ada went to Scarborough to help settle her mother's affairs, before taking Geoffrey to stay with Mrs. Rudduck in West Mersea.

Then Harry was offered the curacy of All Saints Parish Church in Wellington, Shropshire. The vicar, the Reverend John Hayes, was sympathetic to the family's problems and arranged for Ada to move into the curate's house before the summer holidays, while the owner of the house waived the rent. Ada had had a small legacy of just over one hundred pounds from her mother, on which she was living, and she had to spend most of what was left buying essential furniture for the house. When the children came home for the holidays she emptied her purse and found she had only six[26] and threepence three farthings in the whole world. When she said grace before their lunch of bread and butter she asked God to provide their next meals.

Barely had she finished clearing the table when the vicar appeared. He breezed into the living room, where he laughed and joked with the children. Quite casually, as he was leaving, he put an envelope into Ada's hand saying, "I thought you might need that," before adding, "By the way, when you have settled in, I have a job for you – it'll bring you in thirty pounds a year." Inside the envelope was an advance on Harry's first quarter's salary. Harry was ordained deacon and priest at the same ceremony in Lichfield Cathedral but Ada could not afford the fare to go to the service.

Harry loved working in Wellington, which was a busy and growing market town. He had the responsibility for a small country church about four miles away, where he took the services every Sunday morning. On Sunday afternoons he conducted the "Men Only" service, which grew rapidly until he had a regular attendance of between three and four hundred men. After their second busy Easter there Harry suffered a stroke and although he made a remarkable recovery, whenever he became tired and overworked he was apt to muddle his words and it became increasingly obvious to Ada that the work in that busy parish was too heavy for him.

Ada, in the meantime, had to shoulder more and more responsibility for the family. Gordon had started at Wrekin college, where he had to board, despite it being close to their house. She managed to teach Ronnie enough Latin to have him accepted into St. John's School at Leatherhead. Monica, who was nearly eight, went to the junior section of the Girls High School.

The little curate's house was really too small for the family, and it was damp. Monica developed rheumatism and missed most of two terms at school when a rheumatic complaint was followed by an attack of scarlet fever.

---

[26]   Six shillings £sd

Throughout all this, Mrs. Rudduck was wonderful. She had both Harry and Monica to stay while they were ill. Her house at West Mersea was quiet and comfortable, and she took great care over their diet, but she was far too astringent and tough an old lady to allow anyone to relapse into invalidism.

Harry began to look for a new living, while Ada started attending sales in surrounding country houses, which were being sold up because of the depression, and bought furniture which she thought they might need if they moved into a vicarage. The doctor recommended that they should try to live in the east of the country, where it was drier, because of Monica's health. They were delighted to be offered the incumbency of Kirby Cane, in the Norwich diocese. Ada thought the place was ideal for the children but had misgivings about the income. After the pension had been paid to the retiring rector they had £350 a year to run a twenty-four-roomed house and six acres of garden, as well as find school fees and other expenses.

They moved to Kirby Cane in the early summer of 1931. Harry found it difficult to adjust from a busy town parish to a small and rather stolid country village. He was not a countryman at heart and found it hard to make a connection with the local people, who distrusted the "Foreigner". The parish had become run down and Harry patiently set about organising the redecoration and refurbishment of the old Norman church, while conscientiously carrying out his pastoral visits.

Ada did her best to turn the house into a home. At least she was accustomed to living without proper sanitation, piped water or electricity. She also had to scheme and plan to find enough money for the children's education. She managed to get grants and bursaries to allow Gordon to go on after his matriculation to St. Peter's Hall, Oxford and Ronnie was awarded a scholarship of £250 a year at Trinity College, Cambridge. Monica went to Norwich High School for a year but the daily journey by bicycle and bus was too long and difficult and Mrs. Rudduck eventually offered to pay her fees if she attended a school she chose in Brighton. Geoffrey was taught at home by the niece of a neighbouring Rector. He proved to have an exceptionally good musical ear, so Ada entered him for the voice trials for the choir at St. George's Chapel, Windsor. He was accepted and became a choral scholar.

When the war broke out Harry joined the Home Guard. The men of the parish saw a new side to their scholarly Rector, whose years in the army and as a medical missionary gave him an unexpected competence and authority. Ada took charge of the First Aid. Eventually, forty-eight soldiers were billeted in the top floor of the house and four or five officers had to live with the family. Ada had inadequate help to cope with this number of people but when the officers suggested that their batmen should do more, Granny Gooch, who had worked at the Rectory for many years, nearly went on strike. She went as red as a turkey-cock and said, "I aren't a-oosed to warking with min. I'm a respeckable 'ooman and I aren't a-'aving noo min in my kitchen."

After the invasion scares came the air raids. The village was sur-rounded by air bases and Harry and Ada had to turn out to help man the posts when there was an alert. One day, a huge Liberator bomber flew over making an unusual noise and before Ada could run outside to see what was happening, there was a deafening crash. Instinctively she picked up her first-aid bag and she dashed across the meadow behind the house, to where she could see the torn and twisted fuselage of the plane. Other helpers arrived but there was little they could do for the ten men of the crew, other than administer shots of morphine and paint the large 'M' on their foreheads. The American Air Force rescue squad arrived and the first aid workers were peremptorily ordered off the field, away from the scattered ammunition and the full load of live bombs. Only one man, who had a severe spinal injury, survived.

Ronnie had joined the Fleet Air Arm and was taken prisoner. He had been at a party when scrambled to fly and was shot down wearing evening dress beneath his flying jacket. Ada fretted and worried and made up parcels for him. The village was more united than it had ever been as nearly every family had a man at war, many either taken prisoner or killed.

Harry and Ada were very tired. They felt they could no longer cope with the primitive arrangements in the house and continue to manage the garden with no help. Harry also wanted to move nearer his beloved London so when he was offered a parish near East Grinstead he accepted gladly.

When the churchwarden made a presentation to Harry and Ada before they left Kirby Cane, he made a speech on behalf of all the parishioners. Harry had been Rector for thirteen years and the church-warden said, "We are sorry, Mr. Burroughs, that you are going. We are just getting to know you!"

They moved to Hammerwood in June 1944, the very weekend the V-bombs started and they found they were on the edge of "bomb alley". The vicarage had been occupied by the army but, once Ada had got it clean, she appreciated the running water and electricity, even if the kitchen range was faulty and she had to cook on primus stoves. They had to share the house with two old ladies who had been evacuated from Eastbourne, which was trying for everyone. The roof on Hammerwood church was damaged by flying bombs three times that summer, and Harry had a lucky escape when a terrific blast shook the house, showering his desk with broken glass shortly after he had left the room.

Monica had been invalided out of the V.A.D. and came home to help her parents settle in. Geoffrey, too, was at home a lot. He had joined the air force after leaving school and gone for pilot training in Rhodesia, but came back early as there was no need for further pilots.

In the years after the war, Ada and Harry supported their children as they found their way in the world. Gordon had been ordained into the Anglican Church but, after agonies of decision, he relinquished the priesthood and became a Roman Catholic, which Harry felt very keenly. He became a teacher and eventually was head master of his own school at Formby in Lancashire. Geoffrey, too, after an unsuccessful attempt to become a businessman, went into teaching, but sadly died after many years of illness at the age of forty-nine. Ronnie abandoned his original intention of taking Holy Orders and decided to join the Foreign Office.

After ten years at Hammerwood, Harry wanted to retire but could see no hope of doing so. Monica's husband, Godfrey, was in the Commonwealth Relations Office and, when they were posted to India, they were able to offer their house in Beckenham to Harry and Ada for two or three years. Harry was delighted to be so close to London, able to stroll about the city or visit the British Museum, where he had a reader's ticket.

On one of his visits to London, Harry was sitting on the top deck of a bus when he overheard the two men in front of him speaking Tibetan. He leant forward and spoke to them. When they turned he saw that one of them was the Rev. Tsetan Puntzog from Leh. Harry invited him to visit and so they were able to have first-hand news of their friends.

Rigdzin and Tarchungma had found that, after a while, they were the only practising Christians in Pu, so they had decided to make their way to Leh to join the church there. Yoseb Gergan translated the bible into Tibetan and sent the manuscript to London in 1939 for revision and printing. It was kept safe at Ripon Cathedral then, in 1945, the Bible Society Committee raised the funds and decided to put the printing in hand in Lahore. It had taken ninety years to get the whole Bible printed in Tibetan.

The vicar of St. Mary's at Shortlands, which had been bombed during the war, asked Harry if he would like to assist in the parish and he jumped at the idea, as he could devote himself to visiting and assisting with services without any of the burdens of administration. He became greatly loved in the parish.

When Monica and her family were due to return from India, Harry and Ada found a flat nearby. They were taken ill with flu, however, and had not moved in before the family's return. Despite not being well, Harry went to Liverpool Street Station to meet the boat train.

The next day Monica and Godfrey went to the flat and helped to get it ready so that Harry and Ada could move in after the weekend, and Harry and Ada spent the Saturday arranging their books and china. That evening, when they sat down together for the supper Monica had prepared, Harry said grace, lifted his knife and fork and then laid them down again. He swayed and Monica caught him as he fell. He was dead before the doctor could arrive.

Printed in Great Britain
by Amazon